ALSO BY HOWARD LEVINE

TALKING TECH: A CONVERSATIONAL GUIDE TO SCIENCE AND TECHNOLOGY (WITH HOWARD RHEINGOLD, 1982)

THE INSTANT ACCESS GUIDE TO PORTABLE CALC + PORTABLE SCHEDULER (1984)

LIFE
CHOICES

CONFRONTING THE
LIFE AND DEATH DECISIONS
CREATED BY MODERN MEDICINE

HOWARD LEVINE

SIMON AND SCHUSTER
NEW YORK

PUBLISHED BY SIMON AND SCHUSTER
A DIVISION OF SIMON & SCHUSTER, INC.
SIMON & SCHUSTER BUILDING
ROCKEFELLER CENTER
1230 AVENUE OF THE AMERICAS
NEW YORK, NEW YORK 10020
SIMON AND SCHUSTER AND COLOPHON ARE REGISTERED TRADEMARKS
OF SIMON & SCHUSTER, INC.
DESIGNED BY IRVING PERKINS ASSOCIATES
MANUFACTURED IN THE UNITED STATES OF AMERICA
1 3 5 7 9 10 8 6 4 2
LIBRARY OF CONGRESS CATALOGING IN PUBLICATION DATA

LEVINE, HOWARD, DATE.
LIFE CHOICES.

INCLUDES BIBLIOGRAPHIES AND INDEX.
1. MEDICAL ETHICS.   I. TITLE.   [DNLM: 1. ETHICS,
MEDICAL.   W 50 L6645L]
R724.L457   1986   174'.2   86-6693
ISBN: 0-671-55385-2

ACKNOWLEDGMENTS

IT is now twenty years since I enrolled in my first philosophy class, and a list of all those to whom I am indebted would fill half the present volume. Yet I would be remiss in not thanking the six professors, first at Brandeis and then at Berkeley, who made the greatest contribution to my general philosophical education: Ernest Adams, James Child, Michael Scriven, Barry Stroud, Stephen Toulmin, and Jean van Heijenoort.

While working on this book I was lucky enough to be able to draw on the expertise of Marsden Blois, Ann Davis, Marc Lappé, Marcia H. Rioux, Robert Siegel and Charles Silver. Even with all their help, I must accept full responsibility for any factual errors that remain.

Writing a book and having a book published are two very different activities. I also want to thank everyone who helped me to put my ideas between the covers: Sally Furgeson, David Goodtree, Connie Levine, Peter Livingston, Esther Mitgang, Alice Price, and my "artistic rabbi" Howard Rheingold. My editor, Ann Godoff, deserves special thanks for her encouragement and good sense.

Finally, I want to thank Gerri Deckter Levine, who first suggested this project to me fifteen years ago, and then had the strength and humor to remain close by in order to make sure that it got done.

CONTENTS

IV. LIFE AND DEATH 120

V. EXPERIMENTATION WITH HUMAN BEINGS 166

ETHICS

It appears to me that in Ethics, as in all other philosophical studies, the difficulties and disagreements, of which its history is full, are mainly due to a very simple cause: namely to the attempt to answer questions, without first discovering precisely *what* question it is you desire to answer.

—G. E. MOORE

BIOLOGY

Biology occupies a position among the sciences at once marginal and central. Marginal because—the living world constituting but a tiny and very "special" part of the universe—it does not seem likely that the study of living beings will ever uncover general laws applicable outside the biosphere. But if the ultimate aim of the whole of science is indeed, as I believe, to clarify man's relationship to the universe, then biology must be accorded a central position, since of all the disciplines it is the one that endeavours to go most directly to the heart of the problems that must be resolved before that of "human nature" can even be framed in other than metaphysical terms.

—JACQUES MONOD

BIOETHICS

Mankind is urgently in need of new wisdom that will provide the "knowledge of how to use knowledge" for man's survival and for improvement in the quality of life. This concept of wisdom as a guide for action—the knowledge of how to use knowledge for the social good—might be called *Science of Survival*, surely the prerequisite to improvement in the quality of life. I take the position that the science of survival must be built on the science of biology and enlarged beyond the traditional boundaries to include the most essential elements of the social sciences and the humanities with emphasis on philosophy in the strict sense meaning "love of wisdom." A science of survival must be more than science alone, and I therefore propose the term *Bioethics* in order to emphasize the two most important ingredients in achieving the new wisdom that is so desperately needed: biological knowledge and human values.

—VAN RENSSELAER POTTER

Introduction

A few years ago, a book like *Life Choices* might have been important only to those with a special interest in bioethics. But the sensational media coverage of Elizabeth Bouvia, Barney Clark, Baby Fae, Karen Ann Quinlan and others has widened that narrow focus by providing every citizen with important lessons in bioethical decision making. Today, the ability to make informed judgments about the efficacy and ethics of medical care is a vital survival skill, and *Life Choices* serves well as an essential primer and guide to this new way of thinking.

As a result of the impact of modern medical technology, which profoundly alters our lives from conception to death, medical ethics is no longer simply an academic subject to be debated in scientific journals, university classrooms or hospital conferences. Medical ethics has become a prominent consideration in the day-to-day practice of medical professionals; more importantly, it is an integral and indispensable part of the information needed by anyone who must make choices about medical care for themselves or their loved ones.

Our growing need to be more aware of medical ethics stems from the fundamental democratic idea that each of us has a right to determine what shall be done to his or her own body. That Constitutional right, always an important facet of the doctor-patient relationship, has been dramatized in recent years by the increasing difficulty of making personal choices about scientific advances such as immunizations, antibiotics, medications, surgery, intravenous nutrition, cardiopulmonary resuscitation, intensive care, heart-lung machines, organ transplantation and artificial organs. Each new development raises difficult questions about who, and under what circumstances, should receive the benefits, and be subjected to the risks, of modern technology.

Life choices become more and more difficult. Should little Johnnie be subjected to the recently discovered risks of a DPT immunization shot? Should Janie have her tonsils removed even though the surgery could result in complications, even death? Is the best treatment for mother's breast tumor radical surgery or something less deforming? Should father have a coronary bypass operation or continue treatment with the family doctor? Should grandmother, who can no longer think clearly, receive an artificial hip to relieve her arthritis or should she be placed inn a nursing home to rest?

Many of us will face even more difficult decisions when a child is born with near-lethal birth defects, a woman decides whether to have an abortion, an infertile couple considers having a test-tube baby or using a surrogate mother, a comatose family member is kept alive by a respirator or an elder lies terminally ill in a nursing home being fed with a stomach tube. Others will discover the more acute dilemmas of medical ethics when decisions have to be made about undergoing kidney dialysis, accepting experimental treatment such as artificial heart implantation or being subjected to "heroic" and "extraordinary" measures. Some of us may even have to decide about prolonging the life of someone "hopelessly" ill, suffering from cancer or other debilitating disease, who may ultimately want to die. Modern medical technology, with its risks as well as benefits, will confront each of us with difficult ethical decisions, sometimes testing both our right to live and our right to die.

Yet decisions about medical ethics involve more than our individual selves and families. In a democratic socicty, those we elect to represent us, to enact legislation and to make decisions from the benches of our highest courts, will determine to what degree government will regulate our ethical decisions about such important personal issues as childbirth, control of communicable diseases, death with dignity, human research and genetic engineering.

Whether viewed individually or collectively, these ethical issues are made even more complex by another dramatic shift in our society. American medical care has entered a state of financial crisis. As the cost of medical care rose to nearly 11 percent of the gross national product, all knowledgeable experts agreed that expenditures had to be cut. Facing possible bankruptcy of Medicare and intolerable costs to private health insurance companies, government, together with industry, consumer groups and labor unions, has begun programs to drastically reduce healthcare spending. Medical ethics will take on a whole new dimension as decisions about care depend more and more upon costs.

Life Choices does not pretend to answer all these questions. Instead, Howard Levine—philosopher, educator and author—shows us how to think systematically about such problems. By offering valuable new tools, not only for doctors and other medical professionals, but for all of us who are called upon to make choices about medical care for ourselves, our families and our communities, *Life Choices* begins to bring order to these complexities of modern bioethics.

Michael Denney, M.D., F.A.C.S.
San Francisco, California

I

BIOETHICAL THINKING

MEDICAL MIRACLES: BUT HOW TO PAY THE BILL?
—TIME Cover Story,
December 10, 1984

ABORTION: THE MORAL DILEMMA
—NEWSWEEK Cover Story,
January 14, 1985

PROLONGING LIFE: THE NEW DILEMMA
—NEW YORK TIMES Series,
January 14–18, 1985

PHILOSOPHY is relevant again. Twenty-five centuries
ago in ancient Greece, the most important questions, from
what the world is made of to why people act the way they
do, were decided by philosophers. Just in case you haven't
noticed, things have changed quite a bit since the time of
Plato and Aristotle. Today's "wise men" are the scientists
and physicians who are discovering how to predict and
control nature. In a world obsessed by material results,
"wise" is most often used to describe the individuals who
know how to apply the technology needed to solve our
modern problems. Philosophers, literally "lovers of wisdom," are no longer thought to have much to do with
helping us attain Socrates' "good life." Instead, we expect
our quality of life to be enhanced by laboratory research
and packaged in bright colors on the supermarket shelf.

19

But it is precisely this scientific domination of our modern world that has led to the ultimate irony: the success of biology and medicine has revitalized the long-dormant discipline of ethics. Yet, in this age of technomedicine, it's not only professional philosophers who are once again being asked to answer important questions. With the stakes as high as life and death, each of us must become his own, personal bioethicist.

Although science long ago displaced philosophy as a way of gaining knowledge about the world, the achievements of scientific medicine are now raising questions that only philosophy can answer: When should a fertilized ovum receive all the rights of personhood? To what extent should science alter the biological mechanism of reproduction? When is a person dead? Who has a right to "extraordinary medical means?" How can the rights of human subjects be protected during biomedical experimentation?

If these questions sound too abstract, the kind of problems you might expect to find in a philosophy classroom but not in the real world, then consider the stories of the individuals told in the following pages: Dr. Kenneth Edelin, the Boston physician convicted of terminating the life of a viable fetus after an abortion. The Del Zios, who saw their only hope for a child go literally down the drain when an early test-tube-baby experiment was abruptly terminated. Karen Ann Quinlan, the young New Jersey woman whose ten-year struggle with dying gave the whole country a lesson about a new definition of death, the right to refuse treatment, and the horrors of what can happen when medical technology can forestall death without providing life. Jamie Fiske, the cute little girl who needed a liver transplant and whose media-wise father was able to mobilize the resources of the entire country. And Baby Fae, the California infant with a congenitally deformed heart who received the heart of a baboon.

All of these cases share two common themes. First, they all happened to perfectly ordinary individuals who found themselves in extraordinary circumstances created by advances in biomedicine. Second, they also shared the media spotlight because, in most instances, they were "firsts." Today, the media have moved on to cover AIDS, Alzheimer's, and artificial wombs. In one short decade, the miracles of test tube babies and organ transplants have become commonplace. The media are no longer terribly interested in the agonies of parents who ask to have their child's respirator removed so that she may die in peace. Yet the private ethical decision to have an abortion or participate in a biomedical experiment, as well as the public policies and laws which regulate these activities, are far from resolved.

Nor are bioethical dilemmas solely the result of advances in technology. By focusing strictly on the sci-tech aspects of medicine, the media have missed the essence of the story: ethics, from the Hippocratic Oath onward, has been an integral part of medicine. For the most part, technology serves only to exacerbate already entrenched problems. Every time you decide to donate blood, or use birth control, or sign a petition banning nuclear weapons, you are making a bioethical choice. As the following situations demonstrate, bioethical decision-making is an important, everyday part of modern life.

• During your annual physical checkup the doctor notices a small lump in your breast tissue. Although he cautions that it's nothing to get alarmed about, he advises you to enter the hospital for a biopsy. While in the hospital, a never ending stream of anesthesiologists, surgeons, attending physicians, and allied health professionals stop by to "explain" and to have you fill out permission forms. Are you really informed enough to give your consent to the biopsy procedure? How much of a "right to know" do you have?

• Many states now provide residents the option of signing an organ donor's card which is affixed to the driver's license. This card automatically authorizes the donation of needed body organs if you happen to die in an auto accident. What should you consider before signing such a card? Who owns your body while you're alive? After you die?

• After two years of failing to conceive a child, you and your wife undergo a complete series of tests. The verdict: your wife is sterile and cannot conceive. You both still want children and reason that if the child can't share your genes, it can at least have the father's genes if a surrogate mother (a practice as old as the Bible) can be found. What scientific, legal, and bioethical questions need to be addressed?

Real-life examples like these demonstrate why we can no longer allow scientists, lawyers, or even professional philosophers to do all of our bioethical thinking for us. Bioethical decisions are simply too serious, personal, and important to be left in the total control of strangers. In fact, a working knowledge of bioethics is one of the survival skills for a new age. If you're concerned about the care of an aged parent or a premature infant, if you're worried about incompetent medical care or the taking of a newly released drug, or if you're thinking about artificial insemination or trying to predetermine the sex of your next child, you must be versed in the techniques of *bioethical thinking*—a melding of scientific fact, law, public policy, value judgment, and ethical principle to yield a coherent, sensible, action-oriented decision.

This skill requires two distinct abilities: first, an overall synthetic capacity allowing you to judge objective information as it relates to your own, subjective value system; second, the analytical skill necessary to understand the diverse scientific and legal information surrounding specific bioethical decisions. Lacking the first, bioethical thinking is merely technocracy run amok; lacking the second, it is uninformed, wishful thinking. *Life Choices* is designed to help you steer a proper path between these two, and to provide you with the tools necessary to attain a portion of your own, modern version of Socrates' "good life."

PRIVATE VALUES: DETERMINING YOUR BIOETHICAL PROFILE

It was no less an authority than Socrates, the greatest bioethicist of all time, who set forth the First Law of Bioethics: "Know thyself." Sadly, in the 2500 years since his death, societies (and ours in particular) have done little to prepare their citizens to cope with questions of self-knowledge. If we are lucky, we had a conscientious Sunday-school teacher; if not, we're pretty much on our own. Far from helping their children understand the values needed to deal with bioethical issues, parents generally shield their children from the hospitalization of a grandparent, or even the death of a pet (e.g., "Fluffy ran away"). Schools are even less likely to deal with values education. As a result, we have a nation of twenty-one-year-old value illiterates, young adults who know nothing of themselves.

Unfortunately, bioethical dilemmas don't usually wait for on-the-job training. Many times, they are loaded toward the front end of life: the unmarried, pregnant teenager wondering what to do, the depressed graduate student contemplating suicide, and the married couple who cannot conceive are all facing the toughest choices of their lives, and all without any preparation. Nor does the pace of bioethical decision-making abate as we grow older: dealing with a dying parent, or a cult-addled grandchild, or even our own mortality is a crisis to test the strongest among us.

Yet crises need not be perceived as totally negative. The

Chinese idiograph for the word "crisis" combines the symbols for the words "threatening" and "opportunity." If bioethical crises are viewed as deferred chances to come to know oneself, then they are, indeed, threatening opportunities. In fact, in a society racked by bioethical crises, the first step toward group resolution must be an appreciation of the need to understand our own, individual values.

Life Choices provides you with just such an opportunity. In particular, because bioethical choices are value dependent, it is essential that (1) we have self-knowledge of our own values and (2) we understand how to use that information when making these important decisions. This section will help you determine your own *bioethical profile*— the central core of values which must be consulted each time a bioethical choice is made. Subsequent sections, in fact the entire book, will help you apply this self-knowledge.

While "Know thyself" sounds like easy advice to follow, all the research on values indicates just how easily we can be self-deceived. For example, consider all those citizens who profess to value highly the U.S. Constitution, yet, when presented with the particulars of the Bill of Rights, find it much too radical. Bioethics is no less immune from such self-deception: patients profess complete trust in their doctor's judgment only to subvert that judgment by ignoring instructions; citizens claim to value the individual's right to control his own body, yet lobby for laws preventing suicide; and dyed-in-the-wool right-to-lifers also support the death penalty. When it comes to bioethical matters, "Know thyself" is no easy prescription to follow.

The Bioethical Profile Assessment is a three-part procedure designed to eliminate self-deception and to help you better understand your private value structure. It is an instrument that measures your abstract self-image against your underlying value profile. If done conscientiously, it should take only about thirty minutes. However, it will provide you with the knowledge of a lifetime.

1. Study the Bioethical Profile Chart on page 29 and place a mark on each scale designating your self-perception.
2. Turn back to this page and take the Bioethical Profile Assessment. This twenty-five-item instrument contains both fact- and value-based questions. There are no right or wrong answers, only honest or dishonest ones.
3. Put a second mark on each scale of the Bioethical Profile Chart, designating your assessment score. The distance between the two marks is your "value space." A short value space indicates a consistency between what you say and what you do; you possess a great deal of self-knowledge. A large value space indicates a sizable gap between your self-image and your actual actions. Regardless of the size of your value space, the material in this volume is designed to help you clarify your personal values and to provide you with the important analytical information (e.g., legal, political, ethical) needed to make good bioethical decisions.

Confucius, the great Chinese bioethicist, knew quite a bit about threatening opportunities. It was he who wrote, "All great journeys begin with the first step." In a life filled with bioethical decisions, knowing ourselves is that big first step.

BIOETHICAL PROFILE ASSESSMENT

Circle the *one* answer that comes nearest to representing your best response; add the points and enter the totals in the appropriate spaces.

CHAPTER II. THE DOCTOR–PATIENT RELATIONSHIP

1. I seek second medical opinions
   0. never.
   1. seldom.

    2. frequently.

2. I believe that iatrogenic (i.e. physician-caused) disease is
    0. an insignificant problem.
    1. a limited, but real, problem.
    2. a significant problem.

3. When I need a new doctor or specialist, I
    0. pick one from the Yellow Pages.
    1. rely on my current doctor.
    2. research it as if my life depended on it.

4. Compared to other professions, I trust doctors
    0. much more.
    1. about the same.
    2. much less.

5. I keep my own medical and drug records
    0. never.
    1. catch-as-catch-can.
    2. as complete as possible.

TOTAL SCORE FOR CHAPTER II SCALE ____

CHAPTER III. ALLOCATING MEDICAL RESOURCES

6. I donate blood
    0. never.
    1. once a year.
    2. more than once a year.

7. The English system of socialized medicine
    0. has little to recommend it.
    1. has some good points.
    2. should be copied in the United States.

8. I support medical charities (e.g., Heart Fund, MDA)
    0. never.
    1. occasionally.
    2. frequently.

9. Government spending on health is
    0. too much.
    1. about right.
    2. too little.

10. Regarding organ donor cards, I

0. don't have one.
1. am considering it.
2. have one.

TOTAL SCORE FOR CHAPTER III SCALE ____

CHAPTER IV. LIFE AND DEATH

11. I believe the death penalty is
    0. needed as a deterrent.
    1. justified in special circumstances.
    2. never justified.
12. Regarding a living will, I
    0. have one.
    1. intend to write one.
    2. don't have one and don't intend to write one.
13. The decision to "pull the plug" should be made by
    0. next of kin.
    1. doctors.
    2. courts.
14. Regarding right-to-life groups, I
    0. don't belong to one.
    1. would consider joining one.
    2. belong to one.
15. I believe suicide is
    0. the sole right of the individual.
    1. justified in certain circumstances.
    2. never justified.

TOTAL SCORE FOR CHAPTER IV SCALE ____

CHAPTER V. EXPERIMENTATION WITH HUMAN BEINGS

16. When given a prescription, I
    0. take it as prescribed without any questions.
    1. occasionally ask a question.
    2. ask both doctor and pharmacist about alternatives and side effects.
17. Biomedical testing on animals is
    0. necessary to protect humans.
    1. justified only in certain circumstances.
    2. arrogant speciesism on the part of humans.

18. When I'm asked to participate in a survey,
    0. I comply.
    1. I ask questions.
    2. I refuse.
19. Prisoners should be able to participate in drug trials
    0. as part of their punishment.
    1. as a trade for prison time.
    2. only if they are truly informed and not coerced.
20. In my home medicine chest I have
    0. more than 20 over-the-counter drugs.
    1. between 10 and 20 over-the-counter drugs.
    2. fewer than 10 over-the-counter drugs.

                    TOTAL SCORE FOR CHAPTER V SCALE ____

CHAPTER VI. GENETIC INTERVENTION AND REPRODUCTIVE TECHNOLOGIES

21. I use birth control devices
    0. never.
    1. usually.
    2. always.
22. Testing for genetically transmitted disease (e.g., sickle cell anemia, Tay-Sachs)
    0. will only lead to more abortions.
    1. is occasionally appropriate.
    2. is a great medical advance.
23. Regarding sex selection of a child, my spouse and I
    0. would never try it.
    1. might try it.
    2. have tried it.
24. Couples who can't conceive should
    0. adopt.
    1. try limited intervention (e.g., fertility drugs).
    2. keep trying, using new technologies (e.g., *in vitro* fertilization).
25. Regarding genetic screening, I
    0. would never try it.
    1. have considered it.

2. have done it.

TOTAL SCORE FOR CHAPTER VI SCALE ____

BIOETHICAL PROFILE CHART

CHAPTER II. THE DOCTOR–PATIENT RELATIONSHIP

0	5	10
doctor knows best		patient knows best

CHAPTER III. ALLOCATING MEDICAL RESOURCES

0	5	10
medical care is a privilege		medical care is a right

CHAPTER IV. LIFE AND DEATH

0	5	10
quality of life has highest priority		maintaining life has highest priority

CHAPTER V. EXPERIMENTATION WITH HUMAN BEINGS

0	5	10
medical establishment acts in the public's best interest		public must always be completely informed

CHAPTER VI. GENETIC INTERVENTION AND REPRODUCTIVE TECHNOLOGIES

0	5	10
shouldn't fool with Mother Nature		science can make a significant contribution

PUBLIC VALUES: FROM FACTS TO JUDGMENTS

If bioethical decision-making involved only private, subjective values, society would be facing few bioethical dilemmas. Instead of creating so much social turmoil, many of the great issues of our day (e.g., abortion, the use of reproductive technologies, euthanasia) would simply evaporate. Rather than being the foci of intense debates, these issues would be resolved by appealing to each individual's personal preferences. Ethics in general, and bioethics in particular, would be no more difficult or contentious than deciding on your favorite flavor of ice cream.

As inviting as this might be, the ethical theory called *personal relativism*, the belief that the correctness of an action is a mere consequence of its approval by a single individual (i.e., "I believe in action x, so action x must be ethically right"), creates more problems than it solves. First, many bioethical problems are not personal at all, they involve every member of society. The right to health care, the use of human beings in biomedical experimentation, and the propriety of genetic engineering are issues that cannot be adequately dealt with at the level of personal choice. Second, such a theory has no way of resolving the inevitable disputes between individuals with different beliefs. And, third, the words "right" and "wrong" as employed in law, ethics, and moral theory certainly mean more than "I believe in x." Private, subjective values are the place from which we should begin our bioethical thinking, but they cannot also be the final destination.

Personal relativism has often seemed appealing, especially during the "Me decade" of the 1970s, because of the widely misunderstood nature of value judgments. This misunderstanding may be encapsulated as the *fallacy of valuation*: if there is no one correct answer, then all answers must be equally correct; if there is no one group of experts who can give the correct answer, then everyone's opinion must be equally valid. The foundation for this fallacy is an erroneous view of the distinction between facts and values.

For many, values (or value judgments) are always subjective. They are mere matters of opinion that are inherently unreliable and open to bias. This belief about values is generally contrasted with the belief that facts must be objective, reliable, and confirmable. For someone holding this view, the world of information is comprised only of subjective values and objective facts. But the problem with this simple dichotomy is that it totally neglects one of our most important forms of information, the *public value statement*—a judgment of worth or merit that is supportable by objective fact.

Anyone who has read *Consumer Reports* is familiar with the logical form of public value statements: the Sportmobile is the best car in its class, the ZapIt microwave oven is a best buy, the EZsound speaker is significantly lower in quality than other speakers in its price range. No one can doubt that these are value claims—claims regarding worth and merit—and no one can doubt that they are much different from mere matters of personal preference.

Less obvious, but no less important, is the use science (that supposed bastion of fact) makes of value judgments: the special theory of relativity is the best explanation of space–time phenomena, there is a good chance of rain tomorrow, the most likely explanation of acid rain is industrial pollution. Whether the scientist's task is theory construction, prediction, or explanation, public value judgments have an important role to play in our quest for scientific knowledge and technological progress.

The current creationist argument against the theory of evolution is just one example of the confused thinking that can occur when the importance of public value judgments in the scientific domain is overlooked. In arguing that evolution is "just a theory" and "not a fact," the creationists wish to conclude that the theory must be only a matter of opinion. But a well-supported theory, like the theory of evolution or the germ theory of disease, is justified by an interlocking web of hundreds of independent facts. As such, it is much more likely to be correct than any single fact in isolation.

This point is made even clearer when one considers that facts themselves may not even be value neutral. According to some philosophers of science, the very act of observation itself is value laden. For them, believing that observation is divorced from values requires a belief in the *doctrine of immaculate perception*—the idea that observational facts exist independently from each other and from the theories that support them.

Finally, and most importantly for bioethics, medicine deals almost exclusively in value judgments: that rash is probably eczema, the best drug for the treatment of diarrhea is Low-Flow, you have a 90 percent chance for a complete recovery. Although there are certainly differences between the public value claims for a good automobile, a good theory, and a good diagnosis, they all share the same crucial feature that serves to sharply distinguish them from private value choices: they are all justified by factual information. We can give good reasons in support of public value claims.

Just how we bridge the gap between facts and values is a key element in bioethical thinking. In fact, it is also so much a part of everyday life that few of us ever stop to analyze exactly how we do it. Whether it's only choosing a tomato at the market, or selecting a company to work for, or deciding along with your doctor which therapy to undertake, we live in a sea of value judgments. The interesting point is that whether it's tomatoes or medical treatments, the valuing process remains much the same.

Although it is only within the past few years that the human valuing process has become an object of scientific study, a simplified model of how we make value judgments has begun to emerge:

1. *Identify the criteria of merit*—select those features that seem germane to assessing performance. For example, in evaluating the Sportmobile we might consider gas mileage, acceleration, braking distance, and expected rate of

repair, among others. Quite clearly, the more comprehensive the list of criteria, the more accurate the evaluation. At this stage of the valuing process, expert knowledge of factual information is crucial. One difference between a simply adequate doctor and a good doctor is the number of possible diagnoses and treatment options that he considers. It is also one reason why, in an era of exploding medical information, it is often wise to consult a specialist for a second opinion.

2. *Weight the criteria of merit*—decide on the relative importance of each criterion for your specific needs. It is at this stage that private and public values meet. Some individuals may consider economy of operation the key criterion and give gas mileage a double weighting. Others might be more interested in performance and simply reject any automobile that failed to go from 0 to 60 mph in under ten seconds. Still others might have a more complicated view of the matter and choose to weight the four stated criteria as a mathematical relationship (e.g., 10:2:2:5, mileage is five times as important as acceleration and braking and twice as important as rate of repair).

In the case of medical care, some individuals might put a premium on sanctity of life and be willing to undergo any treatment that had even the smallest chance of prolonging life. Others might value quality of life more highly and reject certain treatments (e.g., chemotherapy) that could severely limit that quality. By combining personal values and objective facts, we arrive at a weighted-criteria of merit scale.

3. *Collect the relevant data*—assemble the facts that correspond to the weighted criteria of merit. In the case of the Sportmobile, this might involve driving the car yourself, or relying on published figures, or talking to Sportmobile owners. The results of these data-collection efforts might determine that the car gets 35 mpg, accelerates from 0 to 60 mph in 10.2 seconds, brakes from 50 to 0 mph in 165 feet, and has an above-average rate of repair.

In the medical context, collecting information usually means talking to doctors or other health professionals, contacting a special medical organization like the heart or cancer fund, or consulting a reference book to find out about the side effects of a drug, or the relative survival rates of two different forms of treatment, or the effectiveness of different forms of contraception. Again, this step benefits from expert knowledge. The more accurate the data we collect, the more likely it is that our evaluation will be sound.

4. *Prepare a performance profile*—combine the weighted criteria of merit with the collected data in order to determine how well the object being evaluated meets your needs. This stage of the process is strictly mechanical. It simply involves charting the assembled facts (e.g., Sportmobile acceleration is 10.2) against the weighted merit scale (e.g., disregard any automobile that fails to accelerate from 0 to 60 mph in under ten seconds). Whether the object being evaluated is a car, a drug, or a personal physician, this step synthesizes the information generated in steps 1–3.

5. *Compare performance profiles*—repeat steps 1–4 for each of the objects under consideration. The object with the strongest overall performance profile is the best choice.

This procedure may seem tedious, but it is a procedure we carry out almost subconsciously every day. Usually, we feel no need to follow it in a lockstep manner. An experienced shopper has internalized so much information that choosing a ripe tomato seems almost intuitive. But in the case of bioethical thinking, the stakes are much higher than salad-making, and the information to be assessed is much more difficult to grasp. It then becomes essential that we consciously identify the legal and medical facts, objectively assess the public value claims, consult our private values, and combine them all into a good bioethical decision that we can support with reasons and use as a guide for our actions.

As the result of performing a public valuing procedure, we are often able to select the best choice from among competing options; which insurance plan to purchase, the best method of treating an ulcer, whom to choose as a personal physician. Many times, our thinking about medical care need go no further than determining efficacy and cost effectiveness.

Sometimes, however, the questions that need answering do not end with the selection of a choice based solely on worth or merit. Bioethical thinking also involves choices that must consider the ethics—the rightness or wrongness—of certain choices or actions. For example, it is a well-justified public value claim that laetrile is ineffective in treating cancer. Does it follow that anyone offering laetrile for sale is unethical? Is someone who is using laetrile acting unethically? Should the government promulgate a public policy that bans the sale of laetrile? Alternatively, we also know that smoking is a cause of lung cancer. Does that mean that farming tobacco is unethical? Is it unethical to ask a health insurer to pay for cancer care when that condition was self-induced through smoking? Is the government's policy of tobacco supports unethical? The twin problems of determining private ethical conduct and deciding when the government should regulate that conduct through public policies are the most difficult and central problems in bioethics.

PRIVATE ETHICS AND PUBLIC POLICIES

The practice of medicine has always involved the practice of ethics. Almost 2500 years ago, the Hippocratic Oath established specific rules of conduct (e.g., "Whatever house I may visit, I will come for the benefit of the sick, remaining free of all intentional injustice, of all mischief, and in particular of sexual relations with both male and female persons, be they free or slaves.") that a physician was expected to follow. As the earliest professional code of medical ethics, the Hippocratic Oath was concerned solely with the relationship between doctors and patients (see Chapter II for a thorough discussion of the doctor–patient relationship). There were no canons of behavior suggesting that the physician's ethical responsibilities might extend beyond his patient, and there were certainly no indications that the state might have some bioethical rights or duties. The oath's major substantive legacy is the establishment of two main ethical principles of physician conduct toward a patient that have survived to this day: the duty to benefit the patient and the obligation to avoid doing him harm.

Bioethics remained strictly focused on this doctor–patient relationship until well into this century. Then, within a period of roughly fifty years, two social revolutions occurred that forced its scope to widen dramatically. The first revolution greatly empowered the medical profession; the second increased the importance of medicine for all citizens. As a result of these revolutions, bioethics is concerned today with much more than the singular relationship between doctors and their patients. It is also concerned with the many and varied societal consequences of a multi-billion-dollar medical enterprise. Bioethics has been transformed from a strictly private concern into one that includes many prominent public questions.

The first, little-noticed revolution took place early in this century and resulted in an enormous increase in power and prestige for the medical community. Doctors now have so much influence and importance in our society that it is difficult to remember that not so long ago the barber and the surgeon were one and the same person. As with any powerful institution, the effects of wielding that power often have societal consequences. To its credit, the American Medical Association has recognized that medical ethics must now go beyond the doctor–patient relationship, and it has codified this responsibility in its 1980 Principles of Medical Ethics: "The medical profession has long subscribed to a body of ethical statements developed primarily for the benefit of the patient. As a member of this profession, a physician must recognize responsibility not only to patients, but also to society, to other health professionals, and to self."

The second revolution, the medicalization of society, has been greatly noticed. Whether it's the rising bill for national health care, the new treatment options that have developed as a consequence of spectacular medical technologies, or the perceived right of every citizen to adequate health care, no one can doubt that medicine now plays a central role in our society (see Chapter III for a discussion of this revolution and its consequences for our health care system). But that central role, coupled with the state's interest in it, is creating new bioethical dilemmas that Hippocrates could not have even imagined.

Although physicians have always had to deal with death, a dramatic new definition of death linked to brain function, coupled with some remarkable technological advances, has fostered a whole group of totally unexpected bioethical enigmas: Does the prospective quality of life of some "born at risk" infants ever justify not treating them and letting them die? Should there be a public policy that allows certain terminally ill patients to be euthanized? If we now have an accepted definition of the end of life, why don't we also have an accepted definition of the beginning of life? Wouldn't such a definition solve the abortion debate? Issues of life and death are discussed in Chapter IV.

Medicine has become a modern science only in this century and primarily because it developed a process of experimentation that resulted in a great increase in its knowledge base. Yet medicine's use of experiments that involve human beings raises a whole different set of bioethical problems: How can a single physician balance his responsibilities to his patients with his desire to create knowledge through research? What steps must be taken to insure that all participants in human experiments are truly informed volunteers? Who should decide how the billions of dollars targeted for biomedical research are actually spent? Problems concerning experimentation with human beings are discussed in Chapter V.

Finally, recent discoveries explaining the genetic basis of all life have precipitated bioethical issues that no one could have imagined even a few decades ago: Does the state have any right to information concerning its citizens' genetic constitution? Will the use of reproductive technologies like *in vitro* fertilization really lead to a "Brave New World"? Should there be any public policies limiting the scope and nature of genetic engineering? These issues are treated in Chapter VI, "Genetic Intervention and Reproductive Technologies."

With so many diverse and seemingly unique issues, it may seem as if there is no universal strategy to guide our bioethical thinking. Fortunately, however, this complex of issues shares two common features that enable us to generalize our bioethical thinking skills. The first feature is procedural: it is the nature of all ethical deliberation to begin with a set of closely held, core beliefs (e.g., truthtelling, promise-keeping), and to proceed to reason by applying them to general principles of action (e.g., the right action is the one that produces the greatest good for the greatest number, do unto others as you would have them do unto you). Finally, we apply some specific rule of conduct (e.g., thou shalt not kill, you must tell the truth when under oath in a court of law) to bridge the gap between core beliefs, general ethical principles, and individual cases and actions. Like public value judgments, ethical judgments also incorporate our private values (i.e., closely held core beliefs). But by following this justification procedure, we are also able to go beyond our personal beliefs and provide reasons for our ethical judgments.

The second shared feature is substantive. Although the issues in this volume may seem unrelated, their dilemmatic nature may be traced directly to one of three major unresolved themes that underscore all of bioethical thinking:

1. *Patient Decision-making*: Are there any limits to a patient's autonomy? Is it ever ethical for a physician or the state to act paternalistically toward a patient? This theme revolves about the tension between respecting a patient's decision to do whatever he perceives to be in his own best interest and overriding that decision in order to promote the patient's physical well-being.

2. *Physician Responsibility*: Can a physician be both a scientist and a doctor? How can a physician choose between the health needs of an individual patient and the health needs of the larger society? The tension in this theme is between the physician's responsibility to his patient and his responsibility to the profession, the state of medical knowledge, and the greater society.

3. *Societal Justice*: Is it fair if all citizens have access to equal amounts of health care? How are decisions to allocate scarce resources to be made? The tension in this theme is created by two competing views of social justice: first, that justice is obtained simply by treating all people equally; second, that justice is obtained by rewarding those who deserve it

There may be no definitive resolution to any of these themes, and it is certainly impossible to resolve them in the abstract. But bioethical thinking proceeds on a case-by-case basis, and, as the cases in this volume demonstrate, it is often possible to determine the proper course of action given a particular set of circumstances. Ultimately, this is the final, important message when it comes to doing our own bioethical thinking: our solutions do not have to be universal; they only have to reflect our own personal needs and situations.

II

THE DOCTOR–PATIENT RELATIONSHIP

HIGH-TECH scanners, artificial hearts, and "magic bullet" inoculations may all be front-page news, but they are far from the most vital elements in quality medical care. Even though we are living in the "golden age of medical technology," it is comforting to know that an old-fashioned interpersonal skill over which we exert some control— the communication between doctor and patient—is still the most important medical commodity. No machine can replace your brain's ability to monitor your body. No machine can substitute for the richness of language when it comes to giving a comprehensive description of your physical condition. And no machine can match the ability of a skilled clinician when it comes to making diagnoses based on the information you provide. Your ability to communicate completely and precisely with your doctor is a necessary condition for receiving quality medical care.

But what about your doctor's obligation to provide you with information? After all, communication implies a two-way channel—it's meant to be dialogue, not monologue. Traditionally, doctors have been quite reticent to discuss medical information with their patients. Whether it was because they felt that their patients wouldn't understand, or believed that the patients didn't want to know, or be-cause they just didn't want to take the time, many doctors did not accept a doctor–patient dialogue as part of their professional duties.

Today, this attitude is beginning to change. As the consumer movement has made inroads into medicine, patients have begun to demand more information. Lawsuits brought by patients have resulted in doctors now having certain legal obligations regarding the disclosure of medical information. And medical research has shown that the time doctors spend talking and explaining to patients has therapeutic value. Yet this change is not without controversy.

As the historical function of the doctor–patient relationship evolves, three issues surrounding a patient's informational rights are at the core of that change. The first issue is *confidentiality*: when, if ever, is a doctor justified in revealing your medical information to a third party? The second issue is *informed consent*: what procedural information must a doctor provide to a patient? The third issue is *therapeutic information*: what diagnostic information may a doctor conceal from a patient, and under what conditions? As the cases below illustrate, these questions are not so easy to resolve. Yet the answers cannot be found in any medical textbook. The issues are all ethical, not medical.

CASE 1: THE DOCTOR AS INFORMANT

Gina F. is a seventeen-year-old woman who goes to a Planned Parenthood clinic seeking a prescription for oral contraceptives. While at the clinic, she signs a form authorizing Planned Parenthood to notify her doctor that she is taking birth control pills. The doctor, without receiving her permission, repeats this information to her parents. Is this a breach of doctor–patient confidentiality? Where should the line between a patient's right to confidentiality and a doctor's responsibility to reveal a confidence be drawn?

CASE 2: THE DOCTOR AS DECISION ARROGATOR

Sally G. is a sixty-three-year-old woman considered by her physician to be in the high-risk group for respiratory disease: she is underweight, suffers from mild heart disease, and is a smoker. When the Centers for Disease Control announces that a new flu strain may be epidemic this coming winter, and that a vaccine is available, Sally's doctor advises her to be inoculated. What information, if any, must the doctor provide Sally about the procedure? May the doctor unilaterally decide to inoculate her, or must Sally give her informed consent before being vaccinated?

CASE 3: THE DOCTOR AS PREVARICATOR

Barney D. is a fifty-two-year-old man who is admitted to the hospital after suffering a mild stroke. During routine surgery to remove the pressure on his brain, an inoperable, malignant cerebral tumor is discovered. While the patient is in the recovery room, the surgeon approaches the family with the bad news: the patient has no more than six months to live. The family pleads with him not to tell the patient of his condition, arguing that he is the kind of man who reacts to stress by "denying reality" and that telling him he has terminal cancer will only serve to make his last months miserable. Is not telling the patient the truth about his condition acceptable medical practice? Where should the line between a patient's right to be told the truth and a doctor's responsibility to withhold it be drawn?

These three cases all demonstrate an important fact ignored by most of the media: bioethical problems did not develop spontaneously along with kidney dialysis, or organ transplants, or with the advent of test-tube babies. As long as there have been doctors and patients, there have been bioethical questions regarding confidentiality and patients' informational rights. While the new technologies have certainly accelerated the growth of bioethical problems, the issues surrounding the doctor–patient relationship have always formed the values environment for the entirety of medical practice.

At the heart of this environment is the tension between responsibilities and rights—both on the part of the doctor to the patient and, more recently, on that of the patient to the doctor. Furthermore, the model we use to explicate this relationship—

Paternal: we entrust the doctor to act in our best interests; or

Professional: the doctor follows a set of principles generated by the profession; or

Participatory: both the doctor and the patient have specified areas of rights and responsibilities—

will have important ramifications for the law and public policy, as well as for the private expectations of a patient toward his physician. But these models are more than abstractions. They are descriptions of the types of relationships you may choose to have with your doctor, and that choice is yours to make.

The ramifications of a particular choice are demonstrated by the case of the seventeen-year-old seeking oral contraceptives. If the relationship she had with her doctor was based on a paternalism model—the patient gives up some possible rights and endows the physician with full responsibility to use his judgment and ability to decide what will best benefit the patient—and if the doctor had some reason for telling her parents (e.g., he thought that her not telling them would develop into a neurosis), then it would seem that no confidentiality had been broken.

Alternatively, if she and her doctor had functioned using

a professional model—the rights of the patient and the responsibilities of the physician are stipulated by the professional code—it seems quite likely that a confidence was breached. This is because the relevant portion of the International Code of Medical Ethics states: "A doctor shall preserve absolute secrecy on all he knows about his patient because of the confidence entrusted in him."[1] A doctor who subscribed to this code would clearly be acting in bad faith by disclosing information about Gina's medical history. Yet, other medical codes of ethics (e.g., the AMA's Principles of Medical Ethics) are not nearly so strict in protecting the patient's right to confidentiality. Any patient who wanted to rely on a professional code of ethics to protect his or her rights would be well served by inquiring about just which code the doctor followed.

If these models seem helpful in adjudicating doctor–patient disputes, they may become less useful when dealing with the exogenous factors of law and public policy. Suppose you and your physician decide to use a participatory model—both doctor and patient specify their specific rights and responsibilities, with the mutual goal of achieving optimal patient care—and you emphasize the need for confidentiality. What should your doctor do when you show up with a case of scarlet fever? By law, it is a contagious disease and must be reported to the Public Health Service; yet such a report may violate your right to confidentiality. Does the doctor's responsibility to a greater public good override his responsibility to an individual patient? In this case, most people would agree that since the patient is not harmed by the disclosure, the doctor's responsibility is to the larger society. But what is the proper decision when the disclosure might also harm the patient (e.g., in the case of psychiatric illness)?

And what about cases where the reason for the law seems less than morally compelling? What if our seventeen-year-old had a participatory relationship with her physician and a law was passed (as almost happened in the Reagan Administration) requiring that all birth control prescriptions to minors be reported to their parents? Should the doctor betray a confidence to obey the law? Even when the law seems to be of no medical value? Is a perceived greater moral purpose (i.e., the promise of confidentiality) adequate reason to disobey a law?

This particular example becomes even more convoluted in our dual system of public and private medicine. Presumably, the Reagan Administration's policy would have been binding only on physicians practicing in public facilities receiving federal funds. Does that mean that private codes of ethical conduct, such as that between physician and patient, are subject to public policies? Does it make sense for the same doctor to treat his private patients differently from his public ones?

Finally, even trickier questions may arise when the law is not clear but withholding confidential information may harm society. Suppose you are diagnosed as suffering from a homicidal psychiatric illness. Should your doctor tell the authorities? Should he attempt to have you institutionalized? If this seems farfetched, remember that the psychiatrist who treated John W. Hinckley, Ronald Reagan's would-be assassin, was sued for not taking steps to restrain his patient. As in all matters bioethical, a patient's right to confidentiality is not as simple as it first seems. Just where to draw the confidential line and how are fully treated in the "Confidentiality" section of this chapter.

If determining what a physician may tell *about* a patient seems confusing, then determining what the doctor should tell *to* the patient is just as problematic. It is also a much more pervasive problem, since questions regarding informational rights arise in almost every doctor–patient communication. In particular, these questions about a patient's right to information occur in three separate contexts:

1. *Informed consent*—the right to have fully described, and the right to give prior agreement before the performance of, medical procedures.
2. *Therapeutic information*—the right to be told the truth regarding your medical condition and prospects for treatment.
3. *Access to records*—the right to study, and to some extent control, your own medical records.

Each of these distinct, informational rights comes with its own set of bioethical dilemmas.

Informed consent, not surprisingly, consists of two distinct rights: the right to consent and your right to information. The principle that patients must give their consent before a physician may treat them was eloquently stated in 1914 by Justice Benjamin Cardozo: "Every human being of adult years and sound mind has a right to determine what shall be done with his own body; and a surgeon who performs an operation without his patient's consent commits an assault, for which he is liable in damages."[2] Case law since that time has developed four tests of valid consent:

1. Consent is given only for a specific, described procedure. A woman who consents to a breast biopsy has *not* consented to a mastectomy, even if the biopsy proves malignant.
2. Consent must be voluntary. Patients must not be coerced into giving their consent.
3. The patient who gives consent must be legally and mentally competent to do so. In cases where this is impossible (e.g., children, mental illness), the court may assign a responsible adult to represent the patient's best interests.
4. Consent must be based on adequate information. Patients must be able to give *informed* consent.

It is this last condition, the condition that consent must be illuminated by information, that has led to a number of engaging and difficult legal and bioethical questions: Does the right to information imply that a patient must understand his course of treatment, and what is the physician's responsibility to provide and explain the medical options and outcomes? Because patients don't have the medical expertise of doctors, the right of informed consent presents some curious policy problems: How much meaningful information is accessible to the patient? Who should decide this—doctors, lay panels, the courts? What right do bodies external to the doctor–patient relationship (e.g., the courts) have to impose themselves on the therapeutic relationship? These questions, as well as a full discussion of the patient's right to informed consent, are included in the "Informed Consent" section of this chapter.

The right to therapeutic information is less involved with law and public policy but virtually encrusted with bioethical choices. Take the case of the fifty-two-year-old man with the brain tumor. His doctor really has three choices: reveal the diagnosis, withhold the diagnosis, or distort the diagnosis. Since there is no relevant professional code to guide his decision, and since the law has not yet entered this realm of the doctor–patient relationship, what criteria should the responsible physician use in deciding such cases?

It is an easy cop-out to state that the doctor–patient relationship should be guided by truth-telling, and that it is the patient's right to know and the doctor's responsibility to tell. It's a cop-out because it ducks all the hard questions. First, as in the case of informed consent, medical truth is not always so easy to ascertain (e.g., how can the physician know that the patient has only six months to live?). Even in cases where the truth is evident, it is not always clear how much information a patient may comprehend. Second, even when the state of medical knowledge is certain, the consequences of disclosing that information may be unknown. In the tumor case, the doctor may wish to conceal or distort his diagnosis because he doesn't wish to confuse his patient, or cause unnecessary pain or discomfort, or leave the patient without hope. While all those motivations are noble, the real issue is whether the physician has the right to make the decision to withhold or distort information.

If the doctor and the patient were functioning under a paternalistic model, then the doctor would clearly have the right to make such a decision for the patient. Conversely, if a participatory model with an emphasis on honesty were followed, it would be the doctor's responsibility to disclose the entire truth. When there is no such doctor–patient understanding, the patient can only rely on the physician's responsibility to do what he feels is therapeutically proper.

The issue of therapeutic information is also involved in two special cases far removed from the solitary doctor–patient relationship. The first of these is the use of placebos (i.e., nonefficacious drugs) in the clinical trial research of new pharmaceuticals. Is the development of a new drug an acceptable reason for not telling patients the complete truth about the medicine they are taking? This issue is discussed fully in Chapter V, "Experimentation with Human Beings." The second instance occurs in malpractice cases when one doctor may be called to testify (tell the truth) about the negligence of another health care professional. Does a doctor's responsibility to tell the truth extend beyond mere therapeutic information? Although the sheer number of these questions may seem formidable, answering them revolves about a single key— your personal view of your own informational needs. Because of this, the "Therapeutic Information" section of this chapter provides all the information necessary to clarify your needs.

The third informational right, the patient's right to his own medical records, is a relatively new "right" growing out of the consumer movement of the 1970s. Just as that movement argued that citizens had a right to see their credit records stored in computer banks, and any files the government might keep about them, so its members also argued that patients had a right of access to their medical records. Although it is clear that the analogy between credit records and medical records is not complete, the justification for access is quite similar in two instances: first, to check the accuracy of personal data; second, to be able to make a knowledgeable decision about authorizing the release of your records to a third party. Medical records, however, can also serve to help the patient to make informed treatment decisions, as well as help him judge the quality of his care. With four strong reasons for access, why has this "right" been so long in developing?

The medical community's major argument against wide-open access is that patients are not equipped to understand their medical records and may become alarmed if the information is not properly explained to them. The AMA's position is that patients should be allowed to see only those portions of the record that their doctor approves. These arguments are quite similar to arguments made regarding the disclosure of therapeutic information, and they are fully discussed in that section.

Yet, unlike the issues surrounding therapeutic information, which are strictly ethical, the right to medical records has moved into the arenas of public policy and law. The best-known recommendations regarding access and confidentiality were devised by the Privacy Protection Study Commission, which found:

- That patients be allowed access to their records and be permitted to copy, amend, and correct them.
- That access to records compiled as part of the treatment process be based clearly on a need to know.
- That no patient-identifiable information be disclosed to third parties without patient authoriza-

tion, except for patient care audit purposes or to meet the requirements of statute or court order.
• That disclosures to third parties include only the information needed for the purpose of the disclosure.
• That each time information is disclosed to a third party a copy of the authorization of such disclosure be made part of the record.[3]

Unfortunately, from the perspective of those seeking greater access, these recommendations have not become national law. Your right to access is currently dependent on state statute, and only about ten states currently have laws protecting some kind of patient right to medical records. Because of this lack of statutory power, patients interested in their medical records must seek out physicians willing to share that information with them.

Understanding the mechanics of any relationship always requires viewing it from the perspectives of both parties, and it is no different with the doctor–patient relationship. Patients must try to understand the doctor's perspective if they are to secure their own rights. Today, this means understanding that doctors' responsibilities extend far beyond the single doctor–patient relationship. Physicians may be researchers, or consultants to pharmaceutical manufacturers, or industrial doctors in the employ of big corporations, and each of these roles carries with it responsibilities which may conflict with individual patient care.

The research role is particularly tricky for the physician, since it casts him into two competing roles: the doctor as healer versus the doctor as medical scientist. In the first role, the goal is treating the patient; in the second, the goal is medical knowledge. The infamous Tuskegee Study on syphilis, in which black men were allowed to suffer without treatment for thirty years so that doctors could obtain a better understanding of the effects of the disease, is a classic example of disregarding patient care for a supposed higher goal. No one would expect such a flagrant violation of a patient's rights today, but who can say that a doctor's participation in a research project would have no effect on his medical judgment? Furthermore, in a society justifiably proud of its medical achievements, is it ever acceptable to sacrifice some individual patient's rights during the course of research so that the greater society may benefit? Because medical research is so pervasive, the entirety of Chapter V is dedicated to the legal, policy, and bioethical questions surrounding that complicated process.

Even if your doctor is never involved in research, there are still many instances in which he may face the trade-off between your rights and the rights of society. One such instance is the aforementioned confidentiality issue: When is a physician justified in betraying a patient's confidence for a societal good? A related issue is this: When is a physician justified in betraying a societal trust for an individual patient's good? Just as a doctor has a general obligation to tell his patient the truth, so he has the same general obligation to society. Yet, during the Vietnam War, it was common knowledge that sympathetic doctors would write letters to draft boards stating reasons for declaring their patients ineligible to serve. Was this acceptable behavior? Is the answer to that question contingent on your view of the war? Are physicians ever justified in lying to protect their patients?

Society is not the only entity in competition with individual patients' rights. Physicians are often employed directly by corporations, or indirectly as consultants, and these arrangements may lead to conflict of interest. For example, imagine the case of a professional football player who sustained minor knee damage in midseason. He has two treatment courses: have immediate surgery and miss the remainder of the year, or use a brace, physical therapy, and painkillers to play out the season before having the operation. Can he really rely on the club physician for unbiased advice? Can a doctor who consults for one drug company be expected to be completely objective when it comes to prescribing a competing drug from another manufacturer? In cases such as these, it is probably prudent to expect that doctors will act just like other individuals—that vested interest plays a role in decision-making whether it is acknowledged or not.

Finally, some of the most difficult questions surrounding physician responsibility involve trading off the rights of individual patients. One classically tough issue is *triage*—making decisions regarding the order of patient treatment. Is the emergency room doctor justified when he stops treating your scalp laceration to begin treating my broken leg? Less traditional, but no less wrenching, are cases involving sexually transmitted diseases. Is a family physician obliged to treat the husband if his wife contracts gonorrhea? Can he do this without betraying the wife's confidence? It is only by understanding the physician's dilemma in cases like these that you, the patient, can secure your rights.

It is your responsibility as the patient to engage your doctor in a dialogue to determine the type of therapeutic relationship you will share. Even today, many doctors are uncomfortable dealing with the personal aspects of medical care. Since it's your health at stake, it's your obligation to begin the discussion. Good medical care involves more than competent technique. It also involves trust and understanding. While the former is the sole responsibility of your doctor, you must share the responsibility for the latter.

CONFIDENTIALITY

CONCEPT: Confidentiality is a medical and legal doctrine which supports the principle that the communications between a doctor and a patient are to remain private and inviolable. The physician's code of ethics has stipulated confidentiality since the Hippocratic Oath: "Whatever, in connection with my professional practice, or not in connection with it, I see or hear, in the life of men, which ought not to be spoken abroad, I will not divulge, as reckoning that all such should be kept secret."[4] The legal basis for confidentiality is the privilege doctrine: the idea that certain relationships require privacy if they are to work (e.g., lawyer–client, priest–penitent, doctor–patient), and that this is fostered by forbidding in-court disclosure of the informational content of the relationship. But like other "absolute" rights in our society—freedom of speech (you can't shout "Fire!" in a crowded theater) or freedom of the press (you can't print the timetable of a troopship in the time of war)—the right of patient confidentiality also has practical limits. Just how to set those limits, and where exactly they are to be placed in order to balance the patient's right to confidentiality against society's need to know, is a continuing ethical and legal dilemma.

PRACTICE: 1984 may have come and gone, but the threat of a Big Brother society lingers. We live in what many have termed the Information Age, and it is clear that if knowledge is power, then power resides with those who have access to the most information. Whole industries from opinion polling and market research to credit banks and data bases make their living solely by providing their clients with special kinds of information. It sometimes seems as if information is considered an unadulterated social good. Far from fostering confidentiality, many laws and policies encourage the free flow of information.

Yet some consumer advocates and policy-makers have argued that too much information in the wrong hands may encourage a type of Big Brotherism (witness the long running debate over a national employment card). Because our cyberculture of computers, satellites, and other technologies has raised the communication, manipulation, and storage of information to a high art, lawmakers have determined that individuals have "informational rights" which need to be protected.

In order to accomplish this policy goal, two landmark federal laws were passed in the 1970s. The first of these, the Freedom of Information Act, gave individuals specific rights regarding access to government information. In this way, an informed citizenry may keep a check on the quantity and quality of information gathered by the government. The second, the Federal Privacy Act, put some limits on the type of personal information the government could collect. Such laws seem to steer a middle path between the advocates of an unlimited information flow and Justice Brandeis, who opined that an individual's right to be left alone is the most valued right of civilized people.

Set against this backdrop of our society's megaflow of information, the principle of doctor–patient confidentiality has a special, personal status. It recognizes that in order to foster communication regarding private, sensitive information, it may be necessary to severely limit its dissemination. The principle works as a sort of promise: in exchange for your frank and complete communication, the doctor (as society's agent) pledges to keep strict control over who may have access to your medical information. Just such a promise is implicit in the AMA's Principles of Medical Ethics: "A physician may not reveal the confidences entrusted to him in the course of medical attendance, or the deficiencies he may observe in the character of his patient, unless he is required to do so by law or unless it becomes necessary in order to protect the welfare of the individual or of the society."[5] In order to see how well society keeps this promise, as well as to determine your own views regarding the absolute limits of patient confidentiality, try role playing the doctor in each of the following three cases.

CASE 4: THE SOCIAL DISEASE

Sheila W. is a twenty-three-year-old secretary. Although she is sexually active, she is far from sexually promiscuous. After trying to self-medicate a vaginal itch for a few weeks, she visits her private physician, who diagnoses her as suffering from gonorrhea. In addition to treating her disease, should the doctor:

A. maintain strict confidentiality but counsel her about sexually transmitted diseases?
B. maintain doctor–patient confidentiality but require Sheila to contact her sexual partners so that they may seek treatment?
C. report Sheila's case to state public-health officials?

The doctor in this case has no choice: he must act in accord with answer C—report Sheila's case to state public-health officials. Although all states recognize the need to foster doctor–patient confidentiality, they also realize that certain types of individual patient health information are necessary in order to maintain the collective health of the greater society. Society's need for access to this information has led to laws *requiring* doctors to report the following types of information:

1. Infectious, contagious, or communicable diseases ranging from anthrax to whooping cough, and including venereal diseases. In fact, doctors need not be under the force of law to release confidential information when a

public danger exists. The landmark case upholding this principle, *Simonsen v. Swenson*,[6] was decided by the Nebraska Supreme Court in 1920 when it upheld a doctor's right to inform the community about a patient's case of syphilis.

2. Birth and death certificates. Although this information seems unexceptionable, public-health-policy battles are frequently fought over just what information is to be included on a birth certificate.[7] For example, is the marriage status of the mother and the father germane? Even though such policy decisions are not made by the delivering doctor, such decisions are one point of tension between the society's desire to build an all-inclusive health data base and an individual's desire to keep private matters private.

3. Cases of child abuse. The major difficulty with this reporting requirement lies in its execution, not its motivation. While we can all agree that physically abused children deserve protection, the diagnosis of such cases is still far from certain. This uncertainty (a medical fact) puts added strain on the doctor's ability to make a diagnosis (a value judgment), and on the ethical decision revolving about how probable the diagnosis need be before a child-abuse report is filed.

4. Cases in which weapons, especially guns, caused the wound. Again, the motivation for this law is clear, but its practice may be quite muddy (e.g., how to determine when a knife wound was the result of a fight rather than a slip).

In each of these four exceptions to the doctor–patient principle of confidentiality, society has made the judgment that it has more to gain from requiring the reporting of such information than it might lose by scaring off potential patients (e.g., if Sheila knew the law, she might continue to self-medicate rather than risk having her condition reported). While one can question that social calculus, or even question some of the ethical problems doctors may have in complying with the law, the law and its effect on the promise of confidentiality are beyond question: patients cannot expect personal information that has a direct bearing on the health of the greater society to be kept confidential.

CASE 5: THE PSYCHIATRIC CONFESSION

Charley C. is a twenty-two-year-old college senior. His girlfriend has recently terminated their relationship, and he has become quite depressed. While undergoing self-initiated therapy at the college counseling service, he repeatedly tells his psychiatrist of his intention to murder his ex-girlfriend. If the psychiatrist is quite convinced that Charley sincerely intends to carry out his threat, should he:

A. maintain confidentiality and try to solve Charley's problem through counseling sessions?
B. continue his therapeutic relationship but warn the campus police of Charley's intentions?
C. continue his therapeutic relationship but warn the ex-girlfriend of Charley's intentions?

Case 5 is a brief description of the influential *Tarasoff v. Board of Regents of the University of California* suit. In that case the California Supreme Court found that the psychiatrist (he was working at UC, hence the regents were sued) should have warned the ex-girlfriend (Tarasoff), who was ultimately killed when the threat was carried out:

> When a therapist determines, or pursuant to the standards of his profession should determine, that his patient presents a serious danger of violence to another, he incurs an obligation to use reasonable care to protect the intended victim against such danger. The discharge of this duty may require the therapist to take one or more various steps, depending upon the nature of the case. Thus it may call for him to warn the intended victim or others likely to apprise

the victim of danger, to notify the police, or to take whatever other steps are reasonably necessary under the circumstances...

We recognize the public interest in supporting effective treatment of mental illness and in protecting the rights of patients to privacy... and the consequent public importance of safeguarding the confidential character of psychotherapeutic communication. Against this interest, however, we must weigh the public interest in safety from violent assault... We conclude that [confidentiality] must yield to the extent to which disclosure is essential to avert dangers to others. The protective privilege ends where the public peril begins.[8]

Although the Tarasoff ruling is law only in California (two other states, New Jersey and Nebraska, have followed its rationale in reaching decisions), the case sent shock waves through the psychiatric community. The major concern was that such a disclosure rule would have a chilling effect on psychiatrist–patient relationships, leading to even more societal violence as potentially violent individuals eschewed counseling for fear of disclosure. Such thinking was evident in the court's dissenting opinion:

Until today's majority opinion, both legal and medical authorities have agreed that confidentiality is essential to effectively treat the mentally ill, and that imposing a duty on doctors to disclose patient threats to potential victims would greatly impair treatment...

Overwhelming policy considerations weigh against imposing a duty on psychotherapists to warn a potential victim against harm. While offering virtually no benefit to society, such a duty will frustrate psychiatric treatment, invade fundamental patient rights and increase violence.[9]

The Tarasoff case is important for two reasons. First, whereas the Simonsen case freed the physician from the confidentiality principle and allowed him to use his own judgment when he felt that the public was endangered, the Tarasoff case *compelled* him to breach confidentiality. Second, Tarasoff dealt with psychiatric, not somatic, information. The extension of the rule of law into such fragile relationships as that between psychiatrist and patient is viewed by some as a serious erosion of the principle of doctor–patient confidentiality.

CASE 6: THE HIGH HEADACHE

Donald B. is a forty-five-year-old sign painter. When he begins to suffer from headaches and spells of dizziness he seeks medical advice. The cause is diagnosed as migraine headaches—a condition for which there is really no cure or even much alleviation of symptoms. The doctor advises Donald to speak to his employer about changing his job, since a migraine episode seventy feet above a freeway could well be fatal. Donald brushes off the advice, saying he likes sign painting, doesn't want an office job, and is afraid he might even be fired if he lets his condition be known. Should the doctor:

A. maintain confidentiality and treat Donald as best he can?
B. contact Donald's wife and hope that she can convince him to seek a change of jobs?
C. contact the employer directly and try to get Donald a change of jobs?

There is no correct legal answer in this case. Because the welfare of the patient is the sole consideration, society has made no laws that prescribe the doctor's actions. This does not mean, however, that there is no correct ethical answer. The AMA's Principles of Medical Ethics allow the breach of confidentiality when "it becomes necessary in order to protect the welfare of the individual," and a doctor who followed those principles as an ethical guide would presumably be justified in contacting Donald's wife or employer.

Yet leaving such an important and controversial decision entirely to the doctor is an abrogation of the patient's responsibility to the doctor–patient relationship. In practice, the principle of confidentiality really revolves about three questions:

1. What types of information should be kept confidential?
2. What are the consequences of disseminating that information?
3. Who will control access to that information?

It should be clear that in all areas of doctor–patient communication except those prescribed by law, it is the patient who has the right and the responsibility to help answer these questions.

INFORMED CONSENT

CONCEPT: Informed consent is a legal doctrine which states that before patients are asked to agree to a risky or invasive diagnostic or treatment procedure, they are entitled to receive the following information: (1) a description of the procedure; (2) any alternatives to it, and their risks; (3) the risks of death or serious bodily disability from the procedure; (4) the probable results of the procedure, including any problems of recuperation and time of recuperation anticipated; and (5) anything else that is generally disclosed to patients who are asked to consent to the procedure. It is vital to note that informed consent is not educated consent. The medical profession need only disclose the above information; it is not required to make certain that the patient understands it. The doctrine of informed consent also has special applications to the refusal of treatment (Chapter IV), and the conduct of human experiments (Chapter V).

PRACTICE: Because informed consent is a legal and not a medical doctrine, it has grown from the body of case law. To find out just how good your legal instincts are, try playing the judge in each of these three famous informed-consent cases:

CASE 7: THE UNWANTED OPERATION

A patient consents to have a doctor perform an operation on her right ear. While she is anesthetized, the surgeon decides to operate on the left ear also. Although the operation is successful, the woman sues, arguing that the additional surgery amounts to battery (i.e., an offensive, intentional, unconsented-to touching of a person). As judge, would you:

A. dismiss the case, finding that the physician might be negligent but not guilty of battery?
B. find for the woman?
C. dismiss the case, since the physician acted in accord with best medical practice?

CASE 8: THE UNSTATED DANGER

A woman has undergone a mastectomy for breast cancer and has followed the surgery with cobalt radiation therapy. As a result of the therapy, she suffered injury to the skin, bone, and cartilage in her chest. Although the therapy was performed properly and without negligence, the radiologist did not inform the woman of the potential risks inherent in the procedure. She is suing for damages. As judge, would you:

   A. rule for the physician on grounds that the treatment was necessary and professionally handled?

   B. rule for the physician on grounds that the risk's potential was so small it did not require disclosure to the patient?

   C. rule for the patient on grounds that the physician was obligated to make a reasonable disclosure of the dangers within his knowledge?

CASE 9: THE ONE PERCENT RISK

The physician informs his patient, a nineteen-year-old suffering from back pain, as well as the patient's mother, that the indicated surgery is "no more serious than any other operation." The doctor does not mention that the procedure carries a one percent risk of paralysis. Following surgery, and a fall from his hospital bed, the youth suffers total paralysis from the waist down. He then sues for damages. As judge, would you:

   A. dismiss the case, finding the fall to be a contributing cause?

   B. find for the physician, since the disclosure of a one percent risk is not medically customary?

   C. find for the patient on grounds that his information needs should not be determined solely by physicians?

If you chose answers 7B, 8C, 9C, you're either a natural-born judge or you know quite a bit about informed consent. For the rest of you who didn't finish first in your law school class, here's the legal reasoning:

Case 7 is the *Mohr v. Williams* case dating all the way back to 1905.[10] It affirms that any surgeon who operates on a patient without permission is legally liable, even if the operation is successful. In such instances, any inquiry into medical need or negligent conduct is irrelevant, since the overriding issue is the disregard of the patient's right to exercise control over his or her body. In short, the surgeon must have the patient's consent.

Case 8 is *Natanson v. Kline*; it dates from 1960 and is one of the first "modern" informed-consent cases.[11] The result of this case is that simple consent alone is no longer adequate. Physicians are now under an obligation to offer to acquaint patients with the important risks and plausible alternatives to the proposed procedure. While making it clear that patients were entitled to important information, it still left the decision about what constitutes "important information" up to physicians. This is known as the *community standard* approach, since the level of information that must be disclosed is set with reference to the general practice of other doctors.

Case 9 is *Canterbury v. Spence*, decided in 1972.[12] It is important because it focuses on the informational needs of patients, rather than on what the medical community may find medically customary. In the court's own words: "Respect for the patient's right of self-determination on particular therapy demands a standard set by law rather than one which physicians may or may not impose upon themselves." This is known as the *prudent-person* approach, since the level of information that must be disclosed is set with reference to its ability to influence a reasonable and prudent person. If the information has that power, then it must be disclosed even if its disclosure is not currently common medical practice. It is within this tension between self-determination and professional judgment that informed consent must operate.

Two important points need to be made about these cases. First, the fact that one court ruled in one specific case in favor of the prudent-person approach does not make it the law of the land. There is still a tremendous legal debate over the appropriate informational standard regarding informed consent. Second, the issue of legality aside, the question of just how much information a physician should provide to a patient is central to the doctor–patient relationship. The law may prescribe the broad outline of an answer, but the specific implementation of that answer is a matter decided between an individual doctor and patient. In particular, it requires that three questions be addressed: What types of medical procedures require consent? Who may give consent? How much information is needed to secure informed consent?

Basically, any procedure that puts the patient at risk (e.g., the prescription of powerful drugs, certain diagnostic tests, all surgeries) requires informed consent. The classic example of a medical procedure that does *not* require consent is the drawing of blood. One interesting effect of the informed-consent doctrine is that it turns out that the more we know, the greater the chance that consent is warranted. In the early 1970s, few "prudent persons" would have thought that Sally G.'s flu shot required consent. After the swine flu outbreak in the mid-70s, and the hundreds of cases of Guillain-Barré syndrome that resulted as an allergic reaction to the vaccine, the granting of consent for inoculations may now seem warranted. Sally and any other persons contemplating such treatment should expect to be informed about both the risks of the vaccination and the risks of getting the flu if they choose not to receive the shot.

Of course, medical procedures don't occur in a vacuum, and there may be circumstances in which risky procedures must be performed without the granting of consent. The law recognizes three major exceptions to the giving of informed consent: first, if an emergency procedure is called for and the patient is unable (e.g., unconscious) to give consent; second, patients may choose not to be apprised of risks and waive their right to an informed consent; third, disclosure of risk need not be made when it would "unduly agitate or undermine an unstable patient." This is known as therapeutic exception, and it raises serious ethical questions regarding a doctor's authority to make in-formational decisions for a patient. Since the patient's right to therapeutic information pervades the entire spectrum of the doctor–patient relationship, the next section is devoted to a full discussion of such issues.

Even when we know what procedures require consent, the doctrine of informed consent makes sense only if there is a rational patient to do the consenting. How does the law handle cases of incompetent patients? In much the same way as the law handles any other affairs (e.g., financial) of a person considered to be incompetent—by appointing a guardian. Generally, no one can make a legally binding decision on behalf of an incompetent adult until appointed as that person's legal guardian as the result of a judicial determination of incompetency.

A different type of problem occurs with minors. While they may well be competent to make decisions about their medical care, the law has long presumed them incompetent in order to protect them from making a poor treatment decision. This works well for young children who require the consent of one parent before they may be treated. However, since the age of eighteen may be arbitrary for certain medical conditions, the law grants more and more exceptions (e.g., treatment for drug dependency, pregnancy, contraceptive counseling) to this general rule as the minor reaches the age of majority.

The final question is the most important: How much information must the physician tell a patient in order to secure informed consent? This is really an issue involving both quantity and quality of information. The standard under common law holds that you are entitled to the following information:

1. The nature of the procedure.
2. The possible risks and complications of the procedure.
3. The prospects for success.

  4. Your prognosis if the procedure is not performed.
  5. Any alternatives and options.

But who determines the quality of that information? There is no hard-and-fast rule that can always be applied. Cases like *Canterbury v. Spence* seem to imply that you are entitled to all the information you feel you need to make an informed decision. Other courts have not interpreted the law so liberally. As a practical strategy, it is best to press for everything you wish to know. If your personal physician does not seem forthcoming, seek a second opinion or talk with the person on the hospital staff who is designated as the patients'-rights advocate.

There are many ethically compelling reasons for the doctrine of informed consent: it promotes individual autonomy; it protects the patient's status as a human being; it facilitates rational decision-making on the part of the patient and encourages self-scrutiny by the physician. Yet these goals can be attained only to the extent that doctor-provided information approaches patient understanding.

A common plea heard from those trying to reform the medical system is that we will receive better medical care when doctors stop playing God and patients get off their knees. Interpreted in this way, the doctrine of informed consent is intended as something of an equalizer—a principle that encourages both patient autonomy and self-scrutiny by the doctor. But the law alone insures only that you be informed, not that you understand. In your quest for quality medical care, there is simply no substitute for doctor–patient communication.

THERAPEUTIC INFORMATION

CONCEPT: Should doctors be obligated to tell patients the complete truth about their medical condition? Neither law nor medical codes of ethics require the full disclosure of therapeutic information. In fact, as this quote from Dr. Oliver Wendell Holmes suggests, there is a long medical tradition which holds that deceiving the sick and the dying may be in their own best interests: "The face of the physician, like that of the diplomatist, should be impenetrable. Nature is a sick and benevolent old hypocrite; she treats the sick and dying with illusions better than any anodynes."[13] Opposed to this "benevolent" dispensing of information is the general obligation to tell the truth, as well as the patient's expectation to be totally informed about his condition. Determining when these principles are in conflict, and how to resolve it, is probably the most straightforward ethical problem in the domain of bioethics.

PRACTICE: The old-fashioned idea that telling the truth is its own virtue has taken quite a beating in the past few years. Of course, it's not as if anyone has stood up in favor of the bald-faced lie; rather, we have witnessed a systematic devaluation of the concept of truthfulness. During Vietnam, we were never told lies. Instead, the situation was always "too complex" for us to understand. If only we had access to the information and perspective of the President and the generals, we too would see that their actions were justified. In short, the rationale was not so much that the government could lie to the people, it was just that given our limited point of view there was really no truth to tell.

A second assault on the idea of truthfulness has been led by some members of corporate America. Whether it's car manufacturers failing to release information about automobile safety, or the nuclear industry hiding incidents of radioactive emissions into the atmosphere, or a pharmaceutical company's reluctance to release studies about new drugs, the attitude often seems to be: Why bother the American people with bad news that they won't understand and don't want to hear anyway? For these companies, the failure to tell the whole truth, by concealing information, is perceived to be radically different from lying.

The final debasement of the concept of truth may also be the most self-serving. During the Watergate hearings, former Attorney General John N. Mitchell, the onetime chief law enforcement officer in the country, was asked how he could condone the break-in and the cover-up that followed. He responded that compared to what else was available (i.e., George McGovern), he thought he was justified in doing anything to insure the reelection of the President. This classic ends-justify-the-means argument has a vicious twist in regard to the truth: it asserts that the truth is just another commodity, like money or power, which may be exchanged for some other putative "good" whenever the need arises.

These three rationales for not telling the truth—(1) the truth is often impossible to convey, because it is uncertain and the audience cannot understand its complexities; (2) people don't want to know the truth when it is bad news; (3) the knowledge of truthful information may actually result in harmful consequences—are exactly the same arguments that the medical profession employs for not being totally truthful with patients. Is there any reason to think that these rationales are any more justified in the medical context than in the three preceding public-policy situations?

CASE 10: THE POSITIVE AIDS TEST

Steve F. is a twenty-seven-year-old man who is constantly "run down." He is always the first person in his office to get the flu and the last person whom it leaves. He usually feels tired and sometimes runs a low-grade fever. After almost a year of "not feeling quite sick enough to see a doctor," Steve schedules an appointment for a complete lab work-up. When Steve's doctor receives the results he is surprised to see that Steve was tested for AIDS (acquired immune deficiency syndrome) and that his blood tested positive for the antibody to the AIDS virus. Because Steve was not in the high-risk group for AIDS (homosexuals and intravenous drug users), and because only a small percentage of those who test positive will ever manifest the disease (Steve may have beaten off the disease or be an asymptomatic carrier, or the test may be inaccurate), the doctor decides not to even mention it as a possibility. After all, there can be no certainty in such a diagnosis, and Steve really doesn't have the background to understand the science that makes the test possible or to interpret the stochastic results. Is the doctor justified in withholding this information?

This rationale attempts to trade on the uncertain, value-laden nature of medicine. It argues that much of medical practice is far from certain, and that the patient is ill-equipped to understand the finer points and probabilities surrounding a given diagnosis or treatment course. Since there is frequently no sharp distinction between true and false in the medical context, doctors are justified in emphasizing the therapeutic uses of information rather than dwelling on the illusory goal of telling the truth. In Steve's case, the doctor might rationalize that the possibility of AIDS is quite remote and, since he can't "know" that Steve has AIDS, it is acceptable not to give him the test results.

Such an argument is flawed on both philosophical and practical grounds. Philosophically, it confuses the idea of truth (a fact-based notion) with the idea of truthfulness (a value-based notion). Just because the doctor cannot be certain of the *truth* of his diagnosis, it does not release him from the obligation of speaking *truthfully* to Steve. Good, well-reasoned evaluative judgments—Dom Perignon is the best champagne, that car is a good buy, aspirin is the drug of choice for mild fever—are the basis of most of our communications. Imagine how impoverished our conversations would be if we could speak only when we were absolutely certain.

Practically, the fight over a patient's right to truthful information has already been fought with regard to informed consent, and the verdict is in: Whether the information is certain or not, and whether or not the patient is intellectually equipped to understand all the medical nuances, the doctor is obligated to explain all facets of the treatment course. In fact, he is legally liable if he does not. It makes no sense to require the truthful exchange of information when consent is needed, but to think that it is acceptable to conceal therapeutic information.

CASE 11: THE DYING EXECUTIVE

John S. is a forty-nine-year-old executive who is one of three finalists for the position of chief executive officer for a Fortune 500 firm. One condition of employment is that he pass a company physical. John figures that this is the least of his worries—he gave up smoking fifteen years ago with the first Surgeon General's report, he jogs and plays handball regularly, he passed his last physical two years ago with flying colors, and he feels as good as he did when he turned forty. All this fitness is apparent to the company doctor, so he is shocked when the lab reports reveal that John's body is riddled with a fast-spreading form of cancer. The prognosis: John is likely to die within six months. Is the doctor obligated to tell John about his condition?

One possible option for the doctor is to simply report his findings to the company and let them decide if they want to tell John why he didn't get the job. The very fact that this option even exists speaks volumes about the changing roles of doctors in our society. A generation ago, most people had a family physician whom they saw for all their medical needs. Today, many doctor–patient interractions—team doctor with athlete, company doctor with employer, insurance doctor with litigant—occur in a third-party context in which the doctor's first allegiance may be to that unseen party. In such cases, the operative word is "interraction" rather than "relationship." Because the patient has not entered into a therapeutic relationship with the doctor, and because the unseen third party is the doctor's employer, patients cannot be certain that their best interests, as they perceive them, are the doctor's number-one concern. Since research studies show that the majority of doctors *within* the doctor–patient relationship do not inform patients of a terminal condition, patients can hardly expect more candor from a mere doctor–patient interraction.[14]

What can account for physicians' reluctance to be truth ful with their terminal patients, especially in light of other research which shows that approximately 85 percent of patients, including cancer patients, are in favor of being told the complete facts surrounding their illness?[15] One answer is surely the simple human desire not to have to be the bearer of bad news. But doctors also believe that information itself may be part of a therapeutic regime: Since medical "truth" is often impossible to ascertain, encouraging optimistic thinking even if it's probably unwarranted may actually improve the chances of cure. Furthermore, telling patients about their terminal conditions may simply wring all hope out of them. For many doctors, the potency of information as part of the healing process takes precedence over the general ethical requirement to always tell the truth.

This rationale for withholding information—telling patients about a terminal condition will wring all hope out of them, it's really telling them information they don't want to hear—flies in the face of what empirical evidence we have. It seems that most patients have more emotional strength than their doctors give them credit for having. But, more importantly, while no one ever *wants* to hear a prognosis like John's, there are many reasons why one *should* hear it: to be able to make decisions about terminal care (e.g., full-scale radio- or chemotherapy, hospice, home care), put one's life affairs in order, say one's proper good-byes. While it is certainly any patient's right to request not to be told about a terminal condition, only a doctor who arrogates to himself a kind of superhuman, mind-reading power could feel comfortable using this rationale for not telling a patient all about his or her condition.

CASE 12: THE ANXIOUS PATIENT

Betty R. is a sixty-seven-year-old suffering from congestive heart disease. She has already suffered three small heart attacks, and her personal physician knows that she is a nervous, high-strung woman in a constant state of anxiety over her medical condition. During her bimonthly checkup the doctor discovers a marked increase in her blood pressure. Since the doctor believes that it is unlikely that Betty will adopt any of the lifestyle changes that might lower it (e.g., diet, quit smoking), and since he believes that discussing the subject will only upset her and might even precipitate another heart attack, the doctor decides to simply increase her blood pressure medication and not mention it at all. Is this withholding of information justifiable?

This version of means–ends reasoning (if giving information to the patient may be harmful it should not be given) is probably the medical community's strongest rationale for withholding or distorting the truth. The Hippocratic Oath's major injunction is to "do no harm," so it seems to follow directly that any doctor who believes that conveying therapeutic information would cause an injurious patient reaction is justified in keeping that information secret. While this argument may seem persuasive in its abstract form, its use in concrete instances is frequently less well justified.

Like the failed argument for not telling terminal patients of their condition, this argument both overestimates the ill that the information can have and underestimates its benefits. In the first place, there is simply no credible evidence that patients commit suicide, or have heart attacks, or completely give up their will to live when presented with bad news. Alternatively, there is ample evidence that patients who are wisely counseled tolerate pain better, recover from surgery more quickly, and are more cooperative with their therapy.[16] Far from shielding patients from harm, using the means–end argument as a rationale for withholding therapeutic information may actually be causing harm. Based on scientific and not anecdotal evidence, it appears that patient knowledge is actually good medicine.

As an individual patient instead of a practicing bioethicist, your major concern must be the particular flow of therapeutic information between you and your doctor. Insuring that this information meets *your needs* involves a three-step process:

1. *Analyze.* Determine how much value you put on knowing the complete details of your medical condition: Are there things you're really not concerned about (e.g., possible yet unlikely diagnoses—"It's probably just the flu, but it could be the Epstein-Barr virus")? Do you generally want to avoid hearing any bad news (e.g., "I don't want to know what it is, just prescribe the medication")? How would you like the doctor to convey the knowledge if your condition were terminal: Tell you? Tell your family? Tell no one?

2. *Interpret.* Consider your position regarding thera-

peutic information in light of your general views about the doctor–patient relationship: How much responsibility for your medical well-being are you willing to assume (e.g., will you be using therapeutic information to make helpful lifestyle changes)? What, besides competent medical skills, do you expect from your doctor (e.g., is communication important, or do you just want proper treatment)?

3. *Communicate.* Recognize that if you don't communicate your wishes to your doctor, the dispensing of therapeutic information is entirely a doctor-dependent decision. Unlike your right to informed consent, which is guaranteed by law, or your privilege of confidentiality, which is circumscribed by the medical code of ethics, the right to therapeutic information exists in an ethical free-fire zone. Without patient communication, doctors have only their own ethical principles to guide them.

III

ALLOCATING MEDICAL RESOURCES

THE most important medical revolution of the post–World War II era has nothing to do with birth control pills, or diagnostic imaging, or monoclonal antibodies. In fact, it has little to do with high-tech medicine at all. Instead, it is a true social revolution, a radical altering of our societal perspective regarding the role of medicine in modern life: health care is now regarded as a right, rather than as a privilege available only to those who can afford it.

In 1940, barely one out of ten Americans was covered by any form of health insurance. Today, government programs like Medicare, Medicaid, and VA benefits, as well as privately funded programs through the workplace provide some kind of health coverage for 90 percent of the population. But this new view of health-care-as-right has not come cheaply. Following World War II, the country spent less than $500 (in 1982 dollars) per capita on health care. By 1982, that figure had nearly tripled, to $1,365. As a percentage of gross national product, we now spend 10.8 percent of our country's wealth on health, more than double the 4.5 percent of twenty years ago, and health continues to be the fastest-growing nondefense sector of the economy.[1] What are the reasons that have fostered this social revolution? What has led to, in social critic Ivan Illich's phrase, the "medicalization of life"?[2] And perhaps most importantly, is the dramatic rise in medical costs threatening the idea that health care should be considered a right?

One major reason for the revolution is the shift in disease burden from "quick-killing" infectious diseases (e.g., pneumonia) to the lifestyle-related, chronic, and degenerative diseases. With heart disease, cancer, and stroke as the three leading killers, citizens realize that coping with these maladies is more expensive (the cost of radio- and chemotherapy as opposed to an antibiotic inoculation), is more of a long-term problem (the physical rehabilitation after a stroke may require years of therapy), and may not even involve a cure so much as a lifelong process of management (dealing with a heart condition). Most of us don't need to be reminded by insurance company ads that a bout with any of these illnesses can be financially devastating.

A second reason is the graying of the population. As a consequence of our success with the scourges (e.g., polio, smallpox, diphtheria) of previous generations, more than half the population now lives into their seventies. But this extension of life also exacts a medical cost. On average, older people require medical treatment twice as frequently as the rest of the population, and there are some estimates that the heroic measures in the last few weeks of life account for as much as 25 percent of our total lifetime medical bill. If old age is to have some measure of dignity and quality of life, then society must insure that these citizens receive adequate health care.

A third reason is the incredible cost of some of the most highly publicized high-tech therapies. The average bill for a heart transplant is $100,000; the Autoplex injections needed to keep a hemophiliac alive run up to $100,000 during a three-month period; and kidney dialysis costs about $20,000 a year. In one much-publicized case, the potential bill for the neonatal care of the Frustaci septuplets was estimated at $700,000. If health care is truly to be a right, then mechanisms must be developed that allow ordinary citizens the opportunity to benefit from these "medical miracles."

The final reason is the modern social framework through which we view our health care system. The rights movements of the 1960s (e.g., blacks, women, consumers) created a tide of social expectations that also affected our attitudes regarding medicine. Health care was no longer viewed as just another commodity. Instead, it became one of a select group of "social goods," like education, to which everyone expected equal access. Public pressure led to the passing of Medicare and Medicaid in 1964 so that the elderly and the poor would have some measure of health protection. By 1983, the social revolution was over and the advocates of health-care-as-right were the victors. The President's Commission for the Study of Ethical Problems in Medicine and Biomedical and Behavioral Research (frequently referred to simply as the President's Bioethics Commission) would declare in their final report:

> ... health care is different from most other goods and services. In a society concerned not only with fairness and equality of opportunity but also with the redemptive powers of science, there is a felt obligation to ensure that some level of health services is available to all.[3]

As we've seen, open access to health care carries with it an enormous price tag. But that access, coupled with rising medical expectations, has also led to a kind of paradox of medical progress: As the population becomes healthier, its quality of life and medical standards improve. The whole notion of what it means to be "healthy" changes, and, as a result, the demand for even more medical services increases. For example, people who would have been happy with eyeglasses a few years ago now expect to have radial keratotomy so that they can see perfectly without glasses. As it turns out, the healthier we become, the more medical services we use.[4]

The effect of this social revolution is an economic drain of unprecedented dimension. Whether it's at the high-cost end of high-tech medicine, or simply the added cost of defensive medicine as a result of our litigious society, many experts claim that we can no longer afford such an extravagant health care system. Whether it's organs for transplant, or doctors for rural areas, or dollars to support exotic lifesaving technologies, we may soon have to face the systematic allocation of our medical resources. The health care revolution that swept this country in the space of a generation is now in jeopardy as the result of its own success. Declaring rights is easy, meeting the obligations those rights imply is often difficult. It is the task of the current generation to explain exactly what it means to say that health care is a right in America.

In *My Petition for More Space*, John Hersey wrote, "There should be more of everything. But there is not more of everything. That is the first fact of existence."[5] How we deal with this fact of existence in the medical sphere is a public policy issue with immense bioethical consequences.

CASE 13: FEWER DOLLARS, HARDER CHOICES

Which of the following individuals has a right to health care:

1. A twenty-three-year-old woman suffering from pneumonia?
2. An infant with hyaline-membrane disease?
3. A thirty-six-year-old man suffering from chronic kidney failure?

4. A seventy-three-year-old man who wants to replace an arthritic hip?
5. A college student with syphilis?
6. An unhappy executive whose job performance is suffering?
7. A child going to summer camp who needs a tetanus booster?
8. A heavy smoker requesting nicotine gum?
9. An unmarried pregnant teenager who wants an abortion?
10. A woman who desires breast augmentation?
11. A terminal cancer patient who develops cataracts?
12. A skier with a broken leg?

Making systematic decisions about who has a right to health care requires answers to three higher-level questions: What is a right? What services are included in the right to health care? What principles can be used to make allocation decisions?

The language of rights is both compelling and confusing, because it straddles the boundary between law and ethics. Frequently, the claim of x as a right means that there is a *legal right* to x. In the case of health care, someone claiming it as a legal right might mean that (1) it is guaranteed by a particular statute (e.g., Medicare provides hospitalization and medical insurance to individuals over sixty-five who are eligible for Social Security[6]); (2) it follows from the application of a particular legal case (e.g., *Wilmington General Hospital v. Manlove* upholds every individual's right to emergency medical care[7]; or (3) it is embodied in a specific interpretation of the Constitution (e.g., although the Constitution does not contain the word "health," some have argued that the equal-protection clause of the Fourteenth Amendment guarantees a right to health care[8]).

Just as often, however, someone claiming x as a right is

making a moral or ethical claim. This is the sense of the Declaration of Independence: "that all Men are created equal, that they are endowed by their Creator with certain unalienable Rights, that among these are Life, Liberty, and the Pursuit of Happiness." The previous chapter dealt with what philosophers call *liberty rights*—the right to conduct one's life according to one's own rules provided that the rights of others are not infringed upon. Informed consent, confidentiality, and access to therapeutic information are important tenets of biomedical ethics precisely because they foster an individual's liberty rights.

The rights revolution of the 1960s has tried to extend the notion of ethical right to include a new type of enfranchisement, the *entitlement right*—a claim that generates an obligation on the part of someone else to provide the resources needed to preserve the fundamental liberty rights. In essence, the argument is that without the necessary resources (e.g., food, housing, medical care) it is impossible to maintain an adequate measure of freedom. The President's Commission on Bioethics seemed to accept an entitlement right to health care when it concluded:

> Society has an ethical obligation to ensure equitable access to health care for all. This obligation rests on the special importance of health care, which derives from its role in relieving suffering, preventing premature death, restoring functioning, increasing opportunity, providing information about an individual's condition, and giving evidence of mutual empathy and compassion.[9]

If the language of rights can be confusing, claims about a right to health care can be downright bewildering. Nowhere is this bewilderment brought into sharper focus than in the case of the unmarried pregnant teenager who wants an abortion. For some people, abortion is murder and not a medical procedure at all; for others, abortions are exactly the type of medical procedure to which every woman should have equal access. For some, there can be no entitlement right even if the Supreme Court has interpreted the Constitution as granting a legal right; for others, the liberty right to an abortion supersedes any ruling regarding legal rights. (The issue of abortion is discussed more fully in Chapter IV.)

The question of competing rights is one of the ethical puzzles of any free society. And the question of what kind of, and how much, health care people should have a right to is a value puzzle of bioethics. What is it exactly that people are claiming a right to: emergency medical care? a personal physician? unlimited hospitalization? free access to all medical procedures? According to the President's Commission,

> Equitable access to health care requires that all citizens be able to secure an adequate level of care without excessive burdens. Discussions of a right to health care have frequently been premised on offering patients access to all beneficial care, to all care that others are receiving, or to all that they need— or want. By creating impossible demands on society's resources for health care, such formulations have risked negating the entire notion of a moral obligation to secure care for those who lack it. In their place, the Commission proposes a standard of "an adequate level of care," which should be thought of as a floor below which no one ought to fall, not a ceiling above which no one may rise.[10]

In essence, the commission never answered the question, What services are included in the right to health care? Instead, they simply adopted a recommendation upholding every citizen's right to "an adequate level of care." Although the commission failed to precisely define this level, they did make clear the direction of the public-policy debate: Since medical resources are scarce and individuals have no entitlement right to as much medical assistance as they might want, what principles should be used to make allocation decisions?

Perhaps the most famous medical-allocation procedure is the system of *triage* developed by the French during World War I. Because there were not enough doctors to treat all the wounded, injured soldiers were divided into three groups: mortally, moderately, and mildly wounded. Those in the middle group received medical attention first, since they were most likely to benefit from the care (the mortally wounded might use a lot of resources without ever recovering, while the mildly wounded would probably recover without medical help). The principle of allocation behind triage is social utility: distribute resources so as to maximize the chances of reaching an avowed social goal. In the case of war, triage is designed to keep the greatest number of soldiers on the battlefield, thereby maximizing the chances of victory.

Philosophers call rules like triage principles of *distributive justice*, because they prescribe methods for allocating goods or services when the demand exceeds the supply. In our free-market economy, one such rule is the *rule of property*: the individual with the greatest resources bids up the price until only he can afford the desired good. But health is not just another commodity, and most of us would not consider it just if the last bed in a hospital were auctioned off as if it were a rare painting. Some other possible principles of distributive justice include:

1. *The principle of randomness*—resources are allocated on the basis of a lottery.
2. *The principle of equality*—resources are allocated on the basis of everyone receiving an equal share.
3. *The principle of social utility*—resources are allocated on the basis of achieving the greatest good for the greatest number.
4. *The principle of just deserts*—resources are allocated on the basis of need, merit, or personal responsibility.

Determining how to apply these rules in order to make just allocation decisions regarding medical services is a major topic of this chapter's "The Right to Health Care" section.

CASE 14: JAMIE FISKE NEEDS A NEW LIVER

In the fall of 1982, Jamie Fiske was a cute little eleven-month-old girl with a critical medical problem. She was suffering from *biliary atresia*—a deadly liver disease that blocked the bile ducts, causing jaundice and, ultimately, death. Her only chance to continue living was a liver transplant, but the odds of finding a compatible organ were not good. At Stanford Research Center, one of this country's premier transplant hospitals, about one out of three candidates for a heart transplant dies before a suitable organ can be located; the odds for other organs like lungs, livers, and kidneys are even worse, and infant donors are the rarest of all.

Fortunately for Jamie, her father was a hospital administrator and knew how to mobilize the medical system. He telegraphed five hundred pediatricians, placed an appeal in a newsletter that reached into one thousand hospitals, and used the political clout of House Speaker Tip O'Neill and Senator Edward M. Kennedy to persuade the American Academy of Pediatrics to allow him to make a personal plea. Then the media took over. Fiske's appeal was covered by the three major TV networks and by newspapers all over the country. The Fiskes were deluged with organ offers and finally found a good match for Jamie. She had the operation in November 1982 and is doing well today.

While everyone can sympathize with parents who will do everything in their power to see that their child receives the best in medical care, there is something ethically unsettling about waging what is essentially an ad campaign to secure a scarce organ for one child while another child, perhaps with parents who are less wise in the ways of our media-addicted society, does not have the same opportunity to receive a lifesaving transplant. How should our society be rationing the scarcest resource of all—body tissues and organs?

There is a dramatic and qualitative difference between speculating about possible, abstract allocation decisions (e.g., should prenatal nutrition be part of the right to health care) and facing the specific decision as it applies to a concrete case (e.g., should Jamie Fiske receive a liver transplant). This difference is best embodied in the distinction between statistical lives and identified lives. For example, we know that because many pregnant women do not receive adequate nutrition, hundreds of *statistical lives*—unknown fetuses in possible future peril—are lost each year. Yet as soon as a baby is born it becomes an *identified life*—a known, named individual—and the medical community is obligated to do everything in its power, including transplants, to keep that individual alive. Given the overall scarcity of medical resources, and the enormous cost of tissue transplants, does it make sense to use those resources to save one identified life if that means sacrificing many statistical lives?

Of course, we are never presented with the choice in the exact form in which it appeared in the preceding sentence. There is a genuine difference between a positive choice to subject someone to a risk, or to take his life, and the passive acquiescence in a system that results in lives being taken when they could be saved at some definable cost. We now have the technological capacity to save lives using organ transplants, and few would argue that we should forsake that opportunity simply because it is very expensive. At the same time, we must recognize that we allocate over 90 percent of our medical expenditures to the health care system and less than 10 percent to other determinants of health such as lifestyle and environment.

Yet the government's own *Forward Plan to Health* states: "Only by preventing disease from occurring, rather than treating it later, can we hope to achieve any major improvement in the Nation's health."[11] Finding a way to save statistical lives without jeopardizing identified lives is the major *macroallocation* challenge for our health policymakers.

The most pressing *microallocation* challenge is the problem of devising a just system for the rationing of scarce organs. In the words of James F. Childress, this amounts to finding an answer to the question "Who shall live when not all can live?"[12] Among the many criteria that have been offered to answer that question are probable success of the operation, life expectancy after the operation, family role, future good for society, past accomplishments, and a lottery. Similar ethical questions apply to the selection of the organ donor: Can one be compelled to donate an organ? Who owns the body after death? What right does the state have to a cadaver? How these issues might be resolved is discussed in "Tissue and Organ Transplants."

CASE 15: THE PHYSICIAN AS GATEKEEPER

Mike L. applies for a position as a refinery technician with Texahoma Oil and Gas. As part of the application process, Mike must undergo a physical examination which, in addition to the usual blood pressure and eye check, involves genetic screening for *glucose-6-phosphate dehydrogenase (G6PD) deficiency* (G6PD is an enzyme that is important for the function of red blood cells). When Mike proves to be G6PD deficient, his application is denied. Although Texahoma never provides Mike with any information about his condition or a reason for their hiring decision, their thinking is: The job requires that Mike be exposed to naphtha, a petroleum distillate. Since it is known that G6PD-deficient individuals exposed to naphtha have a statistically higher risk of acute *hemolysis* (the destruction of red blood cells) than the general population, the company policy is not to hire anyone who has this condition for the refinery technician post. Is Mike entitled to this information about his health status? Shouldn't Mike be the one to determine if he wants to take the risk? Is Texahoma Oil and Gas discriminating against Mike? How much right do (potential) employers have to monitor and regulate their employees' health behavior?

Until recently, little attention was paid to the health impact of the workplace. The health-as-a-right movement, as well as the realization that dollars spent on preventive health care at the job site could be very cost efficient, changed that for both employees and employer. In the face of estimates of 390,000 new caes of occupationally induced diseases annually, 2.3 million disabling work injuries, up to ten times that number of serious injuries, and as many as 100,000 deaths yearly, workers organized around the issue of job health and safety.[13] Employers, worried about their legal liability and goaded on by the Occupational Health and Safety Act of 1970, also took steps to make the workplace healthier. One way to do this that seemed to benefit both workers and management was the institution of health-screening programs.

Such programs could aid in the diagnosis of ill workers, provide important information to researchers trying to establish links between disease and workplace conditions, and enable employees to make personal health decisions based on accurate medical information. All these goals are consistent with the traditional objectives of nonoccupational health screening. What wasn't consistent was the fourth goal of occupational screening: the weeding out of potential workers who are hypersusceptible to workplace risks.

Traditionally, health screening is justified on grounds that there will be direct therapeutic benefits for the participants, that there will be follow-up testing and counseling, and that screening is targeted at the reduction of a specific disease (e.g., hypertension or Tay-Sachs screening). None of these justifications applies in the case of Mike L. Instead, the screening was performed almost entirely for the employer's benefit.

The use of health screening for employee exclusion raises immediate questions about the doctor–patient relationship. How can doctors act as the gatekeepers to employment in the face of an ethic that places their primary obligation with the patient? One answer to this question is that by viewing individuals as "job applicants" rather than patients, the occupational physician may relieve himself of some of the standard doctor–patient obligations. A person cannot claim patient's rights if he is not in that role. But it is also clear that a doctor, even when a company employee, is not just any other employee. Seeing the company doctor is different from seeing the company clerk. The question is, How does that difference manifest itself? What are a doctor's professional obligations to an individual seen during an occupational screening? Although these questions are currently being litigated, this much is clear: the potential employee would be well advised to view the occupational physician as something less than a personal physician.

The potential role confusion for the occupational physician is only one of the interesting bioethical issues illustrated by the case of Mike L. In addition to the twin issues of truth-telling and confidentiality (doesn't the doctor's obligation to the patient require him to tell Mike about his condition while prohibiting him from reporting it to the company?), is it proper for physicians even to be involved in "cleaning up the work force rather than the workplace?" Are they the appropriate people to be making decisions about employee risk?

The growing practice of pre-employment medical

screening is producing a new bioethical dilemma: policy-makers no longer need be solely concerned about the just allocation of health care resources. Instead, they must now worry about the use of health status as an allocation mechanism for other scarce resources (e.g., jobs). Are employers whose screening tests affect only one race or sex guilty of discrimination? Are employers penalizing "genetically robust" workers by screening out those believed to be at risk? Should future health status even be a hiring consideration?

This new dilemma involves ethical issues regarding paternalism and autonomy, fairness and equity, and doctor–patient relationships. How these issues might be resolved is the topic of the final section, "Occupational Health Screening."

THE RIGHT TO HEALTH CARE

CONCEPT: All of us believe we have rights. But what exactly do we mean by claiming a right to free speech, or a right to privacy, or even a right to health care? According to modern ethical theory, the claim "I have a right" may be analyzed as "The moral system [or the legal system, where appropriate] imposes an obligation on someone to act or to refrain from acting so that x is enabled to have y."[14] This analysis makes three important points: First, it recognizes that rights don't appear out of thin air; they must be grounded in moral or legal theory. Second, it translates the passive language of rights into the active language of obligations. Third, it establishes two types of rights: (1) liberty (or negative) rights, which are rights to noninterference—they obligate others to respect our freedom of action; (2) entitlement (or positive) rights, which are rights to benefits—they obligate someone to provide us with goods and services.

With respect to health care, the rights developed within the doctor–patient relationship (e.g., informed consent, confidentiality, therapeutic information) are our most important liberty rights. By obligating the medical community to provide the information required to safeguard the patient's autonomy, they also preserve our personal freedom of action.

Entitlement rights to health care are much more contentious. Even though this country's first such right is over 170 years old (in 1813 Congress passed laws granting a right to effective cowpox vaccine), it is only within the last few decades that much public support has been generated for this right. Just which medical services such a right might entail, and how decisions about the allocation of those services should be made, are key bioethical questions in a growing public policy debate about how this country employs its health care resources.

PRACTICE:

CASE 16: THE SIX-MILLION-DOLLAR MAN

Steve Austin was critically injured when the moon landing craft he was testing crashed into the desert. In a desperate and heroic attempt to save his life, the doctors actually replaced his legs, arm, and eye with atomic-powered electromechanical devices. The operation succeeded, and Steve went on to even greater triumphs as the first bionic—part human, part machine—man.

While this scenario might make a hit TV show (in fact it did; as even casual viewers of television might have guessed, Steve Austin, played by Lee Majors, was the Six-Million-Dollar Man), it also raises serious bioethical questions: Did Steve Austin's right to health care include the right to all extraordinary means? If not, how are we to decide where the "ordinary" ends and the "extraordinary" begins? Would society have been justified in allowing Austin to die simply because the cost of his health care was prohibitive?

These are questions asked by policy-makers who are responsible for the health of the entire country. Their perspective differs sharply from the perspective of a single physician who must "owe to his patient complete loyalty and all the resources of his science."[15] Compared to the physician's concern for one individual, the policy-maker's task is the maximizing of health benefits for all individuals. But how are choices to be made when the demand for health care exceeds the supply? What ethical rules should society apply when it cannot make available to everyone "all the resources of his science"?

Trying to answer these questions on a case-by-case basis is both highly impractical and logically impossible. It is impractical because of the sheer number of individual decisions; it is impossible because the very nature of allocation decisions demands that trade-offs be considered. As long as health care remains a scarce resource, the decision to spend six million dollars on one patient requires asking how many other patients might be helped by that expenditure. As compelling as an individual case may be, making systematic allocation decisions necessitates some general principles.

Hospital committees that must make such decisions are often called "God Squads" because they literally hold the power of life and death in their hands. Although these committees are usually convened to select organ transplant donees, you can obtain a real feeling for the ethical issues involved in allocating health resources by playing the role of a committee member faced with the following task.

CASE 17: THE "GOD SQUAD"

Compare the Steve Austin case with the first eight cases on page 41:

1. A twenty-three-year-old woman suffering from pneumonia.
2. An infant with hyaline-membrane disease.
3. A thirty-six-year-old man suffering from chronic kidney failure.
4. A seventy-three-year-old man who wants to replace an arthritic hip.
5. A college student with syphilis.
6. An unhappy executive whose job performance is suffering.
7. A child going to summer camp who needs a tetanus booster.
8. A heavy smoker requesting nicotine gum.

If six million dollars were the total health resources pool, how should it be spent? What principles would you apply to justify your decisions?

One important feature of any allocation system is fairness, and there are two systems that everyone can agree are fair: a lottery and an equal apportioning. The lottery would insure that everyone had the same chance to "win" the entire six million dollars. Equal apportioning would simply give each patient one eighth of the entire pot. While a lottery may occasionally make sense (e.g., when there is only one transplantable heart and three equally qualified potential recipients), and the principle of equality is the proper strategy in those cases where everyone is at equal risk (e.g., inoculations for contagious diseases), these principles don't provide much assistance with the choices under consideration.

The problem is that guaranteeing "mathematical" fairness does not insure a just system of health care. Because health is not evenly distributed in our society—the infant with hyaline-membrane disease is sick, the prospective camper wants to prevent sickness—any truly fair system of health care would have to address this inequality. In addition to fairness, health resources are just like other resources: we want to get the biggest bang for the buck. There is no good reason to think that a lottery or equal apportioning would yield a maximal allocation of health resources.

A more promising way to view the concept of fairness involves the intuitive notion of equitable allocation. In ethical theory, this idea is called the principle of *distributive justice*: like cases are to be treated alike, and different cases treated differently in direct proportion to the differences between them. While this maxim may capture our commonsense notion of fair play, it is difficult to see how the committee could apply it, since it never specifies what "like cases" means. What are the relevant similarities and differences among individual cases that actually make a difference in medical treatment?

As with any other rationing decision, the place to begin is with costs and benefits. Cost/benefit analysis might provide the committee with the following information: the young woman could be treated very inexpensively with antibiotics, there is an overwhelming success rate for this type of therapy, and there is a correspondingly high chance that she will recover fully and without any lingering effects. The treatment for the infant involves expensive, intensive neonatal care with a significant chance of failure. However, the disease is not chronic, and successful treatment is a one-time expense. The young man with kidney disease will require hemodialysis for the rest of his life, or until a transplant can be performed. Dialysis is an expensive procedure that severely limits the quality of life, while transplantation involves a resource on which we can place no dollar amount. Treatment for the arthritic seventy-three-year-old would require hospitalization, surgery, and physical therapy. While the operation is generally successful, some patients have difficulty relearning how to walk, and, at seventy-three, this patient is near the end of the normal life-expectancy curve. The costs and benefits for the college student with syphilis are almost identical to those of the woman with pneumonia. Treatment for the unhappy executive may not even be considered by everyone as a medical problem—it is long-term, and there is no guarantee of success. Prevention in the case of the camper is inexpensive, but it is not clear that he is really at risk. While the heavy smoker is at risk, it is a self-imposed risk, and it is far from certain that a right to health care should include a right to lifestyle-changing technology.

While such cost/benefit accounting may provide some important factual information, it is a long way from providing the needed rules of allocation. One major problem is that each of us may put a different value on the same benefit. For example, some may consider the relatively few years left to the arthritic seventy-three-year-old as counting heavily against the operation; others may not want to consider anticipated health status at all. Some may believe that preventive medicine is the best possible expenditure of our health resources; others may want to give priority to those who are already ill. And some may think that the knowledge generated by experimenting on Steve Austin justifies the cost, while others may put much less of a premium on research. But even if we could agree on a method for translating a cost/benefit ledger into a value ranking, the problem of how to use that ranking would still remain: What ethical principle should be used to allocate the six million dollars?

One seemingly commonsensical approach advocates the principle of "the greatest good for the greatest number." Since we cannot provide everyone with all the health care resources they desire, this principle directs us to calculate

the costs and the benefits of the various alternatives and
to choose the plan that maximizes net benefits over costs.
This is the utilitarian formula first set forth by Jeremy
Bentham and John Stuart Mill almost two hundred years
ago.

> The principle of utility is the foundation of the
> present work: it will be proper therefore at the outset
> to give an explicit and determinate account of what
> is meant by it. By the principle of utility is meant that
> principle which approves or disapproves of every ac-
> tion whatsoever, according to the tendency which it
> appears to have to augment or diminish the happiness
> of the party whose interest is in question: or, what is
> the same thing in other words, to promote or to op-
> pose that happiness. I say of every action whatsoever;
> and therefore not of every action of a private indi-
> vidual, but of every measure of government."[16]

For strict utilitarians, distributive justice is as easy as: (1)
sum the benefits, (2) sum the costs, and (3) subtract and
choose the course of action with the highest number.

Just as the principle of distributive justice captured some
of our intuitive sense of fairness, the principle of utility
also represents some of the spirit of equitable allocation.
After all, it would be pretty bizarre to choose an allocation
scheme that tried to minimize the amount of good. Yet,
by aggregating all costs and benefits into a single number,
utilitarians lose sight of the individuals their decisions
affect. For example, a utilitarian reckoning might allow
brutal experiments on a few individuals if the results produced a little good for a large number. In the case of the
six million dollars, a utilitarian calculation might justify
Steve Austin being allowed to die so that his organs could
be used as transplants for heart and kidney patients. Although we may ultimately decide that the best allocation
of resources might result in Austin's death, it is ghoulish
to suggest that we should consider the value of his organs

in our deliberation. A human being is the classic example of the whole being worth more than the sum of its parts. Quite clearly, the ethical principle that guides our allocation decisions must look at more than total good. It must also instruct us about how that good is to be distributed.

Principles that focus on individual qualities as the key criteria in allocation decisions might be called principles of just deserts after a famous passage in Aristotle:

> If the persons are not equal, their (just) shares will not be equal; but this is the source of quarrels and recriminations, when equals have and are awarded unequal share or unequals equal shares. The truth of this is further illustrated by the principle "To each according to his deserts." Everyone agrees that in distributions the just share must be given on the basis of what one deserves, though not everyone would name the same criterion of deserving: democrats say it is free birth, oligarchs that it is wealth and noble birth, and aristocrats that it is excellence.[17]

But what criterion makes the most sense for distributing health care?

One candidate that should be considered is need. After all, we would all like to think that we would receive the proper medical care if we really needed it. Our legal right to emergency care is based on this very idea: because an emergency patient is in immediate need of health care, the hospital is obligated to provide it. If we could always distinguish need from want, this criterion would capture a good deal of our sense of fairness in the allocation of health resources. But aside from the paradigm case of emergency care, needs and wants have a tendency to blur together. Which patient is more in need, an old man who wants to replace an arthritic hip or an unhappy executive whose job performance has suffered? Since neither individual's life is in jeopardy, some may feel that they only want, rather than need, medical attention. Others may contend that quality of life is just as important as sanctity of life and that therefore both patients really need medical treatment. Even if we could decide on a precise definition of need, how would we decide in cases of equal need (e.g., both Steve Austin and the infant with hyaline-membrane disease need immediate medical care)? Like the principle of utility, the criterion of need is a consideration that must be taken into account, but it is not the full account.

A much different criterion is merit, where that might be construed as ability, or effort, or societal contribution. No stronger plea can be made for this view than Ayn Rand's:

> A morality that holds *need* as a claim, holds emptiness—nonexistence—as its standard of value; it rewards an absence, a defect: weakness, inability, incompetence, suffering, disease, disaster, the lack, the fault, the flaw—the *zero*.
>
> Who provides the account to pay these claims? Those who are cursed for being non-zeros, each to the extent of his distance from that ideal. Since all values are the product of virtues, the degree of your virtue is used as the measure of your penalty; the degree of your faults is used as the measure of your gain.[18]

While Ms. Rand's writing is eloquent, the suggestion that merit is the key to distributive justice embodies a *circular argument*: you first assume what you want to prove and then, using the conclusion as an assumption, go on to "prove" it.

Remember that we were forced to search for a criterion of "just desert" because the principle of utility was insensitive to the individual case. But what is the criterion of merit if not an appeal to how much good a person can contribute to society? It follows that since any meritarian criterion will be based upon utilitarianism, such an appeal must be circular. In other words, merit cannot replace utility because it is simply a variant on the utilitarian theme. The President receives the best available health care because it is in all our best interests to keep him healthy (the principle of utility), and not because he possesses some intrinsic quality of merit not shared by the rest of us.

Of course, there is really no need to rely upon philosophical argumentation. While merit may be the proper test for making certain allocation decisions (e.g., that's why some ball players are worth more than others), health care is not the type of service that can be justly apportioned on such grounds.

A third criterion, responsibility for your personal medical condition, is really an ancient idea with a new, scientific underpinning. For thousands of years, sickness was considered a matter of strict personal liability. If you became ill, it was because of something you did, or didn't do, and the sickness was your punishment. Sick people were bad people, and "medicine" consisted chiefly of trying to drive out the evil spirits. If you were unfortunate, medical techniques like burning and drowning ended up killing you.

As medicine became more scientific and physicians started to understand bodily mechanisms and disease processes, the idea that the individual was responsible for his illness fell into disrepute. With the ascendancy of the germ theory of disease a mere one hundred years ago, any vestige of personal responsibility was replaced by microorganisms of all shapes and kinds. Disease was something that happened to people, not something that they brought on themselves. As such, it was not a reflection of personal "goodness," and not a matter of personal liability.

Recent work in environmental health and in the relationship between lifestyle and disease have begun to swing the pendulum back toward the idea that people are, at least partly, responsible for their health status. Smoking, drinking, compulsive eating, lack of exercise, and a host of risky hobbies (e.g., skydiving, skiing) are all behaviors within our control that may have deleterious health consequences. Any modern view of health must recognize that while there are instances of illness to which the patient in no way contributed (e.g., the infant with hyaline-membrane disease), there are others (e.g., the college student with syphilis) with a direct patient link. How should this modern view of health affect our allocation decisions? While it might be difficult for the committee to deny the college student access to penicillin on grounds that the disease is self-caused, ideas such as special health taxes on risky behaviors (e.g., cigarettes, ski-lift tickets) and the creation of special insurance pools for people at greater risk (e.g., obese, alcoholic) are beginning to receive national attention.[19]

By now it should be clear that there is no single "golden rule" for the committee to apply; there are only important considerations. In fact, the committee's charge is so broad—allocating among cases of preventive, research, lifestyle, crisis, and optional medicine—that it is unlikely that any rational ranking could ever be produced. Role-playing a committee member was just a "thought experiment," a method for coming to understand the various competing claims to health care resources as well as the different ethical principles for allocating those resources.

Given the complexity of making such decisions, the presidential commission's appeal to "an adequate level of care" is good common sense:

> Although neither "everything needed" nor "everything beneficial" nor "everything that anyone else is getting" are defensible ways of understanding equitable access, the special nature of health care dictates that everyone have access to *some* level of care:

enough care to achieve sufficient welfare, opportunity, information, and evidence of interpersonal concern to facilitate a reasonably full and satisfying life.

...the concept of adequacy, as the Commission understands it, is society-relative. The content of adequate care will depend upon the overall resources available in a given society, and can take into account a consensus of expectations about what is adequate in a particular society at a particular time in its historical development. This permits the definition of adequacy to be altered as societal resources and expectations change.[20]

Society may never be able to totally systematize the allocation of health resources. But having a reasonable goal and a few important rules—like cases should be treated alike, the principle of utility, the principle of need, the principle of responsibility—means that those decisions have a good chance of being made fairly and equitably.

TISSUE AND ORGAN TRANSPLANTS

CONCEPT: It is normal to think that solutions solve problems. Yet, in the complex world of biotechnology, solutions to old problems often end up precipitating new ones. Nowhere is this more evident than in the issues surrounding tissue and organ transplants—the removal of one of the body's tissues (e.g., skin or blood) or organs (e.g., heart or kidney) and its placement into the same or a different site on the same individual (donor) or a different individual (donee). Because donors may be either living (as in the case of blood transfusions) or cadavers (as in the case of heart transplants), transplantation is intimately linked to the problem of defining death (Chapter IV). But even when the status of a deceased donor is not in question,

the practice involves interesting and difficult questions—
scientific (How to combat tissue rejection?), legal (What
is the status of living donors?), and bioethical (Who decides which donees may receive transplants?).

PRACTICE: True or false: Dr. Christiaan Barnard was the
first physician to perform human transplant surgery. Actually, Barnard was neither the first to transplant human
tissue (there is evidence that Indian doctors performed
skin grafts 2500 years ago), nor the first to transplant a
human organ (kidney transplants had begun in 1951), nor
even the first to transplant a heart (Dr. J. D. Hardy transplanted a chimpanzee heart into a human in 1964). Barnard's operation on Lewis Washkansky in December 1967
was noteworthy because it was the first attempt at transplanting a human heart, an organ with important historical
and symbolic value. Although Washkansky died eighteen
days later, Barnard had proven human heart transplants
feasible, and this stimulated both the public's imagination
and the biomedical research community. Today there are
more than six thousand kidney transplants and about two
hundred heart transplants yearly in the United States alone
(with a one-year success rate of about 75 percent), and the
list of transplantable tissues and organs include blood,
blood vessels, bone marrow, cartilage, fingers, glands,
heart, kidneys, liver, muscles, ovaries, pancreas, skin, ten-
dons, testicles, and toes.

Although transplantation has a venerable history—Me-
dea is supposed to have arranged a blood transfusion between Jason and his father—most of our modern
techniques were developed in the past thirty-five years.
The most visible of these advances is the improvement
of critical-patient care and the progress in surgical technique: kidney dialysis machines insure that kidney transplant recipients are in good medical condition prior to the
transplant; microsurgery techniques allow skilled sur-

ALLOCATING MEDICAL RESOURCES

geons to connect tiny arteries and vessels when transplanting fingers and toes; artificial respirators can keep the heart and kidneys of brain-dead patients perfused with blood and oxygen until the optimal time for transplant (though not without raising difficult bioethical questions about "harvesting" dead patients and turning them into "organ farms"). Because of breakthroughs like these, the actual surgery is often the least risky part of the transplant procedure.

The second area of scientific advance has received less publicity (surgeons seem to corner the spotlight: Barnard, Shumway, Cooley, De Bakey, De Vries), but may be even more important. It is the explanation of the body's defense, or immune, system. Happily for us most of the time, our bodies are capable of destroying foreign materials (e.g., dirt, virus) when they are introduced into the body. The problem, of course, is that in the case of a tissue transplant we don't want the body to attack the new tissue. Discovering how to turn the immune system off, how to overcome tissue rejection, is the greatest medical problem surrounding transplants.

Before researchers could control the immune system, they first had to understand how it operates. Although many questions still remain, the basics are now fairly well understood: The body defends itself through an extensive network of *lymphoid tissues*. This tissue travels through the body searching for invaders, which it recognizes because the invaders contain foreign proteins called *antigens*. Once these antigens are recognized, the lymphoid cells respond by producing *antibodies*, and the rest of the body's defense mechanisms are marshaled. In the case of a tissue transplant, the cells at the graft site (where the new tissue is attached to the body) are attacked and the blood supply to the transplant is choked off. As a result, the new tissue dies and the transplant is rejected.

In order to overcome this immune response, researchers

have developed a series of antirejection, or immuno-suppressive, drugs. Twenty-five years ago, when these drugs were first discovered, they worked by neutralizing the body's entire immune system. This had the unfortunate side effect of leaving the entire body open to infection. Today, more selective drugs such as *Cyclosporin*, as well as *antilymphocyte globulin* (a serum which attacks only the lymphocyte scouts, leaving the rest of the immune system intact), and radiation of the graft do a much more effective job of combating infection.

Ideally, the whole problem of immune response could be circumvented if the new tissue was a perfect match for our own. While this is impossible except for the cases of autografts and grafts from identical twins, it is the goal of tissue typing to insure that transplants come from the most compatible donors. Just as blood has types, we can now type tissues based on their antigen responses. By matching donor and donee tissue types, physicians greatly reduce the odds of rejection.

No transplant operation is assured of success, but scientific advances like these have made some transplants (e.g., bone marrow, kidney) very good risks. In fact, it is precisely the success of science which has led to some of society's most vexing and perplexing legal problems.

All the legal issues surrounding transplants really revolve about one simple-to-state question: Do you own your own body? As you might expect, the law does not view this as a simple question, and, as a result, there are numerous laws and rulings which attempt to answer it for all possible situations. While only a dedicated lawyer could keep track, understanding just two rulings should serve to give you a working knowledge of your body property rights.

CASE 18: HIS COUSIN'S KEEPER

In 1978, Robert McFall was a thirty-nine-year-old bachelor suffering from acute *aplastic anemia*—a failure of the bone marrow to produce red blood cells. His diagnosis was almost certain death within six months unless he received a transplant of compatible bone marrow. With such a transplant, he had a good chance of a complete recovery.

Because the likelihood of finding a compatible donor was about one in sixty thousand, McFall solicited the aid of his relatives. A first cousin, David Shimp, was tested and proved to be a perfect match. At this point, Shimp decided not to go through with the transplant. McFall sued to compel his cooperation. As judge, would you:

A. find for McFall on grounds that bodily integrity may be overriden in cases of overwhelming social need (e.g., public-health vaccinations, marital blood tests, quarantines)?

B. find for McFall on grounds that Shimp had begun a rescue procedure with very little risk to his own well-being and was, therefore, fully obligated (like a boater coming to another's aid) to continue to assist?

C. find for Shimp on grounds that there is no legal compulsion to aid another who is in distress or danger?

Although the court found Shimp's refusal to be "morally indefensible," it decided for him, stating that compelling bodily intrusion "would defeat the sanctity of the individual and would impose a rule that would know no limits. ...Forceable extraction of living body tissue causes revulsion to the judicial mind. Such would raise the spectre of the Swastika and the Inquisition, reminiscent of the horrors this portends." McFall died three weeks later.[21] If the law is clear—competent individuals have complete right to deny others access to their body parts for purposes of transplantation—the ethics of the case certainly are not.

CASE 19: DONATING THE GIFT OF LIFE

Douglas B., a healthy nineteen-year-old, was critically injured in a motorcycle accident. Upon arriving at the hospital, he underwent emergency surgery to relieve pressure on his brain. Because of a perceived lack of brain function, he was kept alive postoperatively with intravenous feeding and by a respirator. The next day an electroencephelogram (EEG) was obtained and showed no evidence of viability and no evidence of cortical activity. In short, Douglas was "brain dead." Under what conditions can the hospital disconnect him from the respirator, declare him dead, and proceed to use his organs in transplant operations?

The Uniform Anatomical Gift Act[22] is the law in every state, and it details your rights regarding your body's disposition after death. The important clauses are as follows:

1. Any individual of sound mind and eighteen years of age may give all or any part of his body upon death.
2. In the absence of a gift by the deceased, and in cases where the deceased made no known objection, his relatives have the power to give the body or any of its contents.
3. The recipients of a gift are restricted to hospitals, doctors, medical and dental schools, universities, tissue banks, and a specified individual in need of treatment. The purposes are restricted to transplantation, therapy, research, education, and the advancement of medical or dental science.
4. A gift may be made by will, card, or other document.
5. A gift may be revoked at any time.
6. A donee may accept or reject a gift.

The key concept embodied by the act is that of consent. Without Douglas' expressed permission, or the permission of his relatives, the hospital may not consider using any of his organs for transplant. That may be the current law, but does it make sense when seven thousand people are currently awaiting kidney transplants while undergoing dialysis that is costing the government $140 million a year? One alternative approach, currently being considered in Europe, would allow the state to use the organs of a deceased person *unless* that person had expressly vetoed it during his or her lifetime. The trade-offs between the social utility of that plan and the autonomy of the individual, even when no longer living, will be a major public-policy battleground for the foreseeable future.

As a consequence of our inability to provide a transplantable organ for every patient who needs one, we are faced with one of bioethics' cruelest decisions: choosing who may live when not all can live. For some, this is a Godlike power that man has no right to wield. Their solution is that all must die (e.g., no organs are to be transplanted) until it is within our power to save everyone. Most of us, however, would rather try to act justly in order to preserve the life of a few than doom everyone because we thought ourselves insufficiently wise to make such choices. But by what criteria can those decisions be made?

The option adopted by the British National Health Service is triage by delay. Heart transplants are available at government expense to everyone who qualifies medically, but the procedure is performed on a first-come, first-served basis. This means that as soon as your doctor approves the procedure, your name is added to the bottom of the list of candidates. As operations are performed, or other candidates die, you slowly move to the top until you occupy the number-one position. While this system preserves a sense of fairness, it does so at the expense of the sickest patients. Shouldn't one criterion for using our scarcest resource be that it must go to the patient in greatest medical need?

Just such an approach is advocated by the American Medical Association. Their guidelines state that organs must be allocated to patients on a medical basis alone, and that the key criteria must be medical need and likelihood of success. While these criteria seem simple and fair, critics have pointed out two major deficiencies. First, instead of the decision being based strictly on medical facts, the criteria for "likelihood of success" may include many value judgments. For example, Stanford University's heart transplant program requires that potential donees have a supportive family, a job to return to, and the financial resources needed (about $10,000) to enable them to live in the Stanford vicinity well before and after the actual operation. The critics point out that all the candidates who meet these qualifications are likely to be from the same socioeconomic group; and that if value judgments are to be applied, society, and not just doctors, should have a role in deciding them. Secondly, even if everyone could agree on the two AMA criteria, the problem of choosing among patients with equal needs would remain. If we agree that the Fiske family's media blitz or a rich oil sheik's donation of a hospital wing should not immediately move them to the head of the line, we still need to offer positive suggestions for an equitable selection procedure.

Current ethical thinking is united on the broad outline of the approach to take but sharply divided on the details. Most believe that the AMA approach has some merit but should be used only as a *rule of exclusion*—a set of criteria to determine who should be eligible for a transplant operation. These criteria should be public, objective, and easy to apply. Examples include age (the unofficial cutoff age for transplants is fifty) and general physical condition (e.g., there is no sense in transplanting a heart into a patient with lung cancer).

Once the pool of medically acceptable candidates is chosen, it is time to apply the *rules of final selection*—a set of criteria to determine who will actually receive the transplant. It's here that the bioethicists split into two warring camps. One group holds that it is appropriate at this stage to apply some kind of social-worth criteria like past achievements or future contributions. Such a utilitarian rule is argued for by Nicholas Rescher:

> In "choosing to save" one life rather than another, "the society," through the mediation of the particular medical institution in question—which should certainly look upon itself as a trustee for the social interest—is clearly warranted in considering the likely pattern of future *services to be rendered* by the patient (adequate recovery assumed), considering his age, talent, training, and past record of performance. In its allocations..., society "invests" a scarce resource in one person as against another and is thus entitled to the probable prospective "return" on its investment.[23]

For supporters of this view, failure to make the hard choices is socially irresponsible.

Opponents of the utilitarian rule object to it on grounds that it is impossible to objectively rank social values and that even if we could, we could not predict, with any accuracy, people's future contributions. They also make a telling moral objection: The equality of human life is a natural right. It makes no sense to attempt to judge which lives are more valuable and, hence, more worth saving. For these ethicists, the only fair system must involve randomness:

> My proposal is that we use some form of randomness or chance (either natural, such as "first come,

first served," or artificial, such as a lottery) to determine who shall be saved....

Serious study would, I think, point towards its implementation in certain conflict situations, primarily
because it preserves a significant degree of *personal
dignity by providing equality* of opportunity....

The individual's personal and transcendent dignity, which on the utilitarian approach would be sub-
merged in his social role and function, can be
protected and witnessed to by a recognition of his
equal right to be saved.[24]

Is there any chance that these two views might be rec-
onciled? One possibility is a system that requires the utilitarians to recognize the limits of their social calculus,
while requiring the randomizers to understand that utilitarianism is making judgments only about a person's potential contribution to society, and not about his ultimate
worth as a human being. If the important distinction between human worth and human contribution can be maintained, then the only differences that need be resolved
are contingent: What criteria of social contribution should
be used and how are they to be generated?

The most pluralistic plan would engage the entire society in a dialogue to determine exactly which criteria of
contribution are to be given weight. We might decide that,
though the criterion of financial asset may be distasteful,
the oil sheik who will donate $5 million for a new hospital
wing will ultimately create more social good than a gro-
cery clerk. We might also decide that transplant surgeons
should receive a special priority.

For their part in the compromise, the utilitarians must
accept that only the agreed-upon criteria are to be used.
In cases in which the pool of potential donees was still
too large, a randomizing procedure would be followed.
Forcing choices when there are no acceptable criteria is
also socially irresponsible. If society cannot agree on any

criteria, then randomization, rather than the current unspoken, value-laden approach, seems the only just procedure to follow.

Because transplants give us a chance to play God, there
will always be bioethical questions which neither science
nor law can answer: Is it ethical to sell one's body parts
for money? How is selling blood different from selling a
kidney? Is it ethical to keep a brain-dead patient "alive"
so that we can use him as an organ farm? Ultimately, what
are our responsibilities to our fellow human beings? The
only certain conclusion is that until everyone who needs
an organ can get one, we will be faced with these bioethical dilemmas.

OCCUPATIONAL HEALTH SCREENING

CONCEPT: The realization that there may be a connection
between your health and how you earn your living is not
a particularly modern notion. As early as the first century
A. D., Roman physicians noted a "sickness of the lungs"
(which we now call *asbestosis*) in slaves who wove asbestos into cloth. Chimney sweeps in Dickens' London
suffered an inordinate amount of scrotal cancer as the result of shimmying up soot-encrusted flues. And the phrase
"mad as a hatter" didn't begin with *Alice in Wonderland*.
Many hatters actually went mad (brain injured) from in-
haling fumes from the mercury used in their trade.

What is modern is our recognition of the scope of the
problem. With one hundred million Americans spending
half their waking hours on the job, and with increasing
evidence that the workplace contains many health hazards
(e.g., everything from [still] asbestos to radiation to toxic
chemicals), the Centers for Disease Control warns that
the United States is "on the threshold of an epidemic of
occupational illness."[25]

One major response to this threat has focused on the workplace. By banning the use of certain hazardous agents (e.g., DDT), lessening their concentration in other products (e.g., less lead in gasoline and paint), and fostering safety standards for individual industries (e.g., limiting the consecutive hours a trucker may drive, regulating the amount of cotton dust in a mill), the government is trying to reduce the number of workers who suffer injury or job-related illness.

A radically different approach is being taken by some employers. Rather than concentrating exclusively on the workplace, they have begun to screen out prospective employees who might be susceptible to certain job-related hazards. By identifying and removing these employees from the worker population, they seek to reduce the average level of job-related health risk. But this screening raises many serious bioethical questions: How is a particular risk to be determined? Who is responsible for bearing that risk? How can we balance employer and employee rights? Ultimately, what should the role of a medical procedure be in determining the makeup of the workforce?

PRACTICE: Ben Franklin's aphorism "An ounce of prevention is worth a pound of cure" has become a key strategy for modern public health. The allocation of health resources for sanitation, nutrition, and immunization has proven our most effective, as well as most cost-effective, deterrent to disease. By following this strategy,

> we have conquered those infectious diseases that were the major killers of the last century, and we now face the challenges of today's chronic illnesses. How well do our previous models help us?
>
> The challenge is to determine what factors increase the probability of disease, to quantify as accurately as possible the increase in probability of disease due to the specific factor, and then finally to determine

how to decrease or eliminate the identified risk. Our
goal is to identify, assess, and manage risk.[26]

Yet risk, like the concept of health itself, has an important subjective component. It may be defined as "a measure of the probability and sensitivity of harm to human health. *A thing is safe if its risks are deemed to be acceptable.*"[27] But acceptable to whom: the employer? employee? union? panel of doctors? Quite clearly, science acting alone cannot determine what is safe, or when there is an unacceptable risk. Risk assessment occurs at the intersection of science and values, and that always raises the question of whose values. How is a society to decide between an employee's right to work at any job for which he qualifies and an employer's right to hire safe, healthy workers? Is it acceptable to include health status as a job qualification? What about a projection for future health status based on a genetic test? While there are no precise answers to these questions, deciding each of the following three cases of occupational risk assessment should help to illuminate your values regarding these issues.

CASE 20: THE FAIR-SKINNED ROOFER

Sven W. responded to an ad in the employment section of the paper for an experienced roofer. When he explained his qualifications over the phone (six years' experience, state contractor's license), he was told that if his references matched his credentials he would be hired. A few days later the company called Sven and told him he could report for work the following day. When Sven appeared, the foreman took one look at him, apologized, and told him the job offer was rescinded. He explained that it was company policy not to hire any blond, fair-skinned roofers, because of the potential of skin cancer from the combined exposure to the sun and the roofing materials. If Sven wanted to bring a discrimination suit, would you:

A. agree with the employer on grounds that Sven's susceptibility to skin cancer could lead to workers' compensation claims, higher insurance premiums, and increased absenteeism?

B. agree with Sven because his skin coloring has nothing to do with his qualifications as a roofer?

C. find for Sven on grounds that even though his skin coloring could lead to health problems, he is capable of taking preventive measures (e.g., wear a hat, apply sun blockers) that effectively reduce the risk?

Because the roofing company is denying Sven a job based on his membership in a class (i.e., all fair-skinned people, which includes most individuals of Scandinavian descent), the relevant law is Title VII of the Civil Rights Act of 1964. This act bans workplace discrimination unless the employer can demonstrate that the group fails to meet a *bona-fide occupational qualification* (BFOQ), or that a *business necessity* requires that the group be excluded.

A BFOQ is simply a specific, required job duty. For example, a BFOQ for the position of female impersonator is that the applicant be a male. Although this qualification excludes the class of all women, it does so legally, since only men qualify as female impersonators. In the roofing trade, a BFOQ may be the ability to lug a fifty-pound bundle of shingles or to scamper up a twenty-foot ladder. Because Sven's complexion is irrelevant to his performance as a roofer, appealing to a BFOQ offers no defense.

The appeal to "business necessity" permits an employer to establish class-specific criteria for workplace exclusion when he can demonstrate that it is necessary for the safe and efficient operation of the business. For example, a hospital may exclude all pregnant women from the post of X-ray technician, since X rays are especially dangerous to fetuses. Given that Sven has already worked as a roofer for six years and that he can take preventive measures against the putative health risk, the company's policy does not appear to be a business necessity.

The appropriate legal answer in Sven's case is B. The law supports the ethical position that individual workers must be allowed to assume minor health risks as long as, in so doing, they are not putting others at risk.

CASE 21: THE FETAL "CANARY"

In 1979 Barbara Cantwell was a thirty-one-year old divorced mother of two, working in the lead pigments department of American Cyanamid's Willow Island, West Virginia, plant. In order to protect fetuses that might be harmed by prenatal exposure to lead dust, the company adopted a policy banning all women of childbearing age (not just those who were, or intended to become, pregnant) from working in that department. The policy left Barbara with a dilemma: give up her relatively high-paying job for a lower paying one or agree to a sterilization procedure. Barbara chose the latter.[28] If Barbara had brought a discrimination suit, would you:

A. find for American Cyanamid on grounds that the protection of a potential fetus deserves top priority?
B. find for American Cyanamid on grounds that such discrimination is allowed under Title VII?
C. find for Barbara on grounds that excluding women is unfair since lead is also known to affect adversely the reproductive systems of males?

Unlike Sven W.'s case, where the minimal nature of the health risk led to a clear ruling of discrimination, this case has no simple ruling, only complicated considerations. The employer's argument for excluding female workers begins with the recognition that many substances in the workplace (e.g., lead, carbon monoxide, radiation) can be hazardous to a fetus without having any effect on normal, healthy adults. In a very real sense, fetuses are like the caged canaries that miners used to take with them down into the pits; by monitoring the canary (fetus), we can assess the health quality of the work environment.

Since employers want to insure that absolutely no fetal exposure occurs, their policy is all-inclusive: ban all fertile females from the workplace. Less restrictive alternatives such as worker self-monitoring for pregnancy are rejected on two grounds: first, pregnancy testing is not foolproof and the fetus is most susceptible in the earliest stages of pregnancy, even before the tests are likely to be valid; second, since the potential fetus is in no position to give its consent to be put at risk, the female worker should not be allowed to unilaterally make the decision to continue working.

In addition to such ethical arguments, the recent ruling in the *Wright v. Olin Corporation* case seems to indicate that employers may also attempt to legally justify their policy on the grounds of business necessity: "...under appropriate circumstances an employer may, as a matter of business necessity, impose otherwise impermissible restrictions on employment opportunities that are reasonably required to protect the health of unborn children of women workers against hazards of the workplace."[29] Besides opening the business-necessity defense, the court also offered guidelines for its use: the burden of proof is on the employer to demonstrate that a risk to the fetus exists; this proof must be scientific and not business related or anecdotal; and the evidence must also indicate that the risk is substantially confined to women workers.

No matter what the justification, the employer's strategy may be summed up as a willingness to err on the side of safety. According to a business executive quoted in a widely reported Occupational Safety and Health Administration document, "Industry would rather face a charge of sex discrimination than run the risk of a deformed baby."

The counterarguments of the one million female workers of childbearing age who are exposed to fetotoxins hardly make them appear reckless. They first point out that it is the height of paternalism to claim that women cannot monitor their own bodies, discover their own pregnancies, and voluntarily withdraw from positions that put their fetuses at risk. They also dispute any defense based on Title VII; there can be no BFOQ defense, because of an Equal Employment Opportunity Commission ruling:

> ... that narrow exception pertains only to situations where all or substantially all of a protected class is unable to perform the duties of the job in question. Such cannot be the case in the reproductive hazards setting, where exclusions are based on the premise of danger to the employee or fetus and not the ability to perform.[30]

Much more important and contentious is their attack on the business-necessity defense. Since it is well documented that exposure to lead may cause infertility or reduced sperm production, as well as chromosomal mutations, the potential offspring of male workers are also at risk. It follows that allowing only men and sterilized women to hold these positions is an unfair distribution of risk. The women argue that excluding them from these positions only delays and denies the employer's responsibility to make the workplace safe for everyone. Such an argument seems consistent with the court's guidelines for use of the business-necessity defense: plaintiffs, the court said, may rebut this defense by showing "that there are acceptable alternative policies or practices which would better accomplish the business purpose" of protecting against the risk of harm, "or accomplish it equally well with a lesser differential... impact" between women and men workers.[31]

Barbara Cantwell's case is a classic example of competing interests, all of whom may lay claim to some portion of the ethical and legal high ground. The real tragedy is that instead of finding a solution that maximizes each party's rights and benefits, our system of employee–employer relations is fixed on assessing blame and costs. The employer must choose between sex discrimination suits and possible health risks to future generations. The female employees must choose between loss of a high-paying job and sterilization. As long as the goal of equal employment opportunity is seen as competing with the goal of a safe, healthy workplace, the choices will continue to be negative ones.

CASE 22: THE BLACK AIR FORCE CADET

In 1979 Stephen Pullens was on top of the world. A young black man and a gifted athlete, Pullens had just received an appointment to the Air Force Academy. Yet when his physical exam revealed that he was a carrier of sickle cell trait (he did not have the disease), the Air Force withdrew his appointment, explaining that just having the trait jeopardized his life at the high altitude of the academy and certainly would interfere with his pilot training. In response to this policy, Pullens filed a class action suit on behalf of all cadets expelled for the same reason.[32] Would you:

A. find for the academy on grounds that national defense legitimizes a strict exclusion policy?

B. find for Pullens on grounds that the policy is discriminatory, inasmuch as sickle cell trait occurs almost exclusively in blacks and approximately 8 percent of black males exhibit it?

C. find for Pullens on grounds that there is no scientific evidence linking trait carriers with the actual disease symptoms?

The correct decision in the Pullens case, C, is easy to make, because the academy's policy has no scientific backing. In the face of this lack of evidence, the armed services reversed a ten-year policy of putting restrictions on trait carriers. (It is interesting to note that the commercial airlines never instituted such a policy.) But the ease of resolution in this case only serves to hide a thicket of bioethical problems surrounding the use of genetic testing as a means of determining differential sensitivity to occupational hazards, and then using those test results to exclude those judged to be at risk.

Some of these problems are variants on familiar themes. For example, the issue of confidentiality is prominent because medical information usually remains within the doctor—patient relationship. Yet, for occupational screening to work, some medical information must receive wider dissemination. Deciding which records, for what purposes, and for whose knowledge such information may be distributed is one major problem area. If potential employees are willing to give up some confidentiality, then employers must be willing to give them assurances that their private medical records will be handled in a secure manner, and that the dissemination of information between companies or through national data banks will be strictly prohibited. The last thing we need is a national genetic data bank with its potential for abuse.

Another familiar ethical problem arises because of the possible use of employees in human experiments. Since few of the specific genetic tests have yet been validated, it is quite likely that early screening programs (in a 1982 congressional survey, sixty of America's largest corporations indicated that they were considering genetic screening, and seventeen had actually done it in the previous ten years) will simply be gathering baseline data for future use. Such nontherapeutic experiments raise immediate

questions of informed consent and value to the participants (see Chapter V).

A whole other set of problems is unique to occupational
screening. Because no medical tests are ever 100 percent
foolproof, the prospect of test error raises a number of
serious issues: What happens when a person's test is a
false positive—i.e., he tests positive for some defect but
does not actually have that defect? What redress will workers have in appealing test results? What happens when it
is a false negative—i.e., the person has the defect but it
does not show on the test? If this person is hired and
ultimately contracts a genetically linked disease, will he
be able to sue the employer for putting him at risk? Finally, how are we to decide when a specific genetic defect
should be considered serious enough to put a worker at
risk? In other words, how can we be sure that nothing
like the Pullens case happens again?

A third class of problems flows from the application of
genetic-screening technology. The most important of these
is the potential for discrimination. Since genetic characteristics often follow racial lines (e.g., G6PD deficiency
is heavily weighted toward blacks and Filipinos), excluding these workers is a form of discrimination. In fact, in
this particular case it is a form of double discrimination,
because these worker groups are traditionally discrimi-
nated against in our society. Any attempt to use genetic
screening in such a group context is likely to run into the
same negative choices as were encountered in the Barbara
Cantwell case.

Because the employer has the ability to coerce the (potential) worker into participating in a genetic-screening
program, it is necessary that policies that protect the worker's rights be developed. A recent Congressional Office
of Technology Assessment report suggested the following
eleven criteria for the just application of such programs:

1. An attainable purpose
2. Community (workforce) participation
3. Equal access to testing
4. Adequate testing procedures
5. Absence of compulsion
6. Informed consent
7. Protection of subjects
8. Access to information
9. Provision of counseling/follow-up
10. Understandable relationship to therapy, if any
11. Protection of the right to privacy[33]

Most of those criteria apply to any medical procedure. They also rightly apply to genetic screening, regardless of whether the individual being screened is protected by the full doctor–patient relationship. In addition we might amplify "adequate testing procedure" to include: the factor tested for must be a BFOQ, the factor must relate to safety on the job, and the test must be a valid and reliable screen for that factor.

We now know that all disease depends on the interaction between an organism and its environment. We also know that in a world of scarce resources, we can usually spend those resources on one (e.g., the worker) or the other (e.g., the workplace), but not both. We are learning that in such a world making those choices is a social and political act with important bioethical consequences. We must realize that the choices we make today will shape the health care of tomorrow.

IV

LIFE AND DEATH

AS inhabitants of the modern world, we are no longer amazed by technological accomplishment. Whether it's a walk in space, the discovery of the newest subatomic particle, or the latest refinement in cell biology, we have come to expect rapid scientific advance. Perhaps, as a coping mechanism to avoid "future shock," most of us simply accept the inevitability of technological change without so much as a second thought. After all, recovering a wayward satellite, or building the world's largest cyclotron, or having the capacity to grow specialized human cells in the laboratory does not intrude upon our lives in any obvious way. It does not require that we alter any of our core values or ethical beliefs, only that we stretch our already flexible notion of what is scientifically possible.

Occasionally, however, a technological achievement appears with consequences far beyond its immediate scientific application. These technologies not only have the power to change the way we live, they also have the power to change the ways we think about life itself. During the fifteen-year period between 1953 and 1967, two technologies appeared with this power to alter our conceptual scheme. In giving men new medical powers over the dying

120

process, they also caused all of us to reassess the ethical meaning of life and death.

The first was the *heart-lung machine*—a device that supplies and distributes oxygen to the body when the natural circulation system is incapacitated. Finally perfected in 1953 after a nearly one-hundred-year-long quest, this machine enabled surgeons to perform open-heart surgery for the first time. But such operations, which require that the patient's heart be stopped, that the machine perform human circulatory functions, and that then the heart be restarted, created a macabre paradox. For hundreds of years, a beating heart and breathing lungs were the criteria used to determine life. The standard legal definition of death, based on these medical criteria, was "a total stoppage of the circulation of the blood, and a cessation of the animal and vital functions consequent thereon, such as respiration, pulsation, etc."[1] Did that mean that all open-heart patients had died and been brought back to life? The more sensational tabloids seemed to think so, and the public was treated to first-person accounts of what it was like on the "other side." But, for the medical community and some forward-looking members of the public, it was more a case of the need for redefinition rather than reincarnation.

If most of America was too busy in 1953 to notice that it was now possible to be alive without a heartbeat (a beating heart is not a *necessary* condition of life), the whole world took notice in 1967 when Christiaan Barnard demonstrated the implications of believing the converse: it is also possible to have a strongly beating heart but yet be clinically dead (a beating heart is not a *sufficient* condition of life). The success of heart transplantation had two dramatic effects on our conception of the criteria of death. First, as a practical matter, if organ transplants were to proceed, we needed criteria of death that did not require

the death of the donor organ. Second, and more importantly, if the cessation of heartbeat was no longer to be
the criterion of death, we would have to rethink our long
cultural legacy that placed the heart at the "seat of life."
Long before William Harvey finally explained the circulatory system in the seventeenth century, man had considered the heart as the "vital organ." But if the heart is
neither a necessary nor a sufficient condition for life, what
new criteria might we use to replace it?

One clue to answering this question is the history of
medicine. Scientists have a long history of explaining human bodily functions in terms of state-of-the-art technology. In fact, one major reason Harvey was able to succeed
where all others had failed was the recent invention of
the pump. By drawing an analogy between mechanical
pumping systems and the human circulatory system,
Harvey was finally able to explain how the blood was
propelled through the body. In a like manner, modern
scientists are tempted to explain the workings of the human brain by analogy to our state-of-the-art technology—
the computer (often referred to as an electronic brain).
Although the analogy is far from straightforward, the dominant view today is certainly that the brain controls bodily
functions in much the same way that a computer controls
an automated factory. So it was only natural to look to the
brain (the master controller) for a new definition of death.

By 1968, the cumulative effects of the heart-lung machine, organ transplants, and developments in intensive-
care medicine that allowed us to keep comatose patients
alive indefinitely had led to a medical crisis. Using the
old criteria of death, cessation of heart and lung function,
many patients were being kept "alive" artificially by mechanical means even though they had no possibility of
ever recovering. This created an unendurable hardship
for their families, as well as overloading the medical sys-

tem and draining resources from the care of patients who
might recover.

The solution to this crisis was a set of new criteria of
death. In the less than twenty years since the "Report of
the Ad Hoc Committee of the Harvard Medical School to
Examine the Definition of Brain Death" was first published, most of us have incorporated the notion of "brain
death" into our own value structure. Sometimes conceptual revolution is just that easy. But imagine trying to explain the concept to a nineteenth-century relative, someone
imbued with mechanical rather than electrical models;
someone who had never heard of the information revolution, or cybernetics, or computers. While we may not
precisely understand all the medical niceties, we understand enough (not only about medicine but about the model
of scientific explanation in our modern world) that we are
willing to accept the notion that it is the brain, and not
the heart, which directly controls life.

The Harvard committee's report was really quite simple
given the momentousness of its task. The first line stated
that the report's primary purpose was to define irreversible coma as a new criterion of death. The report then
listed the features of irreversible coma:

1. *Unreceptivity and Unresponsivity.* There is a total
unawareness to externally applied stimuli and inner need
and complete unresponsiveness—our definition of irreversible coma. Even the most intensely painful stimuli
evoke no vocal or other response, not even a groan, withdrawal of a limb, or quickening of respiration.

2. *No Movements or Breathing.* Observation covering
a period of at least one hour by physicians is adequate to
satisfy the criteria of no spontaneous muscular movements
or spontaneous respiration.... After the patient is on the
mechanical respirator, the total absence of spontaneous
breathing may be established by turning off the respirator

for three minutes and observing whether there is any effort
on the part of the subject to breathe spontaneously.

3. *No Reflexes.* Irreversible coma with abolition of central nervous system activity is evidenced in part by the
absence of elicitable reflexes. The pupil will be fixed and
dilated and will not respond to a direct source of bright
light.[2]

In addition, the report included three rules of application,
actual procedures for the attending physician to follow:
(1) a "flat" electroencephelogram (EEG) was of "great con-
firmatory value"; (2) the three criteria should be checked
after a twenty-four-hour waiting period to determine if
any change had occurred; (3) *hypothermia*—severe lowering of body temperature—and barbiturate coma were
two conditions which vitiated these criteria.

Since the Harvard Report first appeared, twenty-seven
states have adopted some variation of the "brain death"
criteria. But this hodgepodge approach has led to some
peculiar legal and bioethical questions: Is there more than
one kind of death? Can a person be declared dead in New
York but alive in New Jersey? Can a killer use the defense
that the doctor who shuts off the ventilator, rather than
the person who fired the bullet, is the real murderer?
Because the answer to each of these questions must be
no, the first task of the President's Commission for the
Study of Ethical Problems in Medicine and Biomedical
and Behavioral Research was a detailed study of the definition of death.

After reviewing all the competing statutes, conducting
an empirical study of comatose and artificially respirated
patients, and hearing testimony from all the appropriate
groups (e.g., doctors [AMA], lawyers [American Bar Association, ethicists, policy-makers], the commission produced a model Uniform Determination of Death Act:

> An individual who has sustained either (1) irre-
> versible cessation of circulatory or respiratory func-

tions, or (2) irreversible cessation of all functions of the entire brain, including the brain stem, is dead. A determination of death must be made in accordance with accepted medical standards.[3]

This proposed legislation has already met with much approval. Both the AMA and the ABA have dropped their own proposals and accepted the commission's, and many states have adopted or are considering the adoption of this statute.

If a conceptual revolution has taken place and the nation is now approaching a consensus about the definition of death, the same can hardly be said about the bioethical issues that revolve around it and around the technologies that precipitated it. Whether the issue involves the beginning of human life or the conditions under which it may be permissible to allow a life to end, questions of life and death are always among the most gripping and contentious of bioethical dilemmas.

CASE 23: DR. EDELIN AND "BABY BOY"

In October 1973 Dr. Kenneth Edelin was a well-regarded physician at Boston City Hospital. As chief resident in obstetrics and gynecology his duties included performing abortions, and he subsequently performed one on a woman estimated to be about six months pregnant. After attempts to induce the abortion by infusion of a saline solution had failed, Edelin performed a *hysterotomy*—a procedure similar to a cesarean section in which the fetus is removed through an incision in the mother's abdomen. The operation seemed to be uneventful, and, during its course, the fetus died.

Six months later, while the hospital was undergoing an investigation that had nothing to do with Edelin, the body of a "well nourished black male fetus" was discovered in the hospital morgue. It was the fetus Edelin had aborted.

After further inquiries, the district attorney charged him with manslaughter, claiming that he "did assault and beat a certain person, to wit: a male child described to said jurors as Baby Boy and by such assault and beating did kill the said person." Although there was no doubt the abortion was legal, the DA charged that the aborted fetus had been born alive and that Edelin, far from taking positive actions to nurture that life, had actually acted to kill it.

In early 1975 a jury found Edelin guilty of homicide. There was an immediate appeal, and on December 17, 1976, the Massachusetts Supreme Court overturned the jury verdict on grounds that there was insufficient evidence to find Edelin guilty.[4] While that ruling ended the legal wrangling, it did nothing to answer any of the gut-wrenching bioethical questions: Does abortion imply death of a fetus or just the termination of a pregnancy? What are the physician's obligations to the fetus during late-term abortions? Ultimately, when does a fetus become a person with all the rights and protections that that status confers?

The proximate legal cause of the Edelin case was the now famous *Roe v. Wade*[5] and *Doe v. Bolton*[6] decisions handed down by the U.S. Supreme Court in January 1973. In building on the concept of a citizen's right to privacy, a notion that had recently been established by some landmark family-planning cases, the Court recognized

> that a right of personal privacy, or a guarantee of certain areas or zones of privacy, does exist under the Constitution.... This right of privacy, whether it be founded in the Fourteenth Amendment's concept of personal liberty and restrictions upon state action... or... in the Ninth Amendment's reservation of rights to the people, is broad enough to encompass a woman's decision whether or not to terminate her pregnancy.[7]

Of course, the privacy right is not absolute and the Court
had to weigh it against the potentially stronger claim that
a fetus is a person entitled to all legal protections. In citing
constitutional language holding that a citizen is a "person
born or naturalized in the United States," the Court effectively rejected that claim; a fetus, being unborn, could
not be a citizen.

But the Court did try to accommodate the state's right
to regulate abortion, through its trimester criteria based
on stages of fetal development:

1. For the first trimester, all abortion decisions are
   to be made by the pregnant woman in consultation
   with her physician.
2. For the second trimester, the state may regulate
   abortion in order to promote maternal health.
3. For the third trimester, the state, in order to protect
   its interest in the potentiality of human life, may
   regulate or even proscribe abortion except when
   it is necessary for the preservation of the life or
   health of the mother.

By leaving the moment and definition of fetal viability un-
clear, not to mention the scope of physician responsibility to the near-term fetus, the Court had provided the
legal opening for the Edelin case. It is probable that the
nine justices never envisioned a case that would, at the
same time, involve the questions of when does a life begin
and when does it end.

As we now know, the Edelin case was only the opening
salvo in the "moral war" that surrounds the aftermath of
the "Roe and Doe" cases. By attempting to set legal limits
on what is essentially a moral problem, the Court spawned
the most socially divisive issue since the Vietnam War.
But abortion is hardly the only such personal issue that
the Court has ruled upon. Until the Court's *Griswold v.
Connecticut*[8] decision (which introduced the concept of
a "right to privacy") in 1965, it was illegal for married

couples to receive contraceptive information and materials. And that decision wasn't extended to include unmarried individuals until 1972. Balancing the state and individual rights in the area of family planning is the topic of the section of this chapter that begins on page 135.

CASE 24: BABY DOE AND BIG BROTHER IN THE NURSERY

On April 9, 1982, Dr. Walter Owens expected to deliver another normal, healthy baby into the world. Unfortunately, the baby he did deliver suffered from *Down's syndrome*—a chromosomal disorder resulting in mental retardation—and an *esophogeal atresia*, a blockage of the tube that leads from the mouth to the stomach. Although such birth defects are not uncommon—one in seven hundred babies is born with Down's syndrome, which is usually accompanied by other defects—the facts in this case, and the attendant publicity, led to a genuine national soul searching.

The baby's most immediate need was surgery to correct the atresia. Without it, nutrition could be administered only intravenously, and the backing up of stomach acid into the lungs would almost surely result in death from pneumonia within a few days. Because the small Bloomington, Indiana, hospital was not equipped to perform this operation, or other diagnostic procedures that the baby required, one suggested course of treatment involved transferring the baby to a hospital with a full-scale neonatal-care unit. This was the recommendation made by Dr. James Schaffer, a consulting physician, when he asked the parents to consent to the surgery for their child.

However, Dr. Owens presented another option to the parents. He explained that while the operation would save their baby's life, it would cause pain, would probably lead to the need for additional surgeries, and would do nothing about the mental retardation. His alternative: refuse to consent to the procedure, prohibit intravenous feeding, keep the baby sedated and comfortable, but let it die in peace. When the parents sided with Owens, the stage was set for a tragic modern morality play.

The hospital, worried about its legal liability in letting a baby die, immediately began a series of legal maneuvers. They first asked for a judicial hearing in order to determine whether the parents had the right to refuse treatment for their child. The judge ruled that they did, citing an honest divergence of medical opinion and the parents' right to choose between the two competing recommendations. Attempts to appoint a legal guardian through the county's Child Protection Committee and Indiana's Child in Need of Services statute met with a similar result. When the Indiana Court of Appeals and the State Supreme Court refused to hear the case, the only avenue left open was the U.S. Supreme Court.

But by now the case had left the back-fence-gossip mills of a small American town for the front pages of major metropolitan newspapers. The National Right-to-Life Association filed suit on behalf of a couple who wanted to adopt the child. The Reagan Administration was besieged by phone calls from groups and individuals who wanted something to be done. And the fate of a small child known only as "Baby Doe" consumed the nation.[9] The baby died on April 15, before the case could be presented to the Supreme Court, but not before the nation was given a dramatic lesson in the bioethical dilemmas of neonatal medicine: How can a distinction be made between sanctity of life and quality of life? How can the rights of the state, the rights of the parents, and the rights of the baby be fairly represented? Who should make the decisions about the baby's care?

Perhaps the most provocative item to emerge from the whole incident was the fact that, medically and ethically, Baby Doe was far from unique. Writing ten years earlier in *The New England Journal of Medicine*, Drs. Raymond

Duff and Alexander Campbell had revealed how 43 out of the 299 deaths occurring in the intensive-care nursery at Yale–New Haven Hospital had resulted from similar withdrawal of treatment.[10] Another article, appearing in 1983 in the journal *Pediatrics*, detailed the results of a five-year experiment in the management of infants born with *spina bifida*—a condition in which the spinal cord fails to seal over with protective tissue, resulting in the infant being born with the cord encased in a sac and protruding through an opening in the lower back. One management option was supportive care only; in other words, the condition would not be repaired. All 24 infants whose parents chose this option subsequently died.[11] But if the only thing unique about the Baby Doe case was the publicity surrounding it, that opened America's eyes to an issue that could no longer be ignored.

The Reagan Administration's immediate response was to promulgate what became known as the "Baby Doe Rule": using Section 504 of the Rehabilitation Act of 1973, the Department of Health and Human Services notified all medical institutions receiving federal funds that it was unlawful to withhold nourishment or medical treatment from a handicapped infant simply because that infant was handicapped. Along with the rule was an 800 telephone number, the Handicapped Infant Hotline, so that concerned citizens could notify the government of suspected violations. Big Brother had invaded the nursery. Although the courts eventually ruled against this Baby Doe Rule (a modified rule went into effect in 1984), finding it "arbitrary and capricious" as well as "hasty and ill-considered," the Administration had made its intent clear: all infants, no matter what their medical condition, were entitled to aggressive lifesaving medical treatment.

The courts were not the only party to find fault with the Administration's actions. Civil libertarians saw them as a massive intrusion of the state into decisions that were better made by the families in consultation with their physicians. The medical profession rebelled at the idea that Washington was going to tell them how to best treat their patients. And the President's Bioethics Commission—a body begun under Jimmy Carter but just then (1983) issuing its report regarding care for seriously ill newborns—declared that

> the adversarial atmosphere generated by this approach is unlikely to lead to infants receiving the most suitable care. The same problem arises with the regulations issued by the Department of Health and Human Services in the wake of the *Infant Doe* case.... Instead of adding further uncertainty to an already complex situation, the Federal government would do better to encourage hospitals to improve their procedures for overseeing life-and-death decisions, especially regarding seriously ill newborns. Using financial sanctions to punish an "incorrect" decision in particular cases is likely to be ineffective and to lead to excessively detailed regulations that would involve government reimbursement officials in bedside decisionmaking.[12]

But those protestations were mainly procedural, and the major ethical questions surrounding the neonatal dilemma still remained: Is there something really wrong with requiring that all infants be given lifesaving medical treatment? If there is, what criteria will be used to decide who is to die? And who is to apply the criteria? These questions are addressed in the "Beginnings of Life" section of this chapter.

CASE 25: KAREN ANN QUINLAN AND THE RIGHT TO DIE

On April 15, 1975, Karen Ann Quinlan ceased living; unfortunately, her process of dying would continue for ten years. During that time period, all of America received a firsthand lesson in the promises and drawbacks of technomedicine, the vagaries of constitutional law, and the bioethical dilemmas of life and death.

Karen was a healthy twenty-two-year-old who simply stopped breathing. By the time resuscitation was begun and she arrived at the hospital, she was comatose. After she was put on a ventilator to assist her breathing, an electroencephalogram showed that while her brain activity was abnormal, she did have some brain activity. Instead of being "brain dead," Karen was in what the medical profession calls a *chronic persistent vegetative state*—a condition in which lower-level brain functions may be carried out (e.g., breathing, swallowing) but there is no sign of higher functions (e.g., cognition, consciousness). Although the certain prognosis was that there was no chance of recovery, it seemed that she might live indefinitely on the ventilator.

After months of agonizing over this situation, her father filed suit to become her legal guardian. He intended to use this power to terminate the "extraordinary means" that were being used in Karen's care. He wanted her returned "to her natural state so that we could place her body and soul in the tender loving hands of the Lord." When the hospital objected to this plan, and a lower court refused him, he appealed to the New Jersey Supreme Court.

The court first had to decide whether any patient, comatose or not, could have a lifesaving medical procedure terminated. In basing its reasoning on the right-to-privacy argument that had figured so prominently in the *Roe v. Wade* case, the court decided:

> Presumably this right is broad enough to encompass a patient's decision to decline medical treatment under certain circumstances, in much the same way as it is broad enough to encompass a woman's decision to terminate pregnancy under certain conditions.

But the court also recognized that the state may have an interest in continuing treatment. It just believed that the state's interests were not compelling in this case, and it established vague criteria for determining when the state may intervene:

> "We think that the State's interest *contra* weakens and the individual's right of privacy grows as the degree of bodily invasion increases and the prognosis dims. Ultimately there comes a point at which the individual's rights overcome the state interest.

Having determined that a competent Karen would have been able to decide to forgo the ventilator, the court next had to decide whether anyone else could make that decision for her. In ruling that the right to privacy need not be denied simply because the patient is no longer competent, the court relied on the rule of *substituted judgment*: a proxy may make a decision for the incompetent patient based on what that person would choose if he or she were able. Obviously, the more forcefully the incompetent patient had expressed her desires, the easier this rule is to apply. The Quinlans testified that Karen had often expressed her wish not to be kept alive by extraordinary means, and the court had no problem in complying with this wish.

Even with the court decision, Karen's hospital refused to take her off the ventilator. Eventually the family had to have her moved to a nursing home that respected their wishes. But the saga was not over, because Karen began to breathe on her own when the ventilator was withdrawn. By the time Karen Ann Quinlan finally stopped breathing and died peacefully, in the summer of 1985, the whole country was much more aware of the bioethical issues behind buzz words like "right to die," "death with dignity," and "quality of life."[13]

No one has expressed those issues more starkly than

Richard Lamm, the governor of Colorado: "Like leaves which fall off a tree forming the humus in which other plants can grow, we've got a duty to die and get out of the way with all of our machines and artificial hearts, so that our kids can build a reasonable life."[14] Lamm's words, which drew a storm of comment and criticism from around the country, were really designed to draw attention to two groups of facts that form the context of our modern way of dying.

First, just as women no longer routinely give birth on kitchen tables, families no longer gather around the bed of a dying grandparent. The shift in disease burden from quick-killing infectious diseases to slower-working chronic conditions, as well as the perceived right to health care, has resulted in 80 percent of today's deaths occurring in hospitals and nursing homes. But hospitalization carries with it the threat that death will be far from "natural." With all the ventilators, intravenous solutions, cardiac "crash carts," and other high-tech medical options, Lamm is saying hospitalization often only prolongs the dying, rather than enhancing the living.

Second, exercising every medical option for every patient is incredibly costly. The best current estimate is that 28 percent of the nation's $75 billion Medicare budget is spent to maintain patients over the age of sixty-five during their last year of life, and the bulk of those dollars are spent in the last month. While medical insurance hides most of that cost from individuals, its effect on the nation's health bill is staggering. If we are to continue to enjoy a right to health care, tough decisions will have to be made about when that right should be terminated.

While Lamm's speech was directed at the level of public-policy options, no legal or legislative solutions are possible without an understanding of the underlying bioethical issues: Are there any limits to the treatment that a competent patient may refuse? What are the state's rights regarding refusal of treatment? Is there real distinction between withholding a treatment so that the patient dies and taking an action intended to lead directly to the patient's death? These are the issues that are addressed in the "End of Life" section of this chapter.

FAMILY PLANNING

CONCEPT: No area of health behavior seems so personal and private as procreative decision-making. What grounds could the state possibly have to enter a bedroom and prescribe the conditions of lovemaking? Amazingly, it is only within the past twenty years that society has been willing to answer that question with a single word, "None." From 1873 until the *Griswold* decision in 1965, the law of the land was the Comstock Act, officially titled an Act for the Suppression of Trade in and Circulation of Obscene Literature and Articles of Immoral Use. The purpose of the act was to make it a misdemeanor "to sell, lend, give away, exhibit, publish, or possess an obscene book, pamphlet, paper, writing, advertisement, circular, print, picture, drawing, or other representation, figure, or image...or any cast instrument or other article of an immoral nature, or any drug or medicine, or any article whatever, for the prevention of conception, or for causing unlawful abortion."[15]

Today, we live in an era that prizes personal freedom, and a whole series of laws and court decisions have made it clear that "if the right of privacy means anything, it is the right of the *individual*, married or single, to be free from unwarranted governmental intrusion into matters so fundamentally affecting a person as the decision whether to bear or beget a child."[16] As a simple manifestation of personal freedom, the individual's right to contraceptive materials is no longer an issue.

But it is precisely our society's premium on personal freedom that is the driving force behind the abortion issue: Just how far does this freedom extend? Does it include a woman's right to abortion on demand? Does a fetus have any right to personal freedom? What is the connection between personal freedom, abortion, and human life?

PRACTICE: American society is currently trapped in a curious asymmetrical paradox: while we are finally reaching a consensus concerning the definition of human death, no such consensus seems possible regarding the definition of human life. Nor is this paradox merely of academic interest, something that only semanticists or theologians might find interesting. Just as a civilized society must have a recognized definition of death—to answer legal questions (e.g., When should a will be probated?), medical questions (e.g., When should a respirator be unplugged?), and social questions (e.g., When is it appropriate to begin grieving?)—the same is true of a definition of life. Even though a definitional consensus won't immediately resolve the abortion issue, it will allow us to approach the problem rationally. Without a consensus, there is little hope of resolution and we will continue to be racked by bitter social divisiveness.

Unfortunately, neither the courts nor the Congress seem much interested in consensus building. In deciding *Roe v. Wade*, the Supreme Court evaded the entire issue: "We need not resolve the difficult question of when life begins. When those trained in the respective disciplines of medicine, philosophy and theology are unable to arrive at any consensus, the judiciary, at this point in the development of man's knowledge, is not in a position to speculate as to the answer."[17] In ruling that a woman has a legal right to an abortion, the Court based its decision solely on constitutional interpretation, not medical knowledge or moral argument.

But then it immediately turned around and relied on contingent medical fact to limit that right. Because an abortion is safer than pregnancy during the first trimester, the women has a near-absolute right to terminate her pregnancy during that time period; and because a fetus becomes viable during the third trimester, the state has a right to regulate abortions during that time period. Far from constitutional interpretation, this ruling embodies a medical decision: the right to an abortion rests upon choosing the best treatment (abortion or childbirth) for the medical condition known as pregnancy.

Instead of trying to reach a consensus about the definition of human life, the Court chose to compromise on the right to abortion. But this produced a decision that pleased no one. Legal scholars asked where medical diagnosis could be found in the Constitution. Physicians pointed out the imminent collapse of the trimester criteria as abortions became safer and fetal viability occurred earlier. And advocates on both sides of the abortion issue bemoaned a decision that failed to absolutely recognize "their rights."

The Congress, chafing at what it viewed as judicial usurpation of legislative power, has sought several means of "end-running" the Supreme Court. The best-known of these attempts, an amendment to the Constitution prohibiting abortion, suffers from the rigors of the amending process (i.e., the requisite three-fourths vote of all the states). But some congressmen are convinced that the Constitution already prohibits abortion. The problem, as they see it, isn't the law, but the current lack of an agreed-upon definition of human life. They believe that just as science helped in reaching a consensus regarding the definition of death, it can do the same for a definition of life.

And once such a consensus is reached, the Court will have no alternative but to rule abortion unconstitutional.

CASE 26: THE HUMAN LIFE BILL

Suppose you were a U.S. senator concerned about the emotional turmoil being caused by the abortion issue. Some of your colleagues present the following argument to you:

1. Pass a Human Life Statute stating: "The Congress finds that present scientific evidence indicates a significant likelihood that actual human life exists from conception."[18]
2. Conclude that a fetus is a human life and a person, and it is therefore unethical to kill it.
3. As a person, the fetus is entitled to all the protections of the Fourteenth Amendment's due-process clause: "no state shall...deprive any person of life, liberty, or property without due process of law."
4. Conclude that abortion is unconstitutional.

How would you vote on the Human Life Statute:

A. Vote against it, since science cannot determine when a human life begins (deny premise 1)?
B. Vote against it, since the ethicality of abortion is not an issue that science can answer (deny premise 2)?
C. Vote for it, since it appears to be the best way to bring about consensus on the abortion issue?

Whether you are pro-life or pro-choice, it is important to understand why the Human Life Bill is bad legislation. First, because it confuses facts and values. Second, because it relies exclusively on science to solve our bioethical dilemmas. Third, because it attempts to reach consensus by fiat. Understanding more about how this bill fails is a lesson not only about "abortion politics," but about bioethical thinking in the era of technomedicine.

The bill's initial problem is the sponsor's naive belief that science can answer the question of when human life begins. Rather than being capable of answering such a value-laden question, science can only provide us with factual data—with criteria that we may choose to use as indicators of human life:

Fertilization
Fixation of the genetic code (soon after fertilization)
Implantation (about one week)
Last chance for change in the genetic code (two to four weeks)
Central nervous system activity (detectable electroencephalogram at about eight weeks)
Spontaneous movement (ten weeks)
Brain structure complete (twelve weeks)
Cardiac system activity (electrocardiogram at twelve weeks)
Quickening (thirteen to sixteen weeks)
Viability at present point in technology
    (normally twenty-four to twenty-eight weeks; occasionally as early as twenty weeks)
Integrated functioning of the nervous system
Birth
Breathing
Consciousness
Social interaction
Acceptance by other people
Development of language
Development of nervous system complete[10]

It is entirely up to society to decide which of these scientific criteria is going to constitute the definition of human life.

This situation is exactly analogous to the role that science plays in the definition of death. It provides us with many possible criteria—originally putrefaction, then breathing and circulation, and today degree of brain function—and we must choose the one that best reflects our social needs and values. In the case of death, certain technological breakthroughs have allowed our society to reach a consensus in the last few years. In the case of life, however, no consensus has been possible because the definition has been inextricably linked to the abortion issue. Such a connection has led pro-choice advocates to fear that any consensus which defined a fetus as a human life would entail the end of abortion on demand. But this fear is ungrounded. As the second flaw in the Human Life Bill demonstrates, deciding on a definition of human life is logically distinct from determining the criteria for an ethical abortion.

Suppose that society could decide on a definition of human life. For the sake of consistency with our definition of death, which relies on brain function, let's agree that human life begins at the eighth week with recognizable brain function. (In fact, this argument against the bill works just as well with any definition.) The Human Life Bill would have us conclude from this newly established fact that abortions after this time are immoral and unconstitutional. Yet such a conclusion commits what philosophers call the *naturalistic fallacy*—the mistake of inferring an ethical conclusion about what one ought to do from some factual premises about what is the case. For example, scientific evidence demonstrates clearly that excessive alcoholic consumption is a health risk. It does not follow, however, that alcoholic consumption is immoral, or unconstitutional, or even that it should be against the law. Before any such conclusions can be reached, we need to consider the relative values of alcohol and health in our society, as well as who should have the right to make personal decisions about liquor consumption. In 1920 the Congress erred in these value judgments and we ended up with that national folly known as Prohibition.

Although the stakes surrounding abortion are much more serious than bathtub gin, the logical principle is the same. Contrary to the hopes of the bill's supporters, defining an eight-week-old fetus to be a human being is not the same as demonstrating that such fetuses may not be legally or ethically aborted. Instead, the ability to reach a consensus about the definition of human life merely clears the ground so that the crucial questions regarding abortion may be asked: What is the value of a fetal life in our society? What rights does it have? How do those rights compare to the rights of a pregnant woman?

This approach to resolving the abortion issue may seem counterproductive. After all, we've traded one simple-to-state question (When does human life begin?) for three more complex questions. But the simple question was the wrong one to ask, while the complex questions typify a kind of problem our society is frequently asked to solve: deciding between the rights of competing parties. A classic example of this is the taking of a human life. Not all killing is murder. We warrant killing (both morally and legally) in cases of self-defense, capital punishment, and war. These justifications demonstrate that even an individual's most precious right, the right to life, may be overridden by other competing rights. Every right has a limit (your right to swing your arm freely ends at the tip of my nose), and the real abortion issue is where to draw that limiting line between the right of the fetus to live and the right of the woman to have an abortion.

During the past twenty years the National Opinion Research Center has conducted a series of polls in order to determine exactly where the majority of the American people want that limit line placed. Where would you draw the line?

CASE 27: THE ABORTION POLL

It should be possible for a woman to obtain a legal abortion:

    A. if the woman's health is seriously endangered by the pregnancy.
    B. if she became pregnant as a result of rape.
    C. if there is a strong chance of a serious defect in the baby.
    D. if the family has a very low income and cannot afford any more children.
    E. if she is not married and does not want to marry the man.
    F. if she is married and does not want any more children.

The major public benefit of these polls is education, not policy formulation. Even though answers to the NORC questions indicate that a huge majority approve of reasons a–c, with an approximate 50–50 split on reasons d–f, other poll data are much less clear.[20] But even if the data were statistically conclusive, they would only indicate public preference, not the ethical correctness of the views expressed. By providing a list of possible justifications for abortion, the poll takers have provided some potential ethical boundaries, a place to begin a public discussion. What's missing are the ethical principles that might support the setting of such boundary lines.

One principle that almost everyone should be able to agree with is the principle of self-defense. In cases where the life of the mother would be endangered if the fetus were carried to term, it seems just to override the fetus' right to life. It is this maxim that underlies our intuitive reaction to agree with condition A in the NORC poll. Many would also want to extend the principle of self-defense to include cases in which the mother's health, but not her life, was permanently or severely threatened.

Another principle with some *prima facie* ethical claim
is the maxim that people are held accountable only for
actions for which they are responsible. In the abortion
context, this is taken to mean that since a rape victim is
not responsible for her pregnancy, she should have an
absolute right to terminate it.

Each of the other four NORC conditions is also supported by an ethical principle (e.g., the principle of personal
autonomy), and it is easy to imagine other rules—the
Court's medical-decision axiom—that might warrant abortions in other situations. But this richness of possible justifications is hardly surprising. Without some ethical
underpinning, there would be no reason at all to think
that an abortion might be justified. One half of the reason
the abortion issue is so difficult to resolve is that the pro-
choice forces have an impressive array of ethical principles supporting their position.

Yet the fact that a pregnant woman can adduce some
ethical principle is not conclusive reason for believing
that an abortion is justified in a particular circumstance.
That principle, and the moral reasoning that flows from
it, must be weighed against the rights of the fetus and the
force of its only ethical principle—the right to life. This
is the second half of the reason why the abortion issue
seems so intractable: the fetus' right to life is also a compelling ethical axiom. Judging which principle is to have
priority is never an easy task, but it is the crux of ethical
reasoning and the heart of the abortion issue. The philosopher Hegel could have been thinking about abortion
when he wrote that the greatest battles in history aren't
fought between right and wrong but between right and
right.

Finally, just as the Human Life Bill has little to do with
the abortion issue, it is decidedly the wrong approach to
take in reaching a consensus regarding the definition of
human life. If it really is a scientific issue, as the bill

wrongly alleges, then it must be decided by evidence and not by votes. And if it is a moral issue based on scientific criteria, then it must be decided by ethical analysis rather than by votes. Either way, the bill is clearly extraneous to the issue.

Our most difficult bioethical issues cannot be resolved by scientific evidence, or legislative votes, or court decisions. Their resolution requires nothing less than a values revolution of the kind that occurred regarding the definition of human death. Scientists, legislators, and jurists may contribute information and analysis, but the ultimate choice rests with the larger society. When it comes to bioethical decision-making, the people are the cutting edge.

THE BEGINNINGS OF LIFE

CONCEPT: Infanticide, we would like to think, is one definite criterion for distinguishing modern, civilized society from its ancient, brutish precursors. The practice of killing infants may have occurred in Biblical times (e.g., Pharaoh's injunction to the midwives that "if it be a [Hebrew] son, then ye shall kill him"[21]), been supported by both Plato ("Those of the inferior parents and any children of the rest that are born defective will be hidden away..."[22]) and Aristotle ("... let there be a law that no *deformed* child shall live"[23]), and played a prominent role in the founding of Rome (Romulus and Remus were abandoned as infants and reared by wolves), but it is hardly a custom that we would condone today. Or is it?

To be sure, no civilized society would approve of infanticide for political ends (although the "civilized" state of Nazi Germany did exactly that fifty years ago). But what about infanticide for more humane goals, perhaps even for the benefit of the infant? Recent studies have reported that physicians themselves believe that infanticide may be ethically justified under certain medical conditions. All twenty participants at the 1974 Sonoma Conference on Ethical Issues agreed that it is ethically proper to withhold life-sustaining treatment from some severely handicapped newborns, and seventeen of the twenty went so far as to suggest that actively killing such an infant was proper given the prognosis of a lingering, painful death.[24] A much larger poll of doctors in the journal *Pediatrics* found more than 80 percent of the respondents answering "No" to the question "Do you believe that the life of each and every new born infant should be saved if it is in our ability to do so?"[25] Similar physician polls confirm the widespread nature of these beliefs.

Nor are doctors the only ones in our society who justify infanticide under special conditions. A 1983 Gallup poll found that 43 percent of Americans would request that their doctor not act to keep a badly deformed baby in need of treatment alive (40 percent would request that treatment be continued).[26] And previously cited studies demonstrate that both doctors and parents are willing to act on their beliefs. Are we entering a new era of medically justified infanticide? Is withholding treatment the same as actively killing? Is it possible to ethically support such a practice? If it can be justified, under what conditions and who gets to make the decision? Finally, isn't it against the law?

PRACTICE: We are living in the era of *the fallacy of the technological imperative*—a general belief that if it can be done, then it must be done. Whether it's the production of hideous biological weapons or simply the production of an oxymoron like electrical stimulators for "passive exercise," the dominating principle seems to be "If you've got the technological know-how, flaunt it."

Nowhere does this principle run into more problems

than in the neonatal intensive-care nursery. As a result of the revolution in neonatal care, the death rate for infants in the first month of life was halved in the decade of the 1970s. That's the good news. The bad news is that not all infants will benefit from medicine's new technological capacity. Instead, they may undergo needless days or weeks of pain and suffering only to die hooked up to our modern "medical miracles," or they may survive to live a life that many believe is not worth living. The key medical and ethical question is, Which of the roughly 10 percent of infants born at risk (e.g., because of low birth weight or congenital abnormality) will benefit from our new technological capacity?

Almost everyone, including the Reagan Administration, believes that newborns in need of treatment fall into at least two categories. Most belong to the "duty to treat" category. These are infants for whom treatment is clearly beneficial and for whom there is no ethical question that treatment should proceed. A second, much smaller group belongs to the "duty not to treat" category. These are infants for whom any treatment would be futile. The ethical justification for nontreatment is expressed by Dr. C. Everett Koop, Reagan's strongly pro-life Surgeon General:

> Medicine may *never* have all the solutions to all the problems that occur at birth. I personally see no medical solution to a cephalodymus or an anencephalic child. The first is a one headed twin; the second a child with virtually no functioning brain at all. In these cases the prognosis is an early and merciful death by natural causes. There are no so-called "heroic measures" possible and intervention would merely prolong the patient's process of dying. Some of nature's errors are extraordinary and frightening... but nature also has the kindness to take them away. For such infants, neither medicine nor law can be of any help. And neither medicine nor law should prolong these infants' process of dying.[27]

There is no justification, either medical, legal, or ethical, for treating infants who are "born dying."

The real argument among doctors, lawyers, and ethicists begins with the proposal that some infants in need of neonatal care may fall into a third category—"option to treat." Are there infants whom we are capable of keeping alive but for whom the prospective quality of life is so dreadful that they are better off dead? If so, how might these cases be decided, and by whom?

CASE 28: "BABY BOY HOULE" GOES TO COURT

On February 9, 1974, the life of Lorraine and Robert Houle changed forever. Instead of the normal, healthy child they had anticipated, their son was born with multiple deformities: no left eye, a rudimentary left ear, a misshapen left hand, unfused vertebrae, and the strong possibility of brain damage. Although none of these problems was immediately life threatening, the infant also suffered from a *tracheoesophageal fistula*, an abnormal connection between the mouth and the stomach. Without immediate surgery to allow for feeding and to prevent pneumonia from a fluid buildup in the lungs, the infant would soon die.

When the doctors asked Robert Houle for permission to perform the corrective surgery, he refused. They immediately took Houle to court, charging child neglect and seeking judicial permission to perform the surgery.[28] As the judge hearing the case, would you:

A. Find for the doctors, since preserving the infant's life is the only important issue?
B. Find for the parents, since the infant's future quality of life is an important consideration?
C. Find for the parents, since they are responsible for making decisions regarding their child?

Judge David Roberts, unaware of the bioethical problems that would result from the revolution in neonatal care, had little trouble choosing option A. In a straightforward opinion he ruled:

> The most basic right enjoyed by every human being is the right to life itself.... The issue before the court is not the prospective quality of life to be preserved, but the medical feasibility of the proposed treatment compared with the almost certain risk of death should treatment be withheld. Being satisfied that corrective surgery is medically necessary and medically feasible, the court finds that the defendants herein have no right to withhold such treatment and that to do so constitutes neglect in the legal sense.... Therefore, the court will authorize the guardian *ad litem* to consent to the surgical correction.[29]

Because "Baby Boy Houle" died the day after the operation, no one ever had the opportunity to judge what his quality of life would have been like. But even if the law is clear in this case—quality of life is not a legal consideration—the ethical situation continues to grow murkier as it becomes increasingly possible to save the lives of infants with greater handicaps.

The three judicial options for the above case represent the three major ethical positions regarding treatment for severely handicapped newborns. These are infants who are not "born dying," but for whom there is some good reason to believe that their quality of life will be greatly diminished: lack of physical mobility, inability to feed oneself and manage rudimentary hygiene, little or no socializing capacity, limited mental ability. Is there a point at which so many of these factors are present that death is preferable to life?

Position A answers No, asserting that all nondying infants have a right to treatment. Adherents to this view reject "quality-of-life" reasoning and replace it with an

equality-of-life principle: each life has an equal and independent value. They believe that it is unfair to compare
the future life of a handicapped infant with that of a "normal" infant and to conclude, therefore, that the former's
life is not worth living.

As ethical justification, they appeal to the *principle of
distributive justice*: like cases are to be treated alike. They
believe that this principle supports the claim that two
infants with the same disorder (e.g., tracheoesophogeal
fistula) must be treated in a similar manner. If the operation to repair the fistula is indicated in an otherwise normal baby, then it must be indicated for infants like "Baby
Boy Houle." The ethics of these cases mandate a medical-
decision criterion: focus on the procedure and the chance
for its success, and not on the patient and his chance for
a "meaningful" life.

Those favoring position B find this reasoning unper-
suasive. They believe it is a mistake to claim an ethically
relevant "likeness" between the Houle baby and the normal baby; what is ethically relevant is the dissimilarity
between their future prospects. For supporters of quality-
of-life criteria, the *principle of beneficence*—the duty to
benefit the patient—is the dominant ethical maxim:

> The meaning and criteria of quality of life should
> focus on the *benefit to the patient*, and in some cir-
> cumstances to initiate treatment or to prolong or post-
> pone death can reasonably be seen as non-beneficial
> to the patient. One such circumstance is *excruciating,
> intractable and prolonged pain and suffering*. An-
> other is the lack of capacity for what can be consid-
> ered an inherent feature of human life, namely a
> *minimal capacity to experience, to relate with other
> human beings*. In such instances to preserve life could
> in some cases be a dishonouring of the sanctity of life
> itself, and allowing even death could be a demon-
> stration of respect for the individual and for human
> life in general.[30]

But how are we ever to decide what is an acceptable quality of life? How do we draw the line that means merciful death for some infants?

CASE 29: PLAYING THE NUMBERS GAME

The prognosis for Baby A. was not terribly bright under even the most optimistic assumptions. Born with severe spina bifida, fluid in the skull, and marked *microencephaly*—abnormal smallness of the head—she needed surgery both to relieve the cranial pressure caused by the excess fluid and to seal up the protruding spinal cord. Without an operation, her life expectancy could be measured in weeks, or months at best. With an operation, she might survive twenty years that would probably be characterized by severe mental retardation, epilepsy, paralysis, and constant urinary infection. Does this potential quality of life justify the operation?

One rather bold attempt to apply some quantitative precision to questions like these has been proposed by pediatric surgeon Dr. Anthony Shaw. He suggests that the potential quality of life may be represented by the mathematical formula $QL = NE \times (H + S)$, where NE represents the patient's natural endowment (physical and mental), H the contribution made to the individual by home and family, and S the societal contribution.[31] He does not tell us how to compute NE, or at what value QL justifies an operation. His intent is merely to convey the belief that the future quality of life is dependent upon variables outside the infant's control.

It follows from Shaw's formula that an infant's QL may be raised simply by being born into a family with the financial resources to afford better medical care (i.e., getting a high H value). This conclusion has led social critic Nat Hentoff to accuse Shaw of developing a "means test" for deciding which infants shall live and which shall die. It has also forced many other supporters of the concept of quality-of-life reasoning to sharply restrict the scope and meaning of the term.

It is difficult to disagree with Shaw's major thesis—a handicapped newborn's quality of life will be affected by family and societal contributions. Yet this leads some quality-of-life adherents to what they view as an unethical conclusion: life-and-death decisions regarding the handicapped newborn must be dependent upon the interests of others (e.g., parents, doctors, society). In order to focus the decision directly on the infant, a second school of quality-of-life ethicists propose that the only appropriate question to ask is, What medical option is in the infant's best interests?

Those holding this "best interests" view believe that broad quality-of-life criteria present the wrong decision choice—meaningful life versus death. They find "meaningful life" hopelessly vague as well as dependent on the good graces of others. They seek to replace it with a different decision choice that focuses solely on the newborn—life versus death. Although they are willing to concede that certain medical circumstances make death the preferable choice, they reject the view that life may be categorized into degrees of meaningfulness. All life, except that marked by "excruciating, intractable and prolonged pain and suffering," is inherently worth living.

This turns quality-of-life reasoning on its head. It is no longer appropriate to cast about for criteria that demonstrate a meaningful life; instead, in the absence of medical criteria that indicate that death is the best option, life is presumed the better choice. The ethical justification for this position is the *principle of nonmaleficence*—do no harm. Only when treatment will inflict continuous pain and suffering (harm) is it proper to allow the newborn to die. In all other situations, life must be preserved. But even this strict criterion requires a decision-maker. Who is to decide what is in the infant's best interests?

Option C, allow the parents to make the decision, is really a policy, rather than an ethical, choice. It is the position endorsed by the President's Bioethics Commission:

> Since newborns are unable to make decisions, they will always need a surrogate to decide for them. In nearly all cases, parents are best situated to collaborate with practitioners in making decisions about an infant's care, and the range of choices practitioners offer should normally reflect the parents' preferences regarding treatment. Parents are usually present, concerned, willing to become informed, and cognizant of the values of the culture in which the child will be raised. They can be expected to try to make decisions that advance the newborn's best interests. Health care professionals and institutions, and society generally, bear responsibility to ensure that decisionmaking practices are adequate[32]

Although there is need for a review procedure (e.g., hospital bioethics committee, courts) when it appears that parents are not acting responsibly toward their offspring, this position reflects the widely held societal view that parents generally act in their children's best interests.

The emphasis on decision-making is the hallmark of the commission's work. It recognizes that all bioethical issues involve a philosophical (i.e., What is the right action?) and a policy (How can the right action be fostered?) dimension. By focusing on the decision process, the commission is attempting to bridge the theoretical and practical limits of bioethics in order to provide guidelines for making real-life choices.

It may never be possible to determine which position regarding the treatment of handicapped newborns is ethically "correct." This is another area in which personal values not directly susceptible to logical argument rule. Yet, regardless of the individual value position taken, proper ethical decision-making in these cases requires that the following factors be considered:

1. *The Problem of Prediction.* Accurate diagnosis of the future prospects of a handicapped newborn is notoriously difficult. This is especially true regarding the extent of mental retardation, which is as much a social as a medical condition.

2. *The Problem of Communication.* The issue of therapeutic information is compounded in these cases by the need to convey predictive information and because the ultimate decision will be made by a surrogate who has no firsthand knowledge of the condition being described. Both of these factors mitigate against genuine understanding of the options being described.

3. *The Problem of Emotional Stress.* Critical life-and-death decisions require careful, objective reasoning. Yet this is impossible, for both parents and physicians, in the hours and days following the delivery of a handicapped newborn. The import of these considerations is unmistakable: No matter which ethical position one subscribes to, there must always be a strong presumption on the side of life. All handicapped newborns deserve the benefit of all doubts.

THE END OF LIFE

CONCEPT: Revolution is always dangerous. For in overthrowing the established order we create a vacuum of unknown possibilities. Nowhere is this principle more in evidence than in the ethical dilemmas surrounding dying and death. The conceptual revolution which resulted in a new definition of death was precipitated by the technological achievement of the heart-lung machine and heart transplants. And viewed as a logical consequence of those inventions, the concept of "brain death" makes good sense.

But these technologies, along with dozens more (e.g., artificial respirators, cardiac-resuscitation techniques) are not mere premises in a logical argument. They are actual tools of medicine, and their use is currently creating a crisis in the treatment of patients at the end of life. Society cannot afford to keep every patient alive when there is no chance of recovery. Physicians are unsure how aggressively to treat patients and when that treatment should end. And many patients do not fear death as much as the dread of being "tortured to life."

One much talked-about solution to these problems is the *living will*—a document prepared while the individual is competent and stating what medical procedures he does and does not want taken if he becomes terminally ill. But the living will suffers from two major deficiencies. The first is practical: because it is impossible to specifically list all the medical procedures that the will-maker wishes to exclude from his care, he must rely on general terms such as "heroic measures" or "extraordinary care." Yet it is possible to disagree about how these terms are to be applied. What is "extraordinary" for the patient may be quite "ordinary" from the perspective of the physician. The second problem is legal: unlike property wills, which are supported by the edifice of probate law, living wills have no legal force. They are merely a statement of an individual's health-care preferences.

In order to rectify this legal problem, some fifteen states have passed *natural-death acts*—statutes designed to provide a legal framework for the execution of a living will. Such laws generally establish the conditions for writing a living will, provide a sample declaration, and explain the rights and responsibilities of all parties involved.[33] As well intentioned as these bills may be, most legal scholars believe they are causing more problems than they solve. By allowing a living-will option, such laws may be interfering with rights that individuals already possess (e.g., how do living wills relate to informed-consent rulings?). In trying to specify the rights of individuals with wills, they may be depreciating the rights of individuals without wills. Is it legitimate to assume that they desire maximum, aggressive care? Finally, as with the interstate hodge-podge of brain death statutes, it makes no sense for the rights of patients to refuse treatment to differ from state to state.

The problems surrounding natural-death acts are just one more example of what can happen when we attempt to legislate ethical dilemmas: Is the competent patient's right to refuse treatment absolute? Even when this borders on suicide? Is refusing treatment ethically different from euthanasia? Is there a "right to die"?

PRACTICE: Approximately two million Americans die every year. Most die in hospitals and as the result of a chronic condition. Few of these patients wish to die, but fewer still wish to be kept "alive" indefinitely by artificial means. It is this prospect of a perpetual "demilife," rather than death itself, that is so distressing to many terminally ill patients. The depth of this feeling is reflected in a 1985 Gallup poll finding that 81 percent of the population favor a *right-to-die statute*—a legal guarantee that patients have the right to have all life-support systems withdrawn.[34] But is there really a need for such a law?

The legal position of the dying patient to refuse treatment is no different from that of the patient who goes to the doctor for any simple procedure. As long as the patient is mentally competent, his right to determine how he will be treated is close to absolute.

> Anglo-American law starts with the premise of thoroughgoing self-determination. It follows that each man is considered to be master of his own body, and he may, if he be of sound mind, expressly prohibit the performance of life-saving surgery, or other med-

ical treatment. A doctor might well believe that an operation or form of treatment is desirable or necessary but the law does not permit him to substitute his own judgement for that of the patient by any form of artifice or deception.[35]

But is this right to refuse treatment the same as the right to die? Are there any limits to this right when, refusing treatment, the patient is condemning himself to die?

CASE 30: ELIZABETH BOUVIA WANTS TO DIE

In 1983 Elizabeth Bouvia was a twenty-six-year-old cerebral-palsy victim who wanted to die. Her handicap had left her with extremely limited muscular control, and, while she could transport herself in a motorized wheelchair, she could do little else by herself. When her marriage ended and she lost her state funds for transportation, she decided she no longer wished to live a life totally dependent on others.

Her solution was to check into a hospital which she instructed to use painkillers to keep her comfortable while she starved herself to death. The hospital wanted no part of this plan and threatened to feed her through a nasogastric tube. She then sought legal protection for her "right to die."[36] As judge, how would you rule:

A. Find for the hospital on grounds that only terminal patients have a right to refuse lifesaving treatment?

B. Find for the hospital because an individual's right to refuse treatment may be overridden by other community interests?

C. Find for Ms. Bouvia because the hospital has no right to force a medical treatment (e.g., nasogastric feeding) on an unconsenting patient?

This well-publicized case is a good example of how ethical distinctions may elude the law. Because Ms. Bouvia was already a patient receiving treatment at the hospital, the law forced the judge to choose between two ethically unpalatable choices: either allow a patient to use the medical establishment to commit slow suicide or permit a hospital to run roughshod over a patient's right to personal autonomy. Given this choice, the judge cited reasons A and B in finding for the hospital. Yet neither of these reasons is adequate legal or ethical justification for the decision to commence nasogastric feeding.

The judge's contention that "forced feeding, however invasive, would be administered for the purpose of saving the life of an otherwise non-terminal patient and should be permitted" is simply an incorrect reading of the law. Numerous cases dealing with the right of a Jehovah's Witness to refuse blood transfusions or a kidney patient to refuse dialysis make it clear that a terminal prognosis is not the litmus test of a patient's right to refuse treatment. Competent patients have the legal right to refuse any treatment, regardless of their health status or the consequences of that refusal.

Moreover, this principle of patient autonomy has a much greater application than an occasional religious objection to being transfused. The ability of the medical establishment to keep alive almost indefinitely patients who are comatose though not terminal—defined by the President's Bioethics Commission as a condition likely to cause death in a very short time—is the potential greatest source of these cases. Karen Ann Quinlan's ten-year struggle with death is proof positive that she was not terminally ill in 1975. Yet the application of a criterion of terminal illness would have prohibited her parents from disconnecting the respirator. Not only is the competent patient's right to refuse treatment independent of medical condition, but new rulings are extending this right to incompetent patients through the process of proxy decision-making and substituted judgment.

Reason B embodies the familiar theme of competing rights: Does the state have any right compelling enough to interfere with the patient's right to refuse treatment? The judge in the Bouvia case evidently thought so when he wrote that allowing her to starve to death would "have a profound effect on the medical staff, nurses, and administration... [and] a devastating effect on other physically handicapped persons who are similarly situated in this nation." But even if Bouvia's actions would have the alleged effects on others, is that adequate reason to override her right to refuse treatment?

The courts have identified four possible state interests that might be taken into consideration in such cases: (1) the preservation of life, (2) the protection of innocent third parties, (3) the maintenance of the ethical integrity of the medical profession, and (4) the prevention of suicide.[37] The preservation of life is obviously the vaguest of the state's interests. It serves to do little more than announce that the state has some interest in life as a human value. As a legal principle, it has consistently been diminished by recent rulings like Quinlan that have almost uniformly extended the right of the patient to refuse treatment.

In contrast, the protection of innocent third parties is a concrete principle that is usually applied to require pregnant women or parents with small children to undergo lifesaving treatment. As such, it does not apply to Ms. Bouvia, and the judicial attempt to extend its scope seems ethically dangerous. By arguing that Bouvia must be treated for the sake of other handicapped individuals, the judge is opening a Pandora's box of competing interests. For if Bouvia may be compelled to accept treatment, then so may any other handicapped person. And such a principle could be applied to require the treatment of any member of any identifiable group. Taken to its logical conclusion, this principle completely vitiates any patient's right to refuse treatment. The best way to protect the rights of a group is by protecting the rights of the individual group members.

From a legal perspective, maintaining the ethical integrity of the medical profession seems to have little applicability to cases of refusing treatment. Simply put, there is no code of medical ethics that requires the forcible treatment of a patient. Of course, individual physicians citing the "Do no harm" injunction may not wish to comply with Ms. Bouvia's wishes. But this is a matter of personal conscience, not professional ethics. Other, no less ethical doctors may cite the principle of beneficence as their reason for wishing to assist Ms. Bouvia in her wishes. While the courts should never force a physician to perform a procedure that is contrary to his personal principles, so it should never violate patient autonomy in the name of medical ethics.

The final state interest, prevention of suicide, is the most germane to this case. In general, the courts and prevailing public policy have sought to distinguish refusal of treatment from suicide.

> In the case of the competent adult's refusing medical treatment such an act does not necessarily constitute suicide since (1) in refusing treatment the patient may not have the specific intent to die, and (2) even if he did, to the extent that the cause of death was from natural causes the patient did not set the death producing agent in motion with the intent of causing his own death. Furthermore, the underlying state interest in this area lies in the prevention of irrational self-destruction.[38]

It is only the unique physical handicap of Ms. Bouvia, as well as her patient status in a hospital, that has managed to confuse the two issues.

Quite clearly, her actions violate both of the above conditions: she has the specific intent to die, and, by her own actions, she is setting the death-producing agent in motion. But does this necessarily mean she is bent on "irrational self-destruction?" Are there quality-of-life considerations that might ethically justify her actions?

The case of Elizabeth Bouvia has no easy legal or ethical solution. As a practical matter, both the hospital and Ms. Bouvia would have been better served by eschewing formal legal action and seeking a compromise based upon their own self-interests. For the hospital, starving a patient, even at her own direction, is a clear case of mistreatment. Since forced feeding is an unacceptable alternative, they might have either transferred her to another facility, perhaps one that would have a better chance to defuse the issue with reason rather than inflame it with brute force, or used their own counseling facility to attain the same end.

For her part, Ms. Bouvia, a bright woman with a college degree, must have known she was making an impossible request of a medical facility. One alternative was to check into the hospital for help in overcoming her suicidal depression (this had worked in the past). Another was to view the problem in social, not medical, terms and to seek means of enhancing her independence through the use of technology, community support, and perhaps even a specially trained dog or monkey. In forcing legal action, both parties to the case were foreclosing these options.

Yet the ultimate ethical questions suggested by this case are those that are currently gripping American society: Does the right to die transcend the right to refuse treatment? Are there quality-of-life conditions that are so painful or debilitating that it becomes acceptable to actively take a life? Is euthanasia an ethical option in this age of technomedicine?

CASE 31: ROSWELL GILBERT LOVED HIS WIFE
Roswell and Emily Gilbert had been happily married for more than forty years when Emily was diagnosed as suffering from *Alzheimer's disease*, a progressive and irreversible deterioration of the brain, and *osteoporosis*, a painful deterioration of the bones. By 1985 her condition was keeping her in constant pain while robbing her of the ability to perform even simple personal-hygiene tasks such as combing her hair. Although her condition grew progressively worse, she continued to live at home with Roswell trying to meet all her personal needs. When she began to outwardly express a desire to die, Roswell decided to end her suffering. He administered a sedative and quietly shot her twice in the head. The Florida jury hearing the case rejected his claim that it was a "mercy killing" and found him guilty of first-degree murder.[39] While his case was being appealed, he requested that the Florida Governor's cabinet vote to allow him out on bail. How would you vote as a member of that cabinet? Are there any circumstances that justify *active euthanasia*— an action purposely taken to end a life?

Those who believe that active euthanasia may be ethical under the proper conditions support their position with three major reasons. First, and perhaps most important, is the *principle of personal autonomy*—individuals should always have the right of free choice so long as their decisions produce no harm to others. Just as patients now have the right to refuse medical treatment in order to hasten their own deaths, this principle seems to support their right to further accelerate the dying process by actively seeking to end their own lives.

If the principle of personal autonomy is a very general ethical maxim, the second reason, the right to die with dignity, is one with specific application to this era of high-technology medicine. As a result of the shift in disease burden to chronic conditions like Alzheimer's and cancer, and the concomitant increase in the power of modern medicine to keep terminal patients alive, the process of dying often becomes a lengthy ordeal. During this process many patients feel that their dignity is being stripped away as they lose one human function and then another. In the face of irreversible deterioration which brings only pain and suffering, it seems extremely cruel to force these patients to await a final disease state that even today's medicine is powerless to overcome. Instead, a principle of mercy seems to justify allowing these patients to choose to end their lives.

The final reason is more of an ethical argument than an appeal to *prima facie* principle. Its major premise is a fact: *passive euthanasia*, omitting actions that may serve to extend a life (e.g., failing to use a respirator or to resuscitate a cardiac patient), is both legal and the avowed policy of the AMA and many religious groups. The second premise is the ethical justification for the fact: passive euthanasia, allowing a patient to die, is ethical because it mitigates suffering and preserves human dignity. Finally, and here comes the force of the argument, it must be just as ethical to take an action designed to relieve suffering as it is to omit an action in order to mitigate the same suffering. It follows, therefore, that active euthanasia must also be ethically justified. Taken together, these three arguments present a formidable case for allowing terminally ill individuals to end their lives.

Those who oppose active euthanasia also rely on three arguments. Their usual starting point is the passive–active distinction, but they reject the above means–end reasoning (e.g., if the justified end is to avoid suffering, then any means used to accomplish it must also be justified). Instead, they see the distinction as embodying a group of subtle distinctions:

1. There is an important psychological difference for the patient, the physician, and the greater society between acting to take a life and allowing a life to expire.

2. The active taking of life would be detrimental to the public perception of the medical profession as well as to the self-image of many physicians.

3. Active euthanasia always involves the intention to take a life; passive euthanasia does not.

4. The actual cause of death will be different. In the case of active euthanasia, the cause will be attributable to a human agent; in passive euthanasia, the cause will be a disease process.

Recognizing that none of these reasons is decisive, Robert Veatch concludes:

> In the end the case for a moral difference between actively killing the dying patient and withdrawing treatment in order that the patient may die will have to rest upon all of these arguments taken together, not on any one of them alone. The individual differences may be subtle, some more persuasive than others. Combined, however, their impact is somewhat more impressive.... There are significant moral distinctions between actively killing and simply omitting an action, no matter how subtle these may be in particular cases.[40]

The second argument employs a technique known as the slippery slope, the wedge, or, more colorfully, the "camel's nose under the tent." In its general form, this argument cautions against taking a first action which may be ethically justified for fear that it will lead to other, supposedly similar actions, that cannot be justified. If the slope is sufficiently slippery, and there is no reason to believe that the slide down it may be halted, then the just course of action is not to venture out on the slope at all.

In the particular case of active euthanasia, this technique is used dramatically by Dr. Leo Alexander, a drafter of the Nuremberg Code. He cautions that the German attitude which led to the death camps

> started with the acceptance of that attitude, basic in the euthanasia movement, that there is such a thing as a life not worthy to be lived. This attitude in its early stages concerned itself merely with the severely and chronically sick. Gradually the sphere of those to be included in this category was enlarged to include the socially unproductive, the racially unwanted, and finally all non-Germans. But it is important to realize that the infinitely small wedged-in lever from which this entire trend of mind received its impetus was the attitude toward the non-rehabilitable sick.[41]

For some, passive euthanasia is already the thin edge of the wedge. Many others fear that if active euthanasia is legitimized for the hopelessly ill, it will inevitably become not only a right to be used at one's discretion, but a duty to die. And still others fear that the kind of scenario painted by Dr. Alexander could happen today. While such arguments are never conclusive, they are no doubt cautionary.

The final argument is less philosophical and more an appeal to public-policy considerations. While it acknowledges the ethical acceptability of active euthanasia under certain tightly controlled conditions (e.g., the patient must be terminally ill, suffering greatly, and expressing an unswerving and rational desire to die), it concludes that the potential abuses of such a policy outweigh any possible benefits. This list of potential abuses pointed to usually includes the difficulty of obtaining true consent from a dying patient, the possibility of coercion from relatives and family, the pressure to request active euthanasia for improper reasons (e.g., financial burden), the possibility that the medical diagnosis may be incorrect, and the hor-

rible chance that a mistake will be made and a patient
desiring to live will be euthanized. Taken as a group, and
in conjunction with the other two arguments against active
euthanasia, all of these reasons form a strong case against
the purposeful taking of a patient's life.

Which side is "more right"? Although there are many
different arguments, they all revolve about a single issue:
how best to protect the rights of the individual. For the
advocates of active euthanasia, those rights are best protected by vesting each individual with the power to decide
whether to end his own life. Opponents of the idea believe
that the total freedom of a society is sometimes enhanced
when the state regulates individual behavior. For them,
active euthanasia must be banned in order to insure that
society's weakest members (e.g., the old, the infirm, the
disabled) are guaranteed their right to life.

Seen in this way, the dispute has less to do with the
ethics of life and death than it does with the art of modern
statecraft. Since maximizing individual rights is the goal
of both sides, the issue is really the pragmatic one of how
best to achieve that goal. Twenty years ago, before the
technological revolution that precipitated the need for a
new definition of death, it seemed plausible to argue that
the vast majority of citizens were best protected by a policy outlawing active euthanasia. Today, however, with the
prospect of ever more Emily Gilberts, we need to recon-
sider that social calculus. A policy allowing the controlled
use of active euthanasia may well be fraught with potential
abuses, but it might also be the case that a policy forbidding it is simply guaranteeing that many actual abuses of
personal freedom will occur.

V

EXPERIMENTATION
WITH HUMAN
BEINGS

NUREMBERG. For the past forty years the grisly disclosures made at the Nuremberg hearings have denoted man's inhumanity to man. Yet if it is possible to comprehend degrees of pure evil, then it is the Nazi "doctors" who experimented on unwilling and unknowing subjects who raised sadism to a new level. The horrific experiments on concentration camp inmates that were the subject of the "Doctors' Trials" showed the world just what can happen when a person is reduced to a research subject, a mere piece of scientific equipment.

> I have personally seen through the observation window of the decompression chamber when a prisoner inside would stand a vacuum until his lungs ruptured... They would go mad and pull out their hair in an effort to relieve the pressure. They would tear their heads and face with their fingers and nails in an attempt to maim themselves in their madness. They would beat the walls with their hands and head and scream in an effort to relieve pressure on their eardrums. These cases usually ended in the death of the subject.[1]

In response to such egregious abuses, the key task for modern biomedicine has been to devise a system that will allow needed human experimentation without sacrificing the integrity of the human subject.

While this task may seem far removed from our common, everyday experience, its solution is one in which each of us has a vested interest. Every new drug, every new surgical procedure requires human experimentation. In fact, sustaining the dramatic growth in the rate of biomedical discovery will demand an ever greater pool of human subjects. Even though most of us never envision volunteering for a medical experiment, the proliferation of new pharmaceuticals and therapeutic techniques, coupled with increased life spans and access to medical care, make it not at all unlikely that such an opportunity will present itself. And for the rest of us, the conduct of such research will surely affect our lives. Without a satisfactory solution to the balancing act between society's need to know and the individual's right to autonomy, biomedical research, and its promise for an improved quality of life, will grind to a halt.

Yet the issue of human experimentation has wider implications than simply the kind of medical care we receive. It speaks directly to the kind of society we live in. Just how much license we grant researchers to further the state of medical knowledge is a profound social question that goes to the very heart of our views of personhood and the individual's role in society. This is because biomedical research is not simply a matter of experimental design (a fact-based decision few of us understand); it is also a matter of personal and societal ethics (a value-based decision to which each of us can contribute).

The far-reaching implications of human experimentation suggest that it is too important to be left solely to the physician-researcher. Not only does it require public comment, but numerous post-Nuremberg cases demonstrate that researchers are sometimes ethically blinded in their pursuit of knowledge. Thirty years ago U.S. Army researchers released various bacteria in the New York City subways and sprayed them into the air over San Francisco Bay to clandestinely study how biological warfare could be used against the population of an urban center. Twenty-five years ago, the Central Intelligence Agency instituted its MKULTRA Program—an investigation of chemicals that could induce "aberrant" mental states. As part of the program, researchers secretly dosed unsuspecting citizens with powerful psychedelic drugs. The experiments ultimately resulted in some suicides. And during a forty-year period beginning in the 1930s, a group of black men in Tuskegee, Alabama, were allowed to continue to suffer and die from syphilis just so that doctors could study the life-cycle of the disease.[2] While it may be easy to spot the ethical flaws in each of these cases, there are may more subtle, difficult, and important ethical issues involved with human experimentation.

CASE 32: BABY FAE AND THE BABOON'S HEART

Baby Fae was born in the fall of 1984 with a congenitally deformed heart. Without either surgery or a transplant her prognosis was certain death within a few months. Rather than choose the conservative course of therapy (an *allograph*, or human heart transplant) or an experimental surgical procedure to correct the defect, her doctors convinced Fae's parents that a *xenograph*, the transplant of a different species' (baboon's) heart into Baby Fae, was the best choice. Was this therapy or experimentation? If it was experimentation, was it justified?

Trying to locate the precise point at which therapy ends and experimentation begins is as hopeless as trying to determine exactly when a boy turns into a man. Ideas like therapy and experiment are known as fuzzy concepts,

since, while they may be well defined at their cores, they
are decidedly blurry around their edges. Yet the job of
providing suitable definitions is no mere academic exercise. The rights of patients are quite different from the
rights of research subjects, and the responsibilities of doctors are quite different from the responsibilities of researchers. Without adequate definitions, both patient care
and scientific advancement are in jeopardy.

Therapy is characterized by its primary focus on the
welfare of the patient: the physician's chief goal is benefiting the patient. The values are those derived from
within the doctor–patient relationship (see Chapter II),
and the dominant ethic is absolute—the Hippocratic
Oath's injunction "Do no harm." *Experimentation* is characterized by its primary focus on the production of knowledge: the researcher's chief goal is to discover new truths.
The values are those of the research community, which
speak more about doing "good science" than about protecting the welfare of the research subject, and the dominant ethic is consequentialist—a weighing of risks versus
benefits so that the greatest good may be produced for the
greatest number. Because of this disparity in goals, values,
and ethics, real conflict may arise, as in the case of Baby
Fae, when the research subject is also a patient. Such
cases of *therapeutic experimentation*—the use of new and
unproved treatments which may benefit the patient, but
will definitely produce new knowledge—form a large,
important, and problematic hybrid between therapy and
experimentation.

One attempt to deal with the vexing ethical problems
that surround human experimentation in general, and
therapeutic experimentation in particular, is the promul-
gation of special codes of conduct to guide researchers in
their performance of such research. All of these codes
(e.g., the World Medical Association's Declaration of Hel-

sinki, the AMA's Ethical Guidelines for Clinical Investigation) embody precepts similar to those of the Nuremberg Code:

1. The voluntary consent of the human subject is absolutely essential.
2. The experiment should be such as to yield fruitful results for the good of society, unprocurable by other methods or means of study, and not random or unnecessary in nature.
3. The experiment should be so designed and based on the results of animal experimentation and a knowledge of the natural history of the disease or other problem under study that the anticipated results will justify the performance of the experiment.
4. The experiment should be so conducted as to avoid all unnecessary physical and mental suffering and injury.
5. No experiment should be conducted when there is an *a priori* reason to believe that death or disabling injury will occur; except, perhaps, in those experiments where the experimental physicians also serve as subjects.
6. The degree of risk to be taken should never exceed that determined by the humanitarian importance of the problem to be solved by the experiment.
7. Proper preparations should be made and adequate facilities provided to protect the experimental subject against even remote possibilities of injury, disability, or death.
8. The experiment should only be conducted by scientifically qualified persons. The highest degree of skill and care should be required through all stages of the experiment of those who conduct or engage in the experiment.
9. During the course of the experiment the human

subject should be at liberty to bring the experiment to an end if he has reached the physical or mental state where continuation of the experiment seems to him to be impossible.

10. During the course of the experiment the scientist in charge must be prepared to terminate the experiment at any stage, if he has probable cause to believe, in the exercise of good faith, superior skill, and careful judgment required of him, that a continuation of the experiment is likely to result in injury, disability, or death to the experimental subject.[3]

While such codes may form the conceptual framework for the protection of human subjects, their generalized language is simply too ambiguous to give much help in guiding actual practice. For example: how is one to determine if consent is really voluntary? What criteria should be used to ascertain if the state-of-medical-art is ready to really benefit from human experimentation? How can we decide at what point the benefits of a therapeutic experiment outweigh the risks for a particular patient? Clearly, human experimentation encompasses much more than technical considerations. It also involves questions concerning human values, and no single group, least of all researchers, has any special claim to knowledge in this area. Just how those value questions might be resolved, and the type of system that might be adopted in order to implement them, is described in the section "Therapeutic Experimentation."

CASE 33: THE CANCER INJECTIONS

The Sloan-Kettering Institute in New York is one of this country's preeminent cancer centers. During the 1950s and 1960s researchers there were involved in a series of experiments to determine whether a relationship existed between cancer and the immune system. The experimental hypothesis was that the immune system of cancer patients is depressed with respect to that specific disease. In order to test the hypothesis, a group of medical researchers devised a three-stage experiment that involved injecting live malignant cells into human subjects:

1. A group of terminal cancer patients was recruited for the gathering of baseline data. After the procedure was fully explained and the patient-subjects had given their consent, each was inoculated with foreign cancer cells. With few exceptions, small nodules appeared at the injection site and continued to grow for four to six weeks. The nodules then slowly regressed and eventually disappeared.

2. The next step was to compare the cancer patient's immune response with that of healthy subjects. A group of fully informed prison inmates volunteered for the research and received the malignant injections. Again, small nodules appeared. But this time they all disappeared within four weeks.

3. The differing speed in the rejection of the cancerous cells suggested that there may be an immunological factor related to cancer. In order to prove that, the experiment needed to be performed on equally debilitated patients with noncancerous conditions. By this time, the researchers no longer felt that the experiment carried any risk, so they dispensed with a full explanation of the procedure and simply asked their patients to undergo a "skin test." When these patient-subjects were inoculated, they rejected the cancer implants just as rapidly as the healthy prisoner-subjects. This fact, along with the knowledge that cancer patients did not lack immune responses to other diseases, allowed the researchers to conclude that cancer did involve a disease-specific immunologic breakdown.[4]

What are the relevant differences between the three subject groups? Is there any ethical problem with securing research volunteers from the patient population? The prison population? Does the supposed lack of risk for the last group justify the researchers' decision not to explain the procedure?

There is no doubt that the Sloan-Kettering study is *non-therapeutic experimentation*—research designed solely to produce new knowledge. Unlike the Baby Fae case, none of the human subjects stands to benefit directly from the research. Instead, the experiment will benefit the whole society while putting only the subjects at risk. It is precisely because such basic research has no therapeutic component that it poses the greatest threat of treating the human subject as a mere object, as a means to an end. In order to avoid this depersonalization and to insure that research subjects are authentic volunteers, the identification, selection, and recruitment of humans to participate in nontherapeutic experiments poses several ethical dilemmas.

Before someone may be considered a volunteer, two conditions must be present: first, the subject must be mentally competent and free (i.e., totally uncoerced) to assent to participation; second, he must have all the information needed to make a rational choice. For each of the three Sloan-Kettering subject groups, there is reason to believe that they were not volunteers in the truest sense of the word.

The use of patients in any nontherapeutic experiment is always ethically dubious. Patients are particularly vulnerable, and the more critical their conditions, the greater their vulnerability. They have invested their trust in the doctor–patient relationship, which makes it particularly difficult for them to refuse a doctor's request to participate in an experiment. Finally, patients may feel that their medical care will suffer if they choose not to participate. All of these factors in the well-documented "sociology of sickness"[5] argue against the ability of patients to freely volunteer and, therefore, against their use as subjects in human experimentation.

Yet there is also a societal perspective that must be addressed. If medical progress is to be made and new treatments developed, then there will be cases when the participation of patients in human experiments will be necessary. How can the rights of those patients be balanced against the needs of society? Half of the solution lies in viewing the research process as a partnership between the subjects and the investigators, instead of as a process controlled by the investigators in which the subjects are simply human "research tools." Such a collegial atmosphere will do much to mitigate the depersonalization of the subjects.

The other half of the solution involves recruiting patient-subjects who can identify with the research. Patients who suffer from the disease are highly motivated to see a cure developed, they understand something about the disease, and they may, in fact, have already participated in therapeutic experiments. The use of these factors—motivation, knowledge, participation—is a positive counterweight to the aforementioned barriers to obtaining patient volunteers, and they seem to have been applied in recruiting the first group of subjects in the Sloan-Kettering research.

Unfortunately, these criteria were totally absent in the selection of the terminal noncancer patients. They could not identify with the cause of the research, had no special knowledge about it, and, because they weren't even given a description of the procedure, were never in a position to give their consent. In other words, they were neither free to volunteer nor cognizant of what it was they were being asked to volunteer for.

While it is always possible to disagree about just how "free" someone must be in order to volunteer, the information requirement seems much less open to debate. In suspending the licenses of the two physicians involved, the New York Board of Regents, the licensing agency for New York doctors, found that whether the procedure carried any risk or not (and that was a point of contention), it was up to the patients, and not the doctors, to decide what factors were relevant in making the decision about consenting. As opposed to consent for diagnostic or therapeutic procedures, consent for nontherapeutic experimentation must be based on subject understanding.

The regents also found against the doctors' claim that since using the word "cancer" would needlessly scare the patient, the doctors were justified in withholding that information in the patient's best interest. The regents' decision held that when the doctor acts as a researcher he gives up any claim to the doctor–patient relationship and its so-called "therapeutic privilege." Both of these rulings, (1) that the research subject is the sole arbiter of what is to count as important information, and (2) that the researcher is obligated to fully inform the subject as to all available information, serve to foster a collegial research atmosphere and protect the rights of the subject.

Since the regents' decision in the mid-1960s, the criteria of informed consent for human subjects in both therapeutic and nontherapeutic experiments have been refined and codified. Today, any federally funded research involving humans is required to provide the subjects with

1. A statement that the study involves research, an explanation of the purposes of the research and the expected duration of the subject's participation, a description of the procedures to be followed, and identification of any procedures that are experimental;
2. A description of any reasonably foreseeable risks or discomforts to the subject;

3. A description of any benefits to the subject or to others, which may reasonably be expected from the research;

4. A disclosure of appropriate alternative procedures or courses of treatment, if any, that might be advantageous to the subject;

5. A statement describing the extent, if any, to which confidentiality of records identifying the subject will be maintained;

6. For research involving more than minimal risk, an explanation as to whether any compensation and an explanation as to whether any medical treatments are available if injury occurs and, if so, what they consist of, or where further information may be obtained;

7. An explanation of whom to contact for answers to pertinent questions about the research and research subjects' rights, and whom to contact in the event of a research-related injury to the subject; and

8. A statement that participation is voluntary, refusal to participate will involve no penalty or loss of benefits to which the subject is otherwise entitled, and the subject may discontinue participation at any time without penalty or loss of benefits to which the subject is otherwise entitled.[6]

All of the problems inherent in using patient-subjects can obviously be avoided if healthy volunteers can be recruited. But where can researchers find a population that is generally healthy, ambulatory, competent, and easy to both control and observe? For thousands of years the answer has been the prisons, and there is a long, dismal record of prisoners being used as expendable experimental material. While few people today would argue that prisoners deserve any less protection than other research subjects, there is a serious debate about whether the coercive nature of the prison environment vitiates the prisoner's ability to freely give consent. Resolving this dispute requires judgments to be made about both the role of humans in experiments and the role of prisons in our society.

Nor are prisoners the only "special group" of potential research subjects that raise unique ethical questions. Human experimentation with children, students, mental incompetents, and fetuses all raise novel ethical dilemmas which will be discussed in the section "Nontherapeutic Experimentation."

CASE 34: THE BIRTH CONTROL PILL WAS A PLACEBO

In 1974 a group of Mexican-American women visited a family-planning clinic in order to receive birth control pills. Although they were not informed, the clinic was participating in an experiment to determine the side effects of oral contraceptives. As part of the experimental design, a control group (a similar group of subjects, who received no contraceptives) was required so that the researchers would have a baseline with which to assess the effects of the contraceptives. Seventy-six of the women who came to the clinic were randomly placed in the control group and unknowingly received *placebos* (noneffifacious pills, sugar pills). As a result ten of them became pregnant.[7] Did the potential social good of this research justify deceiving the subjects? Is the use of placebos in research ever justified? Are the researchers responsible for the care of the pregnant women and their offspring? In general, what are a researcher's responsibilities to injured or harmed subjects?

While the conduct of the researchers in the above case seems impossible to justify, society's need to test the efficacy and safety of new drugs and treatments poses serious ethical dilemmas because of the placebo effect. For the uninitiated, however, assessing just how well a new drug works appears to be a simple process: Divide a group of patient-subjects suffering from the same disease into two halves. The first half receives no treatment, while the second half receives the new, experimental drug. If a goodly number of subjects who get the drug show signs of relief, then it seems reasonable to conclude that it is effective.

Aside from the ethical problem of not treating one half of the subjects, this procedure fails as a scientific test because of the *placebo effect*: Study after study has demonstrated that about 35 percent of all patients receiving a doctor's ministrations will report "satisfactory relief" from a wide range of complaints even though the doctor did nothing but prescribe a placebo, a physiologically inactive pill. In other words, simply believing that a doctor has tended to our condition is often sufficient to stimulate our own bodies to combat the illness.

Although witch doctors and shamans have known about the placebo effect for thousands of years, our more recent, detailed knowledge of the power of placebos makes the testing of new drugs a far more complicated process. Researchers cannot simply show that a drug has a positive effect. They must now demonstrate that any curative effects of experimental therapies are not explained by the placebo effect. The standard method for proving this is the use of *randomized experimental design*—dividing the subjects randomly into two groups and treating one with placebos, or an approved treatment, and the other with the new, experimental treatment. While this is good science, it poses serious ethical conundrums: Since the knowledge that one might receive a placebo could vitiate the placebo effect, how can researchers fully inform their subjects without undermining their experiment? How can researchers justify taking a patient off an approved therapy so that they may investigate an untested, experimental treatment? What happens if early results indicate that the new drug works exceptionally well? Exceptionally poorly? How much responsibility should researchers shoulder for the outcomes of their experiments? Ultimately, who should decide which of the many unsolved scientific problems are actually studied? Resolving these puzzles, as well as other ethical dilemmas of the complex social process we call experimentation with human beings, is discussed in "The Research Process," the final section of this chapter.

THERAPEUTIC EXPERIMENTATION

CONCEPT:

1. In the treatment of the sick person, the doctor must be free to use a new diagnostic and therapeutic measure, if in his or her judgment it offers hope of saving life, reestablishing hope, or alleviating suffering.

6. The doctor can combine medical research with professional care, the objective being the acquisition of new medical knowledge, only to the extent that medical research is justified by its potential diagnostic or therapeutic value for the patient.[8]

These two clauses from the World Medical Association's Declaration of Helsinki provide both the justification for and the goal of *therapeutic experimentation*—the use of new and unproved treatments which may benefit the patient, but will definitely produce new knowledge. What they don't provide is a process for assuring that the goal is achieved in an ethical manner: How is potential value to be assessed? By whom? What are the patient's rights when he becomes a research subject? How can the doctor balance his responsibility to research with his responsibility to the patient?

PRACTICE: Everyone applauds the fruits of biomedical research: powerful new antibiotics and multidisease vaccines, artificial organs and transplant techniques, space-age diagnostic and treatment modalities. Yet few people stop to think that each of these successes involved numerous experiments on human subjects. Occasionally, a Lewis Washkansky (the first successful heart transplant patient) or a Barney Clark (the first permanent-artificial-heart recipient) will burst on the media scene, but these individuals form just the visible tip of a very large and important iceberg. According to the General Accounting Office (GAO), ten years ago the Food and Drug Administration (FDA) was responsible for regulating 1400 sponsors and 9400 clinical investigators who were busy researching 4600 new drugs on 250,000 human subjects (these figures include both therapeutic and nontherapeutic experiments). Sadly, the GAO report also concluded that "federal control of new drug testing is not adequately protecting human test subjects and the public."[9] If our society is to continue harvesting those fruits of research, then it must develop systems for protecting human beings when they become the "animals of necessity" in the process of experimentation.

Our current system of protection for human research subjects began as a response to the barbarisms reported at the Nuremberg trials, and continues to evolve as new abuses and problems are discovered in this country. Today, the system involves three distinct tiers: (1) professional codes of ethics, (2) laws and legislation, (3) regulations promulgated by the funding agencies that support most of our biomedical research. While no individual approach, standing alone, is an adequate protector of human subjects, taken together they provide the guidance, enforcement power, and flexibility needed to keep up with the ethical challenges of biomedical research.

The professional codes are really statements of the principles that *ought* to be followed in research with human subjects. Although they provide an important ethical target to aim at, they provide little guidance about the procedures to follow in order to hit that target. They also carry no penalties when the aim is wide of the mark. It is probably best to think of the professional codes as the human subjects' "Bill of Rights"—a basic statement of the researcher's responsibilities that continues to undergo interpretation as new biomedical facts and theories emerge.

Because it is so difficult to prescribe ethics, law and legislation play a relatively small role in the regulation of human experimentation. Rather than setting trends, the law has reacted by codifying what it viewed as common, established practice. For example, in 1955 a Florida court legitimized the doctor's right to engage in therapeutic experimentation. Prior to that time, any major deviation from standard medical practice was considered as grounds for malpractice. In deciding *Baldor v. Rogers*, the court concluded, "If there is no certain cure and the physician did not indulge in quackery by representing he had one," then the issue of malpractice need not arise.[10] With regard to subjects' rights, the law is most explicit on the question of informed consent. If the professional codes provide the ethical goal, then case law codifies established mechanisms for attaining it.

The most significant legislation is the National Research Act of 1974,[11] which created the National Commission for the Protection of Human Subjects of Biomedical and Behavioral Research and mandated it to recommend appropriate guidelines for the conduct of ethical research. Building on previous legislation, the commission created a system of Institutional Review Boards (IRBs) that would act as the major form of regulation applied by federal funding agencies. IRBs are hospital and research committees with a minimum of five members, at least one of whom must be a nonscientist, charged with reviewing all research projects that receive federal funds. In particular, IRBs must determine that the following criteria of ethical research are going to be met:

1. Risks to subjects are minimized.
2. Risks to subjects are reasonable in relation to anticipated benefits and the importance of the knowledge that may reasonably be expected to result.
3. Selection of subjects is equitable.
4. Informed consent will be sought.
5. Informed consent will be appropriately documented.
6. Where appropriate, the research plan makes adequate provision for monitoring the data collected to insure the safety of subjects.
7. Where appropriate, there are adequate provisions to protect the privacy of subjects and maintain the confidentiality of data.[12]

With billions of research dollars controlled by more than five hundred local IRBs, they really are at the frontier of ethical decision-making. In order to see how well you would do as an ethical "frontiersman," try playing the role of the IRB nonscientist in judging each of the following research proposals.

CASE 35: HERPES AND ACCEPTABLE RISK

A new drug, ara-A, has already been shown to be effective in treating herpes. In addition, the drug has no known toxic side effects. This research proposes testing the drug as a treatment for herpes simplex encephalitis, a disease with a 70 percent mortality rate. The therapeutic experiment will involve two groups of HSE patients: one group, the control, will receive the standard treatment; the experimental group will be treated with ara-A. Informed consent has already been obtained and documented. As an IRB member, would you:

A. approve the research as the necessary next step in evaluating a new drug?
B. request more information about the informed-consent process on the grounds that patients with a disease of the brain may not be capable of giving true consent?
C. Deny the proposal on grounds that the control group is made to assume an unacceptable risk?

The facts of this real-life case support C as the best justified response. In actuality, the experiment was begun (response A), but was eventually stopped in face of the following ethical reasoning. Facts known: the standard treatment is ineffective, this disease carries a high risk of death, and the experimental treatment is nontoxic. Value premise: risks to subjects must be minimized. Ethical solution: rather than subjecting a new group of patients to the standard treatment, this experiment could be conducted with an *historical-control group*—matching the experimental subjects with the records of patients who received the standard treatment—in order to judge the efficacy of ara-A. Even though all the subjects in the experiment eventually received ara-A, it proved too late. Only 20 percent of the subjects who had begun with the standard treatment recovered, while over 50 percent of those who received the experimental treatment from the beginning were able to go on and live a normal life.[13]

This case is interesting because it demonstrates just how difficult and tricky it can be to determine risk. We normally think that the patient-subjects receiving the experimental treatment are the ones at risk, yet this case proves that any participant in an experiment, even one receiving a known treatment, may bear an unacceptable risk. Unfortunately, there is no mechanical procedure for determining an acceptable level of risk (both a scientific and an ethical concept), and neither the professional codes nor the IRB criteria provide much guidance. Yet each of us make evaluations of risk versus benefit every day (that's how we decide to "cross at the green not in between"), and it seems plausible that a similar thought process might be used to assess the risks of therapeutic experimentation.

As a general strategy, the risk potential of any activity may be divided into three categories. Category I includes all those activities (including experiments) in which there is no risk. When there are no cars in sight, or no chance that any patient-subject is assuming a risk, there is no need to be concerned at all with risk. The decision to conduct the experiment will be decided on other grounds (e.g., importance of the information to be obtained).

Category II constitutes all those activities in which the risk is prohibitive. Just as we don't consider running across a busy freeway during commuting hours, we need not consider experiments with unacceptable risks:

1. Poorly designed experiments unlikely to yield worthwhile results.
2. Experiments proposed by researchers lacking the skills or facilities to safely conduct the experiment.
3. Experiments that can be conducted in a manner that exposes the patient-subjects to less risk (this is the rule that would be used to justify decision c. in the ara-A case).

By quickly disposing of research proposals that fall into the first two categories, attention may be focused on Category III—decisions about experiments that contain both identifiable risks and benefits.

Category III contains all the tough cases, and there is no simple decision procedure guaranteed to yield the ethically correct choice. There is, however, a four-step process that guarantees to at least review the proper questions:

1. Make a thorough scientific assessment of both the risks and the benefits. This involves gathering the informed opinions of experts other than the research proposers, who may have a bias and certainly have a conflict of interest. On a personal level, this is equivalent to securing a second opinion.
2. Institute a risk-reduction round to determine whether new procedures might be added that would reduce the level of risk.
3. Since the medical needs of the patient are the primary concern of therapeutic experimentation, compare the benefits and risks of the experimental therapy with those of known therapies. Consider proceeding with the experiment only if it is a clear winner in this comparison.
4. Focus on the informed-consent process to insure that each patient-subject fully understands the risks he or she will be undertaking.

These four steps don't guarantee that the scientifically correct choice will be made (e.g., there could be a crucial error in the risk calculation), but they go a long way toward assuring that the experiment will be ethically justified.

CASE 36: GENE THERAPY AND SCIENTIFIC MATURITY

Cooley's anemia is an especially pernicious, hereditary blood disorder caused by a genetic defect in the hemoglobin gene. The disease results in stunted growth, disfigurement, and usually death before the onset of middle age. Based on preliminary mice studies which showed that selected genes can be transplanted into a living organism and that the new genes might be incorporated by the organism and carry out their function, this research proposes to use a similar gene-transfer technique for the treatment of Cooley's anemia: A small amount of the patient-subject's bone marrow will be withdrawn and mixed with healthy human globin genes. Then the subject's leg will be irradiated in order to kill the existing marrow and create a niche for the globin-enriched marrow that will be reintroduced. The therapeutic hope is that the new marrow will produce healthy red blood cells, thereby stemming, and perhaps reversing, the anemia. The patient is totally informed and eager to undergo the procedure. As an IRB member, would you:

A. Approve the research as the necessary next step in evaluating a new therapeutic procedure?
B. Request more information about the irradiation procedure in order to be certain that the level of risk was acceptable?
C. Deny the proposal on grounds that not enough is yet known about gene transplantation to justify using humans as the "animal of necessity"?

Although the scientific facts and value premises differ greatly between this and the previous case, the proper ethical solution remains the same: option C is the correct choice. The real-life background to the case is this: Martin Cline was a physician at the University of California at Los Angeles specializing in blood disorders. In the late 1970s he did some pioneering work studying the transplanting of genes in mice. Even though the results of his work were disputed within the scientific community, he decided to attempt to use his technique to transplant new genes into patients suffering from sickle cell anemia. When the UCLA IRB denied his proposal, Cline went to Israel and Italy, where he performed the procedure on patients suffering from Cooley's anemia, which is similar to sickle cell. As it turned out, his treatment neither helped nor hurt the patients, who are still alive five years later, and there is no evidence that the transplanted genes were ever incorporated by the patients. When word of Cline's experiments leaked out, the National Institutes of Health

(NIH) performed a thorough review, found him guilty of violating federal guidelines for human experimentation, and cut off all his research funds, and UCLA forced him to resign.[14]

The reasoning that led to these actions proceeded along the following lines. The scientific facts were:

1. The results of Cline's mice studies were disputed.
2. Human globin genes had never been made to function effectively in transformed cells.
3. Cline had been unable to get human genes to work in mice.
4. While Cooley's anemia is a terrible disease, the patients were not in imminent risk of death.

The important value premise was Principle Three of the Nuremberg Code: The experiment should be so designed and based on the results of animal experimentation and a knowledge of the natural history of the disease or other problem under study that the anticipated results will justify the results of the performance of the experiment. The ethical solution: Postpone the experiment using humans until much more is known about the entire process of gene transplantation.

This case is important because it emphasizes the criteria of scientific maturity: Humans are not to be used as the "animal of necessity" until all other research methods are exhausted. Quite clearly in the Cline case the scientific-knowledge base regarding his procedure was not nearly adequate enough to justify experiments on human beings. In such cases, the ethical rule is evident: In order to insure that the experiment has a reasonable prospect of providing valuable information, it must be delayed until a satisfactory base is built from animal or other studies.

It is important to distinguish the Cline case from the recent attempt by an Arizona doctor to implant the un-approved "Phoenix" heart. Had that been an experiment, it obviously would have failed the criteria of scientific maturity. The heart was unapproved precisely because it had not undergone enough animal experimentation. But it was not an experiment, it was a last-ditch therapeutic maneuver by a doctor to save his patient. In life-threatening situations, doctors are ethically bound to try any treatment with a chance of saving the patient.

CASE 37: BABY FAE REVISITED

Using this analysis, what should one conclude about the Baby Fae case—was it an ethically justified use of therapeutic experimentation? Sadly, the case seems to fail each of the ethical criteria. The level of risk was unacceptable because there were two other therapeutic options, a human heart transplant and an experimental surgery with a 60 percent success rate, that had less risk. In addition, both of those therapies included the prospect of a normal life had they succeeded. Even if Fae's body had not rejected the baboon's heart, there is still great debate about whether the heart could have grown with her body. Second, the criterion of scientific maturity was violated. The researcher's previous xenograph work had been done with sheep and goats, a far remove from primates, and the few unsanctioned attempts to transplant primate hearts into humans all ended as tragic failures. Nor was it possible to argue that these criteria didn't apply because Fae's condition was a matter of "life and death." Unlike the patient in the Phoenix heart case, Fae was not in imminent danger of death and there was time to treat her with either of the safer, more conservative therapies. Finally, the informed-consent process seems to have been carelessly handled. Since the doctors and ethicists advising Fae's parents worked at the hospital where the research was to take place, it appears that there may have been a conflict of interests.

Perhaps it is unfair to judge these dedicated scientists when we are secure in the luxury of time that only hindsight can provide. Yet the details of these cases demonstrate a simple fact: ethical analysis is no less difficult a job than scientific research. It is a mistake to think that we can make ethical decisions in hours about experiments which take months to plan and sometimes years to carry out. Protecting both the rights and the health of human subjects is more important than the potential knowledge to be gained, and we must be willing to take all the time needed to insure that that primary goal is attained. If therapeutic experimentation is going to continue to contribute to our quality of life, then particular attention will have to be paid to the ethical conduct of those experiments.

NONTHERAPEUTIC EXPERIMENTATION

CONCEPT:

1. In the purely scientific application of medical research carried out on a human being, it is the duty of the doctor to remain the protector of the life and health of that person on whom biomedical research is being carried out.
2. The subjects should be volunteers—either healthy persons or patients for whom the experimental design is not related to the patient's illness.
3. The investigator or the investigating team should discontinue the research if in his/her or their judgment it may, if continued, be harmful to the individual.
4. In research on man, the interest of science and society should never take precedence over considerations related to the wellbeing of the subject.[15]

These four clauses from the World Medical Association's Declaration of Helsinki emphasize subject safety in *non-*

therapeutic experimentation—research designed solely to produce new knowledge. But aside from specifying that the subjects are to be volunteers, they give no guidance concerning *who* may volunteer, and under *what* conditions. Unless ethical criteria are devised to meet such concerns, the conduct of nontherapeutic experiments, and their potential benefits, will be in serious jeopardy.

PRACTICE: In the preface to his play, *The Doctor's Dilemma,* George Bernard Shaw gives us a classic example of an ethically unacceptable nontherapeutic experiment: "No man is allowed to put his mother in the stove because he desires to know how long an adult woman will survive the temperature of 500 degrees Fahrenheit no matter how important or interesting that particular addition to the store of human knowledge may be."[16] In fact, it was precisely this kind of "experiment," in ovens and iceboxes and pressure chambers, that so shocked the world at Nuremberg.

The immediate response to such horrors was various codes of ethical experimentation. In order to forever ban such abhorrent uses of human beings in the name of science, these codes stipulated principles of conduct for experiments with human subjects:

1. *The criterion of social worth.* Only experiments that promise fruitful results for the good of society are to be undertaken

2. *The criterion of acceptable risk.* The level of risk to the subject must be minimized and commensurate with the anticipated social benefit

3. *The criterion of scientific maturity.* Humans are not to be used as the "animal of necessity" until all other research methods are exhausted

4. *The criterion of informed consent.* The voluntary consent of all subjects is required.

These four criteria apply to all experiments, both therapeutic and nontherapeutic. But because the participants in nontherapeutic experiments do not stand to benefit directly from the research that puts them at risk, it is especially important that the criterion of informed consent be ethically administered.

As already discussed, the ability to give one's informed consent requires at least two conditions. First, the ability to consent. According to *Black's Law Dictionary*, consent is the "voluntary agreement by a person in the possession and exercise of sufficient mentality to make an intelligent choice to do something proposed by another."[17] Since consent that is not voluntary is not consent at all, the ability to consent requires that the consenter be totally free to decide whether or not to participate in an experiment. Do prisoners, medical students, and patients, the three classes of people most frequently used as subjects in nontherapeutic experiments, have the degree of freedom needed to be a true volunteer?

Second, the consent must also be informed. In the experimental context, this means that the subject must be provided with all the information that a reasonable person would deem relevant, and must also be helped to understand the procedure and its risks. Quite clearly, neither children nor mental incompetents nor fetuses have the capacity to be informed. Does this mean that no research may be carried out using them as subjects?

Few topics polarize society as much as crime and punishment. Is it the job of the prison system to punish or to rehabilitate? Does our current system of laws coddle criminals or deprive them of their rights? These questions would be inappropriate in a book about bioethics except that the United States, alone among the countries of the modern, industrialized world, employs prisoners as subjects in biomedical research. In fact, a few years ago over 85 percent of all Phase I drug tests—the initial test used to determine toxicity and safe dosage range—involved prisoners.

Such practices have prompted social critics like Jessica Mitford to charge that prisoners are used in this way simply because they are "cheaper than chimpanzees."[18] On the other hand, biomedical researchers have described the overwhelming willingness of prisoners to participate in experiments and the "genuine esprit de corps" that develops among the subjects.[19] To be sure, prisoners are no longer abused as they were in eighteenth-century England when Caroline, Princess of Wales, "begged the lives" of six condemned criminals so that they might be used as human guinea pigs for an experimental smallpox vaccine before it was administered to her children. And no one is suggesting today that prisoners be treated any less well than other research subjects. Yet ethical questions still remain: Is it ever possible for prisoners to be true volunteers? Does the nature of the prison environment preclude their involvement as subjects in nontherapeutic experiments? Is it fair that prisoners are the usual "animal of necessity"?

In the mid-1970s these decidedly ethical questions became the focus of intense public-policy debate. Under the aegis of the National Commission for the Protection of Human Subjects of Biomedical and Behavioral Research, studies were commissioned and hearings held. Just how philosophical debate was turned into concrete policy is an important lesson for citizens in a country that seems forever moving toward the public regulation of previously private functions.

CASE 38: PRISONERS, POLICY, EXPERIMENTS, AND ETHICS

The Life Extension Drug Company is particularly proud of its new gout medication. It performed well during animal studies and produced few noticeable side effects. Yet before L.E.D. can receive manufacturing approval, they must first test the drug for safety on a human population. The company's standard procedure is to conduct nontherapeutic trials using prisoner-subjects at the state penitentiary. This has worked well in the past and there have been no complaints. This time, however, the Prisoners' Union files a suit to stop the test, arguing that inmates should not be used as "research animals." The company counters that everyone (e.g., society, the prison, the individual subjects) benefits by their research. What other arguments might be made? As judge, how would you decide this case?

Those arguing against the use of prisoners as research subjects claimed that it was impossible for them to give truly informed consent, because of fears of reprisal if they did not participate, because inducements such as monetary compensation (typically ten times more than the standard prison pay), extra privileges, and the promise of early parole amounted to a bribe, and because prisoners would agree to be research subjects simply to be relieved of the boredom of prison life. In short, that the conditions of prison life were so dehumanizing that it was impossible to volunteer from within that environment.

A second type of argument against the use of prisoners traded on the notion of *distributive justice*—the idea that those who shoulder the burdens must receive an equal share of the benefits. Opponents argued that prisoners were shouldering such a disproportionate amount of the research burden that they could not possibly receive their fair share of benefits. If the people want the benefits of continued nontherapeutic experimentation, then it is only fair that they begin to volunteer as research subjects.

Proponents of the status quo, or at least of the idea that prisoners should be allowed to volunteer for experiments, also argued along several lines. First, that because prisoners are confined, controlled, and under constant observation, they are the ideal population for the conduct of experiments that contribute an immense amount of social good. Second, that under the principle of *retributive jus-*

tice—those who commit wrongdoings should be required to make reparations—it seems appropriate that prisoners be allowed to volunteer for experiments. Third, social-science research has demonstrated not only that prisoners believe that their consent is voluntary, but that fully 90 percent of prisoner-subjects would be willing to participate in future experiments.[20] How could the commission decide among the competing claims? What kind of policy could incorporate all these points of view?

The key to resolving these questions was recognizing that none of the competing claims embodied an *in-principle* argument—an argument based entirely on ethical principle (e.g., abortion is in principle wrong because it violates the Commandment Thou Shalt Not Kill). Instead, all the arguments started with a factual premise, coupled it with a value premise, and arrived at an ethical conclusion. For example:

FACT: Prison is a coercive, dehumanizing environment.

VALUE: Freedom is a necessary condition for the granting of informed consent.

CONCLUSION: It is unethical to use prisoners in nontherapeutic experiments.

Since government may seek to regulate behavior but rarely wants to challenge or legislate private ethical beliefs, the commission used the presence of factual premises to recommend a policy based on changing the facts rather than anyone's values or ethics.

The strategy of the commission was clear in its conclusion, "Should coercions be lessened and more equitable systems for the sharing of burdens and benefits be devised, respect for persons and concern for justice would suggest that prisoners not be deprived of the opportunity to participate in research."[21] In other words, if the facts that buttressed the arguments of the opponents to the use of prisoner-subjects could be altered, then their ethical conclusion would lose its force. By recommending a series of improvements in the administration of the prison system (e.g., adequate living conditions, provisions for effective redress of grievances, separation of research participation from parole conditions, and public scrutiny), the commission was providing a set of objective criteria that would allow the ethical use of prisoner-subjects.

As a case study in ethical reasoning, the commission's work is instructive because it highlights an often overlooked point: many ethical disputes hinge not on moral absolutes but on contingent fact. This is especially true in the case of bioethics, where the facts may change as quickly as you can say "artificial heart" or "genetic engineering." Since it is always easier for people and governments to accommodate a change in the facts than in their ethics and values, good ethical analysis should always begin by reviewing the facts.

If the controversy concerning the use of prisoners as research subjects aroused little public interest, the debate regarding experimentation on fetuses was a real attention grabber. After all, it's hard to ignore three-inch-high letters screaming the headline ABORTION CLINICS SELL HUMAN FETUSES TO RESEARCHERS. Partly as a response to such headlines, a moratorium was declared in 1974 on all fetal research pending the recommendations of the National Commission for the Protection of Human Subjects of Biomedical and Behavioral Research. As the real-life cases below demonstrate, this time the commission would have to grapple directly with some explosive value issues.

CASE 39: GERMAN MEASLES AND THE FETUS

Rubella (German measles) causes serious abnormalities in 20 to 40 percent of exposed fetuses. This research proposes a method for studying whether it is safe to vaccinate an already pregnant woman—i.e., whether there is any chance that the vaccine will cross the placenta and invade the fetus. A group of women who had independently reached the decision to obtain an abortion will be recruited and vaccinated. Eleven to thirty days after the inoculation, the women will undergo the abortion procedure and the placenta and abortus will be analyzed for traces of the rubella virus.[22] As a commission member, what would you recommend about such *in utero* research:

A. Approve it in concept as the most efficient way to make needed discoveries about pregnancy and fetal medicine?

B. Deny it in concept on grounds that delaying the abortion for research purposes produced unnecessary risk for the women, and that such an experiment prohibited the women from changing their minds about undergoing an abortion, since the research might harm the fetus?

C. Deny it in concept on grounds that the fetus could not give its informed consent?

CASE 40: THE ARTIFICIAL PLACENTA

Premature birth is one of the greatest causes of infant mortality and retardation. The goal of this research is the development of an artificial placenta so that premature infants may continue to mature in a womblike environment. Women scheduled for a late abortion (well into the second trimester) will be recruited and the abortion performed by *hysterotomy*—a procedure similar to a cesarean section. The fetus will be delivered in the amniotic sac, and the umbilical vein and arteries cannulated (connected by tubes) to permit total perfusion of the blood supply. The research will investigate methods of improving this system that might eventually lead to a procedure for keeping currently unviable deliveries alive.[23] As a commission member, what would you recommend about such *ex utero* research:

    A. Approve it in concept as the most efficient way to make needed discoveries about pregnancy and fetal medicine?

    B. Deny the concept of such research on grounds that it is cruel and unethical to extend the duration of a nonviable fetal life?

    C. Deny it in concept on grounds that nontherapeutic experimentation on fetuses who are ready to die may lead to research on other societal members (e.g., terminal patients, condemned criminals) who are also ready to die?

Although there are some obvious and important differences between the two cases (e.g., *in utero* research must always be concerned with the health of the pregnant woman), the crucial issue the commission had to decide was the ethical status of the fetus. For some, the fetus is little more than a "growth" within a woman; as such, it has no special ethical claim, and questions about fetal research are no more difficult than questions about research on tonsils or tumors. For others, fetuses are considered full members of society with all the rights of any adult citizen. Since this includes the right to consent, and since it is obvious that fetuses cannot consent, those holding this view would in principle ban nontherapeutic research using them as subjects.

The commission was not willing to go as far as the opponents of fetal research wished. Instead, it recognized the work of a previous government report that found that fetal research was necessary in order to secure

    1. Knowledge concerning the transfer of substances across the placenta, the reaction of the fetus to drugs, enzyme activity in the fetus, and the development of fetal organs and systems; and

2. Therapies for preventing or offsetting congenital defects, saving the lives of premature infants, and counteracting the disabilities associated with prematurity.[24]

Once it had made the utilitarian ethical decision that the continuation of fetal research promised the greatest good for the greatest number, the commission promulgated a series of guidelines designed to protect the fetus.

With respect to *in utero* research, the commission recommended: "Nontherapeutic research may be conducted ...provided minimal or no risk to the well-being of the fetus will be imposed by the research."[25] Depending on how the word "minimal" is interpreted, this recommendation would ban the research proposed in Case 39, using reason B as the justification.

With respect to *ex utero* research, the commission recommended: "Nontherapeutic research directed toward the fetus during the abortion procedure and nontherapeutic research directed toward the nonviable fetus may be conducted provided...(f) the fetus is less than 20 weeks gestation, (g) no significant procedural changes are introduced into the abortion procedure in the interest of research alone, and (h) no intrusion into the fetus is made which alters the duration of life."[26]

Because of these three clauses, this recommendation would ban the type of research proposed in Case 40. Any research investigating the artificial maintainence of fetal life would have to be conducted on a therapeutic basis— i.e., conducted on fetal subjects with a chance of surviving, and therefore benefiting from, the experiment.

All human experimentation poses some threat that the subject will be depersonalized, that he will become merely a means to some research end. This threat is further heightened in nontherapeutic experiments, since there can be no pretense that the research being conducted is for the subject's own good. One preemptive approach for stemming any potential abuses would focus on the "Who may participate?" question. By banning certain vulnerable populations, we could eliminate even the prospect of some unethical research practices. But such a drastic solution would put unacceptable limits on our medical knowledge (e.g., children are not simply little adults, some research must use them as subjects if we are to learn about safe dosages of new drugs for the child population), as well as depriving other groups of their right to participate in the research enterprise.

The alternative is to focus on the "What conditions?" question. Rather than prohibiting certain populations from participating in research on *in-principle* grounds, this approach attempts to specify the ethical criteria that must be considered before any particular experiment is conducted, and to implement a review process that will insure that those criteria are met. This contingent approach taken by the National Commission established a National Ethical Review Board to decide difficult cases, specified the actual conditions that would allow vulnerable populations such as prisoners and medical students to volunteer freely, described a system of proxy consent that would permit children and mental incompetents to participate under certain conditions, and defined the criteria for ethical fetal research. By following this strategy, the commission chose to walk a tightrope between the potential for abuse and the constant need to develop new biomedical knowledge. In essence, this strategy accepts the ethical principle that ends sometimes justify means, though clearly not all means.

THE RESEARCH PROCESS

CONCEPT:
   The purpose of biomedical research involving human
   subjects must be to improve diagnostic, therapeutic

and prophylactic procedures and the understanding
of the aetiology and pathogenesis of disease.

Medical progress is based on research which ultimately must rest in part on experimentation involving
human subjects.[27]

These sentences from the Declaration of Helsinki's introduction support the thesis that research is the driving force
behind medicine's transformation from an art to a science.
Even though medical experimentation has a two-thousand-
year-old history associated with names like Aristotle,
Galen, and Harvey, it is only in this century that *biomedical research*, the systematic investigation of body processes and disease mechanisms, has enabled doctors to
make a really effective contribution to human welfare.

Yet the necessity of using human beings in this research,
as well as the very private and value-laden questions that
are being studied, has led to some peculiarly modern and
vexing ethical problems throughout all phases of the research process: Should there be any limits to what may
be studied? How are our research priorities set and who
should get to set them? Who is responsible for the consequences of the research design? When it goes well?
Goes poorly? Should research subjects receive compensation when experiments result in unintended, negative
effects?

PRACTICE: America's attitude toward biomedicine has
shifted dramatically in the past thirty years. The "miracles" of the postwar decade—the Salk and Sabin polio
vaccines, scores of new antibiotics, kidney dialysis—created an initial feeling of laissez-faire goodwill between
researchers and the public. They promised to continue
producing new medicines and therapies that would keep
us all healthier, happier people, and we promised to keep
the research dollars flowing and not ask too many questions about cases like thalidomide. After all, we could

afford to be smug since the drug was never officially released in this country.

Today, one only has to think about the concerns regarding recombinant-DNA research, or the monumental failure of Nixon's "war on cancer," or the numerous troubling stories about incredibly costly technology that may keep us breathing, if not quite living, to realize that biomedicine is no longer viewed as an unadulterated good. In fact, the scientist's image has deteriorated so badly that an article about recombinant DNA in *The Atlantic* portrayed the researcher in almost Frankensteinian terms: "A recondite area of modern biology has become a metaphor: The ultimate question is not whether bacteria may be contained in special laboratories but whether scientists can be contained in an ordinary society."[28]

While no one wants to return to an era of polio epidemics, many worry that biomedical research can no longer be given a blank check. The new attitude in America toward the value of science and high-tech medicine in our society stems not simply from a loss of confidence in researchers or from a decline in the belief that medical discoveries will inevitably improve our lives. Instead, it is fundamentally a dispute about how much influence biomedicine is to have on our lives, and who should be making the decisions about the extent of that influence.

CASE 41: CONTROLLING THE RESEARCH AGENDA

The regents of the University of California control more than the nine-campus system. They also have a contract with the U.S. Department of Energy to manage Lawrence Livermore Laboratory and Los Alamos National Laboratory, this country's premier centers for the design of nuclear weapons. This stewardship has fostered an ongoing debate within the academic community concerning the propriety of a university being engaged in weapons research. Those in favor say that the work will proceed anyway and the university's involvement is a positive force. Those opposed argue that the university should not give its resources and prestige to such research. Whether the issue is nuclear bombs or nuclear medicine, citizens are now asking, Who is controlling the research agenda?

It is dogma within the women's-rights movement that a male contraceptive pill would have been developed long ago if only the research establishment were not male dominated. Whatever the merits of that particular claim, there is little doubt that citizens are now questioning research priorities from a number of perspectives. For some, like those who vigorously campaigned against recombinant-DNA research, the issue is safety. They worry about producing an "Andromeda Strain" organism, a doomsday bug that might be lethal to humans, possess no natural enemies, and be capable of reproducing quickly enough to wipe out the human race or overturn the whole evolutionary process.[29] For others, the issue is just allocation of resources. How can we, they ask, spend millions to produce an artificial heart that will benefit only a few, when a similar expenditure on public-health projects such as prenatal nutrition or increasing the research budget for the study of venereal diseases would benefit many? Finally, still others worry not about the means of research but about its ends. For these individuals, some research topics such as those involving genetic engineering, extending the human lifespan, and sex selection of children are examples of "inopportune knowledge"—knowledge we do not have the wisdom to use properly.[30]

It hardly matters whether such concerns are always justified. What does matter is the public's realization that biomedicine is not value free, that decisions about which research questions to pursue require ethical as well as technical expertise. As long as the public's tax money is used to support the overwhelming majority of research ($5 billion to the National Institutes of Health for fiscal year 1986), and as long as the public is directly impacted by the quality and kinds of research conducted, then it is only ethical to conclude that the public's voice should be heard.

Partly as a response to such arguments, and partly in response to old-fashioned political clout, scientific groups and the government have begun to develop new mechanisms for allowing the public to make its many voices heard. Organizations such as Physicians for Social Responsibility have routinely provided technical expertise to lay groups in order to help them better articulate their concerns. The National Science Foundation's Office of Science and Society and its Ethics and Values in Science and Technology Program fund a number of programs designed to facilitate informed interactions between the public, the government, and the scientific community. Increasing numbers of nonscientists are being appointed as active members of scientific advisory panels (e.g., the National Institutes of Health's Recombinant DNA Advisory Committee), citizen advisory groups (e.g., the National Commission for the Protection of Human Subjects of Biomedical and Behavioral Research), and local Institutional Review Boards. Instead of limiting the public to passive comments after all the nitty-gritty choices have been made, these stratagems are designed to allow public participation during the early, active stages of the decision process.

Yet there are many public voices and only a few influential policy posts. It is also important to recognize that while the desire of affected parties to participate in biomedical decision-making is increasing, unlimited participation may conflict with efficiency, economy, and the need for special, technical knowledge. Finding the appropriate balance between democratic justice and expert competence is an ongoing problem in the applied ethics of choosing research priorities.

CASE 42: ETHICAL RESEARCH DESIGN

Willowbrook State School is a large New York institution for the care of the mentally retarded. Because of overcrowding, understaffing, and the health habits of the children-clients (e.g., most are not toilet trained), infectious diseases such as hepatitis were endemic. In an attempt to develop a method of immunization, a special hepatitis research unit began operation in 1956 and continued to run for fifteen years. One research project involved injecting children-subjects with infected serum in order to produce mild cases of hepatitis that could be studied and treated in isolation from the ongoing epidemic. Although the experiment had the consent of the children's parents and was approved by various local, state, and federal agencies, the key ethical question still remains: Is it ever justifiable to employ a research design that requires the induction of a disease agent?[31]

If overall research policy has important consequences for every member of society, then the specifics of the research design can be a matter of life or death for the individual research subject. Even when the importance of the research is unassailable and the selection of subjects impeccable, problems with the research design, with the actual strategy for conducting the experiment, may lead to ethically unacceptable consequences.

This is precisely what occurred in the study of the side effects of oral contraceptives. By adopting the classic "randomized, controlled, double blind design"—*randomized* because the placement of subjects into the treatment or control group is decided by chance, *controlled* because one subject group receives a well-understood therapy (or no therapy at all), *double blind* because neither the researchers nor the subjects know who is receiving the actual treatment—the researchers chose a design that, in this instance, had two unacceptable ethical consequences.

First, they placed half their subjects at too great a risk, the risk that they might become pregnant. Second, since the researchers knew it would be difficult, if not impossible, to recruit subjects who were fully aware of this risk, they simply declined to tell the women that they would be participating in an experiment and that some of them would receive placebos.

There is little doubt that placebos can play an important role in human experimentation. Yet it must also be made clear to the research community that they should not be used deceptively. In many cases, such as the testing of a new aspirin-type drug for headache pain, the experiment will not be compromised if the subjects are informed that placebos will be used. Since no one, including the on-site researchers, knows who is receiving the treatment and who the placebo, worries about "abnormal" responses and high, variable dropout rates seem overstated.

In other cases, such as the birth control study, the risks of replacing a known, effective therapy with a placebo are simply too great.[39] Such cases require a change to a more ethical research design, perhaps one that uses historical controls or compares the side effects of oral contraceptives to other methods of birth control.[33] Researchers must understand that safety is always the primary priority in any human experiment, and that informed subject consent is the first line of defense. If there is simply no other way to obtain information than by deceiving a subject, then that experiment ought not be performed.

A completely different set of issues involves the ethical obligations that are generated when an experimental therapy proves successful. Twenty-five years ago, comedian Shelley Berman began performing an uproarious routine about a surgeon who wants to repossess a heart pacemaker because his patient is failing to keep up with the payments. The humor developed from the obvious absurdity of a doctor taking positive steps to actually injure a patient because he was two months in arrears. Yet similar situations occur within the context of the research process. Almost by definition, experiments must have unknown consequences, and they must end at a preset time. But what happens to patients involved in therapeutic experiments that demonstrate the curative powers of a new treatment when that research ends? Are the researchers, or the hospital, or society obligated to continue to provide the now proven therapy?

There is no single answer to these questions. Instead, the ethical course of action is determined by both the nature of the experimental treatment and the understanding between subject and researcher. For example, there is no doubt that the recipients of artificial hearts are involved in an experiment that will last their lifetimes. Trying to imagine Berman's scenario ("Hello, this is Dr. De Vries, I'd like to arrange a time when my staff can come by and pick up the heart, the experiment's over.") is an absurdist exercise in life imitating art.

Alternatively, another recent research study has shown that a fifteen-minute telephone call once a week from a nurse-practitioner can have a dramatic effect in lowering high blood pressure. It would seem equally absurd to expect that in conducting such an experiment the researchers have obligated themselves for a lifetime of phone calls. Instead, the ethical obligation might include assisting their subjects in transferring the experimental treatment to a normal part of their health regimen (i.e., help in finding a medical service that will provide the phone call as part of normal patient care).

The ethical solution is not so obvious in cases that don't involve life and death but do involve a scarce drug or treatment. We now know that the growth of some congenitally short children can be dramatically boosted by the use of human growth factor. But HGF is in short supply. Is it right to reward with continued treatment the subjects of the experiments that proved the efficacy of HGF? Doesn't this reward put other afflicted children at a disadvantage? This is a concrete example of a major ethical dilemma in the theory of justice—the dispute between those who view justice as a matter of *equity*, based on merit, and those who view it as a matter of *equality*, based on equal access. While there is no general solution to this dilemma, it may be ethical in this case to expect everyone to compete for HGF on an equal basis, since the research subjects have already received a temporary boon with long-lasting consequences (i.e., their growth has already been stimulated). The point not open to ethical debate is that, regardless of the theory of justice subscribed to, research subjects must never be put at a disadvantage simply because they volunteered to participate in initial experiments.

CASE 43: COMPENSATING RESEARCH SUBJECTS

The ad in the paper seemed innocuous: "Wanted—women between the age of 21 and 45 to act as research subjects for the testing of a new drug designed to reduce the pain of menstrual cramps. Must commit for three months. Modest pay. Reply to Extremely General Hospital."

Ellen D. had often suffered from cramps and saw the ad as an opportunity to make a little money while seeking some medical relief. When she reported to the hospital, she was completely informed about the experiment, including its perceived modest risks, underwent a physical exam, and signed a consent form and a legal release. She was then given some tablets, either the new medicine or a placebo, told to take them whenever she experienced cramps, and asked to report back to the hospital the following week. Unfortunately for Ellen, she experienced a severe allergic reaction to the first tablet and was rushed to the hospital suffering from anaphylactic shock. Even though she had signed a legal release, is the hospital ethically liable for her treatment costs? What about compensation if she is left permanently disabled?

Ethical dilemmas of a different sort occur when an experiment goes poorly. Has a research subject forfeited all rights to compensation when he signs an informed-consent form, or is this subject "owed" compensation by virtue of volunteering for a risky experiment? There are three distinct reasons for thinking that compensation not only is ethical but may actually lead to the conduct of better research.

The first is the fallibility of the informed-consent process. One need not be as cynical as Dr. Henry K. Beecher:

> Ordinary patients will not knowingly risk their health or their life for the sake of "science." Every experienced clinician investigator knows this. When such risks are taken and a considerable number of patients are involved, it may be assumed that informed consent has not been obtained in all cases.[34]

to understand that truly informed consent represents an ideal, rather than the normal state of affairs. Since research subjects can never know the precise extent of their risk, and since researchers can rarely predict the exact consequences of a given experiment (that's why they must experiment), it is unreasonable to suppose that the mere act of signing a form should cause a subject to forfeit all financial protection from unseen consequences.

A second line of argument focuses on the entirety of the research enterprise instead of the individual researcher and his experiment:

> There can hardly be debate about the basic principle that research costs which take the form of injuries to human subjects ought, to the extent possible, to be borne by the research industry, and ultimately by society as a whole, and not by the unlucky subjects themselves.
>
> This principle of societal responsibility makes not

only humanitarian but economic sense, for the research industry will undertake fewer projects that are
not justified by a balancing of risks (and other costs)
against potential benefits if all of the potential costs
must be taken into account. Despite all the precautions in experimental design that ethics prescribes,
the necessary balancing of risks and benefits lacks
needed indices and incentives—and thus sacrifices
attainable precision—unless dollar costs must be
contended with. Whatever compensation system is
devised must not only compensate the unlucky subject but also place the burden on those best able to
evaluate and control the risks attending the experiment.[35]

This argument assumes the moral justice of subject compensation and argues on consequentialist grounds that it
will also lead to better research: first, because it will enable a more precise calculation of the criteria of acceptable
risk; and, second, because it will discourage researchers
from conducting all but the most important experiments.

The final argument for compensation is decidedly ethical. This country has a long tradition of compensating
individuals injured in the service of others (e.g., police,
fire, military). We honor this obligation because (1) those
individuals accept added risk in the performance of their
duties; (2) the services they perform are necessary for the
public good, and (3) society mandates that such activities
occur. Since these three factors are all present in the case
of research subjects (at least the ones engaged in nontherapeutic research), fairness dictates that we also honor
their right to compensation for injuries sustained while
serving the public good.[36]

The U.S. Health, Education and Welfare Secretary's Task
Force on the Compensation of Injured Research Subjects
also reached the same conclusion. While it left in doubt
how serious injuries must be in order to receive compen-

sation, what form that compensation should take, and how the compensation fund should be administered, it left no doubt that compensation of injured subjects should be our national policy.[37]

Experimentation with human beings is an issue that encompasses much more than the behavior of the scientist and his subject. Whether the question is what experiments to conduct, or who is free to volunteer, or how subjects should be compensated, the issues surrounding this type of research are, first and foremost, societal. They speak directly to the innovativeness of available medical care, the manner in which we train our doctors, and the way we spend our public funds. But more importantly, they also speak directly to the quality of our society. The ethics of the human use of human beings are nothing less than the litmus test for a just and free society.

VI

GENETIC INTERVENTION AND REPRODUCTIVE TECHNOLOGIES

LIFE forms have existed on the earth for three billion years; human beings have been attempting to codify their legal and ethical systems for approximately three thousand years; and biotechnology is a scant three decades old. Yet, as the material in this chapter dramatically demonstrates, recent advances in the biological sciences are not only changing our conceptions of life itself and what it means to be a human being, they are also challenging our legal and ethical systems in ways unimaginable even a generation ago.

The scientific foundation of this revolution is the pioneering work of James Watson and Francis Crick. In closing their now famous 1953 paper with the modest line, "It has not escaped our notice that the specific pairing we have postulated immediately suggests a possible copying mechanism for the genetic material,"[1] they signaled to the world the end of the search for the solution to one of mankind's most enduring riddles: What is the invisible mechanism of human renewal?

For more than twenty-five centuries, philosophers and scientists, mystics and churchmen had proposed various theories—*homunculi, epigenesis, preformation*—to account for the fact that children resemble their parents. Watson and Crick's explanation of the workings of the DNA molecule succeeded where all others had failed. By demonstrating how the famed double helix can (1) contain an almost infinite amount of information through the coding property of its individual base pairs, (2) direct the formation of duplicates of itself, a necessary step in building the organism from a single cell into the trillions of cells that comprise a human, and (3) control the synthesis of proteins, the complex building blocks of life, Watson, Crick, and others actually provided the "blueprint of life."[2]

But having that blueprint rekindled another longtime dream that had coincided with the goal of simply understanding the renewal mechanism. This second dream was less concerned with knowledge and more concerned with "Godlike" power. It was the human ability to shape and control that renewal process; to actually determine what kinds of people there should be. Plato had written of such control in the Allegory of the Metals fable in the *Republic*; Jewish legend credits the seventeenth-century Rabbi Judah Loew with creating the *golem*, a huge, dull-witted, semihuman being, to protect his fellow Jews; and Mary Shelley captured the public's imagination with her tale of Dr. Frankenstein's monster.

But the dream was much more than a fictional plot device. Rulers throughout history, both despotic and benevolent, had dreamed of molding their future constituents. Only forty years ago, the Nazi quest for a race of Aryan supermen demonstrated, with gruesome detail, that the dream was still alive. In fact, many of the ghoulish Nazi experiments exposed at the Nuremberg Doctors' Trials were directed at finding methods of genetic manipulation.

Today, because of the work of Watson, Crick, Paul Berg,

Herbert Boyer, and a whole host of prizewinning molecular biologists, we are on the brink of being able to directly manipulate the genetic material of human beings. Yet the power of these techniques is matched only by the importance of the ethical concerns they raise. Any attempt to alter the genetic composition of future generations (e.g., through public policies, eugenic policies, or genetic manipulation) is fraught with peril, and these new technologies are just the third, and newest, method for accomplishing this end.

Although we may not recognize them as such, most social and economic policy changes have an effect on future generations. Whether it's a change in the Medicaid budget, or food stamps, or abortion laws, or tax policy, or the amount spent on medical research, these all have the potential to affect the gene pool. For example, food stamp policy may alter the number of children born to poor parents, either through family planning or through miscarriage as a result of inadequate prenatal nutrition. However, since the effect of such policy change takes many generations to appear, since it is likely to be very small, and since these policies are adopted for reasons other than explicitly affecting the gene pool, little attention is paid to their potential impact in this area.

A second strategy seeks to affect the gene pool by directly altering breeding patterns. Today, while such *eugenic* policies are generally considered unthinkable for humans, they are followed assiduously for livestock and crops. But this does not mean that such a strategy is not applied on a small, private scale: selected infanticide (usually female), compulsory birth control (e.g., China's one-child rule is being used for population, and not genetic, control), mandated sex partners, arranged marriages, and forced sterilization are all directed at influencing the genetic makeup of future generations. Yet any large-scale, governmental attempt to mandate these policies would raise serious bioethical reservations (e.g., who would choose the targeted characteristics?, don't these methods run roughshod over personal autonomy?). In addition, there are also practical reasons why they are not likely to be successful.

First, the outcome is highly uncertain. The "natural lottery" is so varied that it is extremely difficult to accurately predict the characteristics of the offspring. Second, the rate of change in the gene pool would barely exceed that accomplished by having no policy at all. Finally, and most importantly, it is impossible to breed human beings for all-around improvement (whatever that might mean). At best, we could breed for a single characteristic (e.g., height or hair color). But as Nobel laureate Sir Peter Medawar has pointed out, selective breeding rarely gives something for nothing; you can only breed in one characteristic at the expense of others. While that might be acceptable for racehorses, it is not for human beings. Perhaps that is why he concludes, "The genetical manufacture of super-men by a policy of cross-breeding between two or more parental stocks is unacceptable today, and the idea that it might one day become acceptable is unacceptable also."[3]

The genetic interventions (e.g., introducing new genetic material into the cell, repairing flawed DNA) and reproductive technologies (e.g., test tube babies, cloning) based on the new science of molecular biology escape most of these practical and ethical objections. Because they directly manipulate specific genes, the results of gene therapy are highly select and immediate. And because this manipulation is targeted toward an individual and not a population, there is no need to override autonomy by promulgating an ethically dubious eugenics policy. But if these new techniques for shaping human beings escape many of the old concerns, the cost is an entire new set of problems which may ultimately cause us to reassess the very foundations of our ethical thinking.

CASE 44: THE AGGRESSIVE GENE

Mitch C. was the typical problem teenager: he never did well in school, his behavior oscillated between overt social aggression and resolute withdrawal, he was prone to brushes with the law. Finally, after a third vandalism episode at the high school, his parents agreed that they couldn't control him and they consented to send him to the State Home for Delinquent Boys. As part of the home's induction physical and processing, Mitch's chromosomal structure was tested for evidence of an additional Y, or male, chromosome. This testing was conducted because some scientists believe that the extra Y is indicative of "supermales"—males genetically programmed to be socially deviant, with a high proportion engaging in lives of crime. Was this testing procedure justified? Would the state be warranted, on the basis of a positive test result, in starting a regimen of biomedical control (e.g., drugs, therapy, sterilization) for Mitch's "aggressive tendencies"?[4]

CASE 45: RIGGING THE NATURAL LOTTERY

Bob and Martha K. are happy with their two daughters but would like a son to make their family complete. When they approach a fertility counselor with their desire for a male child, they are told that there are at least three techniques that might be tried to tip the scales in favor of a boy: modifications in their normal act of intercourse; sperm separation and artificial insemination; and test tube fertilization and selection of a male embryo for implantation. Further, they are advised that the more radical and riskier the technique, the greater the chance of a boy baby. Once the goal of a male child is decided upon, what are the ethical differences between the means? If sex selection is ethically acceptable, does the question of means even matter?

CASE 46: TO KNOW OR NOT TO KNOW

At the age of twenty-four, Richard N. had already been married for three years. With his career on track and a down payment on a new home, he and his wife were ready to start a family. Then Richard's mother called with the bad news. His father, age forty-four, had just been diagnosed as suffering from *Huntington's chorea*—an inherited disease of the nervous system that usually manifests itself in midlife, leads to progressive mental and physical deterioration, and results in a horrible, lingering death within ten to fifteen years.

Besides grieving for his father, Richard has his own situation to worry about: because the disease is inherited in an *autosomal dominant fashion*, one half of the offspring of an affected individual will carry the gene and ultimately develop the disease. In other words, there is a fifty–fifty chance that Richard's genes have already predestined that he will exhibit Huntington's chorea. When Richard confides this to his family doctor, he is told that there is an accurate test that can determine if he has the lethal gene, but there is nothing that can be done if he tests positive. What use might Richard make of this knowledge? Does it matter that Richard is contemplating children? What are the potential societal abuses of this knowledge?[5]

These three cases demonstrate the major reasons why the twin topics of genetic intervention and reproductive technology have generated so much interest and debate: First, by challenging long-held beliefs with new scientific data and techniques, they have a tendency to expose any weakness or inconsistency in our ethical position. Second, because technology always increases our options and presents us with a continuum of choices, whereas many people think of their ethical beliefs as absolute, our whole ethical structure is being threatened with a relativism that makes many uncomfortable. Finally, the rapid rate of spectacular scientific advance calls into question our time-honored notion of "knowledge as progress." Is it possible that some knowledge should not be acquired? Further, since knowledge inevitably leads to action, how are we to acquire the wisdom to act on this new information?

Ultimately, genetic intervention and reproductive technology are forcing us to rethink the meaning of some very central tenets and doctrines, perhaps the most important being our two-thousand-year-old Judeo-Christian system of moral and ethical reasoning. While it is, of course, an oversimplification to pretend that we all share the same value structure, the history of ethical thought, as well as the cases and discussion in this volume, supports the claim that the ethical system of rational human beings begins with the primacy of some general, closely held core beliefs: truth-telling, promise-keeping, fairness, personal autonomy. Most of our ethical dilemmas arise not because we disagree over the importance of these beliefs, but because certain situations put two or more of these beliefs in conflict.

The system's second component is a general ethical principle for determining what kinds of actions are considered right, and it is at this level that many disagreements begin. For some, that principle should be *consequentialist*—actions are judged just or unjust solely on the basis of their consequences. The most famous of these principles is the Utilitarianism of Mill and Bentham that judges an action right and just when it produces the greatest good for the greatest number.

Others adopt a *formalist* position—actions are to be judged independent of their consequences. Such *deontological* thinking reasons from first principles (e.g., Kant's categorical imperative, "I will never act in such a way that I could not also will that my maxim be a universal law"[6]) without regard to consequences. One of the reasons the abortion dispute is so polarized is that the two dominant groups are operating with different underlying principles. For the freedom-to-choosers, an abortion is justified if the consequences of having it outweigh those of not having it (e.g., as a result of amniocentesis, it is determined that the fetus has Tay-Sachs and will, therefore, die before the age of three). For the right-to-lifers, an abortion is killing, and there are *no* consequences that justify that particular action.

Finally, our ethical systems must also contain some rules of operation (e.g., the Hippocratic Oath, the Nuremberg Code) that allow us to bridge the gap between core beliefs, general ethical principles, and individual cases and actions. These specific rules generally reflect our more deeply held beliefs and try to put them into actionable language.

The new genetic technology is challenging each of these three ethical layers, as well as the way that the whole system is put together. In the words of the philosopher of science Thomas Kuhn, the old paradigm of thought and action is in crisis. Our shared system of ethical beliefs, principles, and rules of conduct no longer seems capable of providing us with the type of guidance we require. If this crisis is genuine, then the goal of ethical thinking can no longer simply be to solve individual problems within the accepted paradigm. Ethical freethinkers must be willing to search for new concepts and ideas as they struggle with increasingly difficult problems.

In fact, there is plenty of evidence to support the view that our ethical system really is in crisis. As demonstrated in the case of Mitch C., adding a new technological layer (chromosome testing) to an already vexing ethical problem (biomedical control) starts out by making recognizable bioethical problems that much tougher, and ends up presenting us with dilemmas at the core of our social and moral philosophy: Is the scraping of a few epithelial cells off a cheek a medical procedure? If it is, doesn't the state need someone's informed consent? Even if Mitch is XYY, does this give the state the right to begin some form of behavior therapy? Finally, if genetic screening can detect the "mark of Cain," what are we to do with this knowledge?

Some of these questions have obvious answers. Not only is testing for XYY a medical procedure, it is also a human biomedical experiment because we do not, as yet, have scientific proof that XYY individuals are especially aggressive or prone to crime. Early studies showed only that men with XYY *genotypes*—an individual's genetic constitution—populated the prisons in far greater numbers than would be expected by chance. It was false media reports in 1968 about Richard Speck, the killer of nine Chicago nurses, being an XYY that popularized the view that XYYs were indeed violent criminals (the media just couldn't resist sensationalizing a mass murderer with the tattoo "Born to raise hell").

To date, that view has not been confirmed. Because there is no proven link between XYY and criminal behavior, Mitch is entitled to all the safeguards designed to protect human subjects. In particular, he may refuse to participate.

But the larger questions still remain. Will we ever be capable of linking genotypes with explicit behaviors? And what should we do, as a society, if we obtain that power? In the case of XYY research, so many questions about both methodology (how can you distinguish the genotypic from the environmental influence?) and political ends (should we be conducting research that may demonstrate that a segment of the population is prone to crime?) were raised that the research was halted.[7] Yet history has demonstrated that it is terribly difficult to direct the flow of scientific research, and we must be ready to face these questions again.

Nor is Mitch's case the only example in which genetic technology adds another dimension of difficulty to already entrenched dilemmas. Virtually every problem already discussed, from the confidentiality of the doctor–patient relationship to the proper allocation of medical resources, to the use of human subjects in medical research, is impacted and made more confusing by the new technology. It's tough enough for a doctor to decide whether he should tell a seventeen-year-old's parents that she is taking birth control pills. But at least it's not a matter of life and death. Suppose a doctor screens a couple for *Tay-Sachs*—a deadly genetic disease that can afflict the children of East European Jews when both parents carry the recessive gene— and finds out that the husband carries the gene but the wife does not. All the potential children of this couple are safe from the disease, but does the doctor's responsibility end there? Should he notify the husband's siblings that they have a good chance of carrying the gene? Is the state an interested party? What would be the effects of a state gene information bank? These questions are addressed in the "Genetic Testing, Screening, and Counseling" section of this chapter.

Further questions, such as whether it is justified to spend scarce medical dollars to help infertile couples (is childlessness even a health problem?), or the status of fetal research (does a fetus have any special rights? how about an abortus?) only point up the fact that it is increasingly difficult to resolve these new, technology-exacerbated problems within our old ethical paradigm. Of course, difficult problems alone would not be reason enough to abandon our time-tested system for making ethical decisions. Yet the growing number and severity of recent ethical crises generated by scientific advance must be taken as a sign that mere patchwork solutions (e.g., adding a new specific rule to deal with a unique case) grafted onto the old paradigm may not be sufficient.

A second type of evidence that our ethical system may need overhauling, and one that points to a more systemic problem than the mere accumulation of individual, technology-aggravated problems, is demonstrated by the case of Bob and Martha K. Twenty-five years ago, sex selection was impossible and our greatest expectation was the birth of a healthy baby regardless of its sex. Today, the three technological choices the couple are given tend to blur or erase ethical boundaries that were previously considered absolute: the value placed on procreation as a sacred act between husband and wife.

Traditionalists fear that, provided with choice where none previously existed, society will go out onto a "slippery slope" of relativistic ethics on which we may lose our balance and tumble to the bottom. They are afraid we may find ourselves in a position where our ability to make ethical decisions is so debilitated that we find we are living in an "ethical free-fire zone" where "anything goes." After all, most people would probably agree that assuming a new sexual position to enhance the joy of loving is perfectly acceptable. But is it acceptable if it is used as a means to an end—the procreation of a male child? And if that's all right, why isn't artificial insemination or egg insertion? How we make ethical distinctions once we're on the slope, once we leave the firm ground of the two-thousand-year-old Judeo-Christian ethic, is the challenge being posed by advances in reproductive technology.

Historically, our ethical system has been structured so that we never venture out onto a slope. Kierkegaard spoke of it as Either/Or: either an action is ethically acceptable or it is not. One need only reflect on the syntactic structure of the Ten Commandments, "Thou shalt not," to see that there are no exceptions, no specific situations where one is granted special permissions. Yet technology is never absolute, and by granting us a continuum of options it is threatening to make obsolete our old, absolute ethical categories. Dilemmas of this sort suggest that repairing our ethical system cannot be accomplished at the level of specific rules. It is the guiding ethical principles (does it ever make sense to consider actions right or wrong independent of context?) that are called into question.

Nowhere is this clearer than in the new techniques that science has devised to help in the making of babies. There are at least seven stages of technological intervention:

1. Infertility clinic—physical exams to make certain that the reproductive organs are operating properly, sex technique counseling, corrective surgery, and drug or hormone therapy.
2. Artificial insemination by the husband—useful when sperm is subfertile or the sperm is having difficulty reaching the ovum during regular intercourse.
3. Artificial insemination by a donor—necessary when the husband cannot produce fertile sperm.
4. Surrogate mothering—artificial insemination of a surrogate mother with the sperm of the husband who has an infertile wife; when the baby is born, it is adopted by the husband (the biological father) and his wife.
5. *In vitro* fertilization—the so-called "test tube baby" procedure in which the egg of a woman is surgically removed, inseminated in the laboratory, and then surgically reimplanted; this is necessary when the fallopian tubes are damaged.
6. Embryo transplants—the same technique as *in vitro* fertilization except that the implanted egg comes from a donor; necessary when the woman is infertile.
7. Cloning—although not a biological reality for humans as yet, this is asexual reproduction in which

exact copies of individuals are produced from their
own cells.

It is not enough that for each, individual technological
advance there are questions regarding how and why it
may be used, what advantages and problems it could bring,
and what ethical problems it fosters. (These questions are
discussed in the "Reproductive Technologies" section of
this chapter.) Once we take that first step out onto the
slope, once we grant that it is ethically acceptable to allow
scientific techniques to contribute to the making of a
healthy baby, we are immediately faced with the question
of where to draw the line. Unfortunately, our current ethical theory is ill-prepared to help us answer that question.
Science and technology continue to provide us with new
choices, but our ethical system cannot help us choose.
The fact that our ethical concepts are so structured that
they are not flexible enough to help us make key life
decisions is yet another indication that we should be considering how to change the paradigm itself.

The final piece of evidence that our ethical system is
in crisis is also the most potent, since it strikes at our
central core of beliefs: recent scientific advances, coupled
with their ethical consequences, are causing us to call into
question other deeply held beliefs. This is clear in the
Huntington's-chorea case which causes us to rethink the
value of knowledge. Would Richard C. be better off not
knowing? As with the sex selection case, is society better
off not knowing how to predetermine the sex of a child
so as not to threaten nature's delicate fifty-fifty balance?
Is it possible that our ability to "know" is outstripping our
ability to "know what to do"?

Such concerns are not new. Every generation since the
Luddites has had its anti-technology voices, but they are
now becoming widespread. When Cambridge, Massachusetts, was debating the control of recombinant-DNA research inside its city limits, page one of its lay panel report

made this startling claim: "The social and ethical implications of genetic research must receive the broadest possible dialogue in our society. That dialogue should address
the issue *whether all knowledge is worth pursuing.* It
should examine whether any particular route to knowledge threatens to transgress upon our precious human
liberties." [emphasis added][8] What's at question now isn't
a human being replaced by a machine, but people being
made to feel less than human as the result of new knowledge.

One area in which this diminishing of personhood is
quite acute is our newly found ability to develop biomedical tests in order to predict everything from behavior to
disease patterns to ultimate causes of death. A central
tenet of our ethical system is that we are all responsible,
as free agents, for our actions. Yet, if the XYY hypothesis
is correct, is Mitch C. really responsible for his actions,
or is behavior predetermined? Tests can now determine
whether a baby has sickle cell anemia, but we don't have
the medical knowledge to affect a cure. Are individuals
better off being told now, on the basis of tests, what their
biological fate is to be? Ultimately, is this type of future
knowledge changing our image of what it means to be a
human being?

An even greater threat to personhood is promised by
advances in gene therapy. While most people would wel-
come the day when doctors could enter an individual's
DNA and "fix" the faulty genes that cause Huntington's,
or sickle cell, or any one of the other hundreds of genetically caused diseases, such a power also poses tremendous ethical dilemmas. We have no problem with using
recombinant-DNA techniques to produce insulin or interferon in laboratory dishes, but do we want to face a
world where our cells may be cloned so that sex itself
becomes unnecessary? These issues are discussed in the
"Genetic Engineering" section of this chapter.

Since genetic interventions and reproductive technologies are actually changing mankind in new ways for the first time in our 4.5 million years of evolution, we've got to stop and ask ourselves just what our status is as a maker of ethics. Bioethics started out using an ethical framework to answer questions about medicine. Now advances in medical science are forcing us to ask, Who is this being that is making ethical choices, and are the old ethical concepts and structures adequate for the job?

GENETIC TESTING, SCREENING, AND COUNSELING

CONCEPT: Ever since the first Mesopotamian farmers invented agriculture ten thousand years ago by selectively sowing the seeds of plumper cereal grains, human beings have known that it was possible to manipulate "nature's lottery." Yet it was not until the mid-nineteenth century that we learned enough about the manipulation process to turn it into the science of *heredity*—the study of the transmission of characteristics from parents to offspring. By carefully choosing traits that displayed themselves in an all-or-none manner, and by working with pea plant populations large enough to display convincing arithmetic trends, the Austrian monk Gregor Mendel was able to demonstrate that the "stuff of heredity" was composed of particles that could be transmitted independently of one another. Mendel's "gardening" had discovered two of the important laws of the process of *meiosis*, the splitting of sex cells: traits could be inherited as complete units, and certain traits were dominant.

It took about another hundred years before scientists could completely explain the process Mendel had described. That explanation involved *chromosomes*, the cellular bodies that contain the genetic material and do the splitting during meiosis; *genes*, the actual carriers of the instructions for the development of specific characteristics; and the DNA molecule. With all the subcellular pieces in place, the science of heredity gave way to the science of *genetics*—the study of the transmission of genetic material, *genotype*, and its relationship to observable characteristics, *phenotype*.[9]

Because genes control literally everything from hair color to specific diseases, the medical community has developed techniques (e.g., *amniocentesis*, analysis of the fetal fluid; *karyotyping*, photomicrography of an individual's chromosomes) that can be used to test the genotype for the presence of disease even before the symptoms become detectable in the phenotype. Today, there are three major levels of genetic screening:

> 1. *Neonatal*—tests of newborns to determine if they carry the genes for certain diseases (e.g., *phenylketonuria* [PKU], a metabolic disease leading to mental retardation) that can be treated if diagnosed early.
> 2. *Prenatal*—tests of fetuses to determine whether they carry the genes or chromosome structure for certain diseases (e.g., *Down's syndrome*—mongolism) so that the parents may decide how to deal with the pregnancy.
> 3. *Carrier*—tests of adults to determine whether they carry the genes for certain diseases (e.g., sickle cell anemia) that put them at risk of having children who would actually manifest the disease.

While each of these three types of genetic screening promises to bring us a healthier society, they all raise serious bioethical dilemmas: Who is entitled to the results of genetic tests? What does it mean to be "genetically healthy"? Who should decide the appropriate action if a fetus is shown to have defective genes? Is abortion an acceptable option? Is it possible to know too much about our genetic makeup? Will all this knowledge change our view of human beings and their place in the world?

PRACTICE: The place: a local singles bar. The time: the not too distant future. The scene: After exchanging furtive glances across the room, he approaches and asks her to dance. While they're dancing, he notices a small mark, actually a tiny tattooed "TS," behind her ear. He has an identical mark which signifies that he carries the gene for Tay-Sachs disease. He knows that should they marry and have children, one fourth of their offspring will suffer from the deadly disease. When the music ends, he thanks her and excuses himself. He thinks to himself, Best not to get involved unless we're genetically compatible.

The idea that we all submit to genetic tattooing was proposed by Nobel laureate Linus Pauling as a means of mitigating the possibility that carriers of recessive genes would become too fond of each other. In this way, such couples could avoid having to face serious bioethical decisions about marriage and children. In a sense, Pauling is proposing a double protection scheme: first, everyone must undergo genetic testing; second, there must be mandatory dissemination of those test results. If taken seriously, his suggestion would lead to a new kind of "truth in packaging" legislation—we would each walk around with a mini-billboard behind our ear declaiming our "inner ingredients."

Pauling's proposal suffers from two types of objections. First, there are a number of policy and bioethical objections (e.g., fear of eugenics programs) that argue against its being implemented in the "not too distant future." Second, the proposal would hardly be very effective in reducing genetic disease, since it deals only with one (i.e., the offspring of parents with matching recessive genes) of the many causes of such disease (e.g., dominant genetic defects, chromosomal abnormality). Understanding the scope and mechanisms of such conditions requires a quick and simplified refresher course in human genetics.

Modern medicine's war against disease is similar to

Hercules' fight with the Hydra. Every time a disease is conquered, it seems that another appears to take its place. Antibiotics have eliminated the infectious scourges of the last century, but they have been replaced by the chronic, degenerative diseases of old age. At the other end of the age continuum, improvements in prenatal care, nutrition, and neonatal medicine mean that fetuses have a greater chance of being carried to term, and that infants have a better chance of survival. Yet, by reducing or eliminating environmental causes of death and disease, we have come to see clearly their genetic component:

—Four to 6 percent of infants are born with clearly defined genetic diseases, chromosome abnormalities, or severe congenital defects.

—When disorders like Huntington's chorea that reveal themselves only later in life are included, an estimated 10 percent of the population carries a potentially handicapping inherited abnormality.

—Inherited diseases and genetically influenced birth defects account for 20 percent of all infants' deaths in the first year of life in the United States, second only to the number caused by birth injuries and premature birth. They are the second leading cause of death in the one-to-four age group and the third in the fifteen-to-nineteen age group.

—An estimated 40 to 60 percent of all human fetuses conceived are lost to miscarriage or spontaneous abortion. At least half of those spontaneously aborted in the first three months of pregnancy have chromosome abnormalities.

—Inherited defects account for 30 percent of pediatric admissions at major hospitals and 13 percent of adult admissions....A 1972 study estimated that hereditary disease and congenital defects caused the hospitalization of 1.2 million people annually in the United States at a cost of more than $800 million.[10]

Pauling's proposal would eliminate only a fraction of this genetically induced carnage.

If we are now coming to comprehend the scope of genetic disease, we are also gaining a greater understanding of the mechanism of genetic transfer: We all have our own, unique genetic blueprint which contains several hundred thousand pairs of genes. Each pair is responsible for some specific trait—eye color, production of a specific enzyme. When we produce *gametes*, sperm or egg cells, the gene pair is split in two. After the egg is fertilized by a sperm, the genes are paired once again and the ovum now contains half of the male's genes and half of the female's. Individual genetic defects are passed on to the ovum, because genes may be faulty in two ways: first, a gene may carry the instruction to produce a defective protein or enzyme; second, a gene may carry no instruction at all.

The genes in the first case are called *dominant* because everyone who inherits that gene will exhibit the trait (e.g., dwarfism, Huntington's chorea, retinal aplasia) regardless of the other gene in the pair. Since dominant genetic traits are always manifested, Pauling's proposal is of no use in such cases. Patrons at the singles bar already know, just by looking, what dominant traits a prospective partner carries. They also know that, given the laws of genetics, half of the offspring of someone with a dominant trait will exhibit that trait. Dominant genes are nature's own "truth in packaging" law. The cruel exception is Huntington's chorea, which doesn't manifest itself till midlife.

Genes that carry no instructions are called *recessive* because they defer to the instructions of their pair-mate. It has been estimated that each of us has approximately five to ten defective, recessive genes, but that they do no damage because they are paired with a "normal" gene capable of providing the needed instructions. Recessive defects occur when both members of the gene pair are recessive. When that happens, the genotype carries no instructions, and an important substance cannot usually be produced.

Because recessive defects hide their trait, most of us don't know whether we are *carriers*, people with one recessive gene, for diseases like sickle cell or Tay-Sachs or PKU. It is only when we mate with people who are also carriers that our genetic blueprint is revealed: The offspring of people who each have one recessive gene will have a one-in-four chance of inheriting the disease, a one-in-four chance of not carrying the gene at all, and a one-in-two chance of being a carrier. It is because of recessive defects that Pauling made his proposal.

The final major cause of genetic disease is chromosome defects. These conditions (e.g., Down's syndrome, defects of the sex chromosomes like the XYY syndrome) are not caused by problems with individual genes. Instead, they happen when errors occur within entire chromosomes and are usually the result of mistakes in the copying mechanism. Since there are no genetic carriers for these conditions, they would not be affected by Pauling's suggestion.

While the burden of genetic disease is great, it is not likely that a free society would willingly submit to a massive program of genetic screening, and its implied risk of state eugenic control, simply to mitigate a small portion of that problem. In fact, as the cases below demonstrate, even "enlightened," small-scale uses of genetic testing can raise some serious bioethical dilemmas.

CASE 47: PLAYING BIOCHEMICAL BINGO

The state legislature is considering a bill to mandate the screening of all newborns for a list of genetic defects including PKU, XYY syndrome, and *alpha-1-antitrypsin deficiency*—a condition that may involve a predisposition to emphysema. Those supporting the bill argue that medical science has now made it possible to obtain genetic information that may be helpful in treating and preventing certain diseases and that not making use of that information would be socially irresponsible. Those opposed to the bill argue that genetic information is very private, that it should be gathered only in special circumstances, and that the state has no legal right to mandate such all inclusive screenings. As a member of the legislature, would you:

A. support the bill on grounds that the health benefits of inexpensive genetic screening are a smart allocation of health resources?
B. oppose the bill on grounds that the state cannot "violate the person" simply to obtain genetic information?
C. postpone the vote and request that the state medical adviser prepare a memo on the costs and benefits of screening for each specific disease or condition?

Screening for PKU became possible twenty-five years ago, and it has served as the model for similar programs. A newborn with PKU lacks the enzyme needed to break down the amino acid *phenylalanine*, a constituent of most proteins. Without the enzyme, phenylalanine accumulates in the brain and causes retardation. By screening all newborns, doctors are able to identify those with PKU and put them on a very restrictive, protein-free diet for the first five years of life. This treatment enables the newborn to avert brain damage and to mature into a healthy adolescent. Since the state would have to shoulder the cost of institutionalizing untreated PKU infants, most states have passed laws mandating PKU screening.

Although there have been some disagreements in the medical community about the actual effectiveness of PKU screening, most agree that it is a worthwhile program. The real arguments begin with what some have called the "disease-of-the-month-club" approach to genetic screening.

The ability of scientists to detect genetic abnormalities is running far ahead of their ability to treat those abnormalities. XYY syndrome is a perfect example. While it is quite easy to identify XYY newborns, it is not even clear if the syndrome has any deleterious consequences, much less what to do about them. Similar questions surround the newborn with alpha-1-antitrypsin deficiency. At best we can say that this individual has a statistically higher-than-normal chance to contract emphysema if exposed to certain environmental conditions. Does this mean he is "sick"? Should such a diagnosis at birth affect his next seventy years? Our ability to test the genes of the newborn has added a new dimension, genetic health, to the already value-laden issue of what constitutes good health.[11]

The most appropriate legislative action would be C, a careful review of the costs and benefits of screening for specific diseases. While there is no in-principle objection to the state mandating health screenings (i.e., this is already done with blood tests for venereal disease before marriage), it should also be clear that genetic information is qualitatively different from information about infectious disease or high blood pressure. To a large extent our individual genetic blueprint determines who we are. Given our right of privacy, the state is not entitled to that information without compelling reasons. The state may screen for genetic abnormalities when they are treatable, when they are a recognized health risk, and when the state has a substantial fiscal interest, but it certainly has no right to play "biochemical bingo" with the lives of its citizens.[12]

CASE 48: SECOND-CLASS BABIES?

Anne A., Betty B., and Carol C. all came to the hospital on the same day for amniocentesis. Each had been identified by her physician as undergong an "at-risk" pregnancy: Anne was thirty-eight and therefore at risk (about one in three hundred) of giving birth to a Down's-syndrome baby. Betty B. was a carrier of the gene for hemophilia, which meant that 50 percent of her male offspring would manifest the disease. Both Carol and her husband were Tay-Sachs carriers; their baby had a one-in-four chance of being afflicted with the disease.

A few weeks later, after the results of the procedure were analyzed, they met individually with genetic counselors. The news was not good: Anne was definitely carrying a Down's baby, Betty was carrying a male, and Carol's baby had Tay-Sachs. Anne was advised that Down's-syndrome children varied widely in their mental retardation and that many Down's children were also born with other congenital defects. Betty was once again told of the fifty–fifty odds of a child with hemophilia, and she was also informed of the breakthroughs in managing the disease, the likely costs, and the outlook for such a child. Carol received the darkest news: her child would die within a few years.

The unspoken word underlining each counseling session was "abortion." While the counselors provided information, the actual decision was up to each couple. Is abortion acceptable in any of these cases? All of them? What are the relevant differences between the cases?

Unless you hold the position that abortion is never justified, these cases provide a classic example of the way in which new medical technologies are aggravating already intractable ethical problems. Twenty-five years ago there was no way to ascertain the genetic health of a fetus. Medical decisions regarding abortions focused solely on the health of the mother. Today, it is possible to make categorical statements about the health of the fetus (e.g., it has Tay-Sachs) as well as probabilistic judgments (e.g., he has a fifty–fifty chance of being a hemophiliac). The key ethical question is how to use this information.

Lurking behind this question is the slippery-slope argument: once we allow the health status of a fetus to be considered, it will be impossible to deny any woman the right to abort on grounds of some genetic defect, even something as speculative and minor as alpha-1-antitrypsin deficiency. The fear is that there will be no stopping the woman out to give birth to the perfect baby.

It is this last worry that may be the greatest issue in fetal screening. According to Dr. Leon Kass, "A child with a genetic defect, born at a time when most of his potential fellow sufferers were destroyed prenatally, is likely to be looked upon by the community as one unfit to be alive, as a second-class (or even lower) human type. He may seem a person who need not have been, and who would not have been if only someone had gotten to him in time."[13] The technology that allows fetal screening has the potential to produce much good, but it will also provide us with a whole series of new ethical choices. Deciding which choices to make will go a long way toward determining the future society we will live in.

CASE 49: THE INVISIBLE TATTOO

When Johnny and Velma R.'s little girl first showed signs of having sickle cell anemia, the family was referred to a local university hospital for treatment. In return for free medical care, the family agreed to become participants in the sickle cell research program. After all the forms had been signed, the first order of business was drawing blood from all three members for a broad spectrum of analytical tests. The results shocked the research team: Velma carried the sickle trait, but Johnny did not. Unless an incredibly rare mutation had taken place, Johnny couldn't possibly be the father. When this information was presented to Velma, she said she was pretty sure Johnny was the father, and she begged the doctor not to tell him of the results. How should the doctor respond? Who is the patient: Velma, Johnny, their daughter, future generations?

Because testing for paternity is asymmetrical—it is very difficult to prove paternity but relatively easy to prove nonpaternity—genetic testing for carrier status has the potential to put the doctor in the middle of a delicate family problem. Similar problems may be caused by the familial nature of genetics. If one of four brothers is a Tay-Sachs carrier, the odds are seven out of eight that another brother is also a carrier. Is a physician obligated to notify these individuals? If so, wouldn't this obligation run counter to the right of confidentiality? There are no clear-cut answers to these questions, only a realization that biotechnology has once again intensified ethical problems of long standing. Genetic testing stresses the doctor–patient relationship because it introduces a new interested party: future generations. How that relationship should change to accommodate both perspectives is an issue that affects all of us.

The ethical dilemmas surrounding all three modes of genetic testing arise because we attempt to use that information to guide actions. As Nobel chemist Dr. Glenn Seaborg has pointed out, it's not the science, but the use we make of it, that has value implications: "People must understand that science is inherently neither a potential for good nor for evil. It is a potential to be harnessed by man to do his bidding. Man will determine its direction and its effects. Man, therefore, must understand science if he is to harness it, to live with it, to grow with it."[14]

Many of the problems surrounding genetic information occur because the public does not understand the basics of biological science (e.g., a confusion between being a carrier and having the disease). In the new age of biotechnology, the doctor must often be as much an educator as a healer. Other problems arise because the "Man" in Seaborg's quote is too often "The Man"—the state or the law—rather than the individual affected by a particular genetic condition. While the state does have some compelling public-health interests, it must always recognize that genetic information is also an individual's most private information. Even in cases where the state has a "need to know," it must take special precautions to insure that the information is used properly. Finally, we must keep the possibilities of genetic knowledge in perspective. As with all other knowledge, most people will use it wisely. A minority may choose to abuse it. But as long as the power to use it resides with individuals, and not states, it should serve as a positive force in our species' continued 4.5 million years of evolution.

REPRODUCTIVE TECHNOLOGIES

CONCEPT: Recent evidence indicates that America may be suffering from an *infertility*—defined as being unable to conceive despite more than one year of concerted effort— epidemic: Nearly 2.5 million couples are infertile. Among women age twenty to twenty-four, the rate of infertility has tripled since 1965. Studies of men's sperm count has shown similar declines, from 100 million per milliliter in 1951 to less than half that in 1979. Some are even calling it the era of "chemical vasectomies."

Fortunately, *reproductive technologies*—any biomedical devices or procedures used to alter, manipulate, hinder, or augment the human reproductive cycle—are coming to the rescue of all those unable to produce children "the old-fashioned way." Female infertility caused by ovarian problems is being cured with fertility drugs that increase ovulation. As a result of this therapy's often spectacular results, quintuplets hardly make the news wire anymore. In cases where the husband's sperm is subfertile, artificial insemination using his enhanced sperm, or the use of a fertile donor's sperm, is accounting for nearly ten thousand babies annually.

More severe problems, such as blocked fallopian tubes, may require *in vitro fertilization*—an ovum is surgically removed, fertilized in a sterile glass dish, and then implanted in the uterus after it has begun to divide. This ability to manipulate sex cells outside the body has led to other biomedical miracles (e.g., embryo transplants) and a whole host of bioethical questions.

For example, *surrogate mothering* involves contracting for the use of a third party's womb, and her agreement to be inseminated by the sperm of the father-to-be, to carry the fetus to term, and to give it up for immediate adoption. This approach to infertility involves little technological intervention but overwhelming legal problems. Add to this the possibility of future technologies such as *ectogenesis*—nurturing of the fetus to term entirely outside the womb—and cloning, and it is easy to see why many have feared the coming of a Brave New World.[15]

Although we are a long way from facing some of the most chilling prospects of Huxley's dystopia—abolition of the family, total asexual reproduction, mass production of human beings to specification—the current success of reproductive technologies does present three types of bioethical dilemmas. Type I problems are technology specific: Is it acceptable to use fertility drugs when we know that their use will result in the deaths of many premature infants? What is the ethical and legal status of frozen embryos? Can surrogate mothers be compelled to give up the babies that they've carried? Type II problems relate to the whole spectrum of these technologies: If it is ever acceptable to scientifically intrude upon the procreative act, how are we to decide upon criteria for the just application of such technologies? Does accepting *in vitro* fertilization under certain conditions really put us on the road to a Brave New World? Type III problems are the most global, involving what philosophers call the "human condition": Does our ability to alter the ways in which we reproduce result in a changing image of the human being? In particular, do the scientific achievements of individual humans lead to a dehumanization of us all?

PRACTICE: The "facts of life" have changed. For millions of years there was only one correct answer to the perennial "Where do babies come from?" question, and parents simply had to decide how much of that answer to divulge. Today, with embryo freezing and transplants, sperm banking, *in vitro* fertilization, and surrogate mothering, a child may have as many as five parents: the egg and sperm donors, the surrogate mother who bears the child, and the couple who rear it. Knowing how to respond to the precocious eight-year-old has gotten a lot tougher.

Nor have things gotten any easier for a society that has to grapple with such biotechnological wizardry. Even the President's Commission for the Study of Ethical Problems in Medicine and Biomedical and Behavioral Research, which recently published seventeen volumes on topics ranging from defining death to whistle-blowing in biomedical research, could only conclude: "Medical interventions over the last several decades in human reproduction have raised a number of issues that have never been fully addressed, much less resolved."[16] Their only recommendation was a suggestion that further studies investigate topics such as *in vitro* fertilization and surrogate motherhood because "the shock many people feel at this development may have contributed to society's failure to produce an ethically and legally coherent response that would provide appropriate protection to the interests of all involved, most particularly any children produced."[17]

One can only speculate about why a society that is willing to redefine death in light of new scientific evidence is so troubled by advances that have the capacity to redefine life. It is not speculation, however, to review the foolish legal and public policies that this head-in-the-sand attitude has allowed to evolve. Thirty years ago, in *Doorn bos v. Doornbos*, a Chicago judge ruled that artificial insemination was adultery and that the offspring was illegitimate.[18] Today, because of a general shift in sexual attitude, the issue has changed from legitimacy to parental rights. But some of the courts' rulings remain just as problematic. A sperm donor in California was recently granted weekly visitation privileges to a three-year-old conceived with his sperm, even though he didn't know the mother or the child. With almost ten thousand children conceived every year through artificial insemination, the need for policies to resolve these problems is apparent.

Yet, current laws regarding issues such as a sperm donor's rights and obligations form a crazy-quilt pattern across America. Only half the states have specific statutes proclaiming that the child born to a couple through aritificial insemination is that couple's legal child. And only eleven state statutes specifically protect an anonymous sperm donor from paternity claims. For some the message is clear: we need new laws, preferably at the national level, to regulate reproductive technologies. But, as surrogate mothering demonstrates, any attempt to legally regulate procreative and family decisions can cause as many problems as it hopes to resolve.

CASE 50: WOMB FOR RENT

After years of frustration trying to conceive a child, a Michigan couple decided to hire a surrogate mother. For a fee of $5,000, the surrogate agreed to be artificially impregnated with the husband's sperm, to carry the baby to term, and to allow the couple to adopt it at birth. Although both parties were happy with this arrangement, it was illegal because of Michigan's baby-broker black-market statutes. These laws make it a misdemeanor or a felony to pay a mother for her consent to or cooperation with the subsequent adoption of her child. Private-adoption statutes further forbid payment of reasonable maternity and living expenses to a mother if contingent on an agreement for adoption.

The couple sued to overturn the law, arguing that the statute (barring the plaintiffs from exchanging $5,000 for their surrogate arrangement) was an overbroad intrusion into the fundamental privacy rights of both the surrogate and the couple.[19] As judge, would you:

A. rule that the concept of surrogate motherhood was illegal?
B. rule that the couple's right to make procreative decisions includes the right to arrange for a surrogate mother?
C. rule that paying a surrogate mother was illegal?

Surrogate mothering is neither very new nor very scientific. In fact, if normal sexual relations are considered as a means of insemination, the earliest recorded case of surrogate mothering occurred in Biblical times when Abraham's barren wife Sarah sent her husband to Hagar, her handmaiden, who bore him Ishmael. Even the standard method of scientific fertilization, artificial insemination, is almost two hundred years old, having first been used in England in 1790. The only recent scientific advances that affect the practice have been in the storage of sperm, where supercooling insures stable storage for long periods, and in the certain diagnosis of medical problems that might make surrogate mothering an attractive option. For example, it is now possible to determine both that the husband's sperm is healthy and that the wife is a poor pregnancy risk due to causes such as defective or damaged fallopian tubes, serious health problems, or genetically transmittable diseases.

Rather than being scientifically driven, the real reasons behind the growth of surrogate mothering (no one knows how widespread the practice is, but estimates range between a total of one hundred and one thousand successful transactions) are social and legal. Social because of the limited number of babies available for adoption, and a desire on the part of couples to have a child that is, in part, genetically theirs. Legal because lawyers have begun to challenge the system of laws that prohibit surrogate mothering, as well as starting to develop procedures which facilitate the practice's use.

This challenge, however, has not always met with success. On January 28, 1980, Circuit Court Judge Roman Gribbs ruled against the Michigan couple, stating that their alleged right to contract for adoption was a privilege "not deserving of, nor within the constitutional protection of the right to privacy."[20] This decision was upheld by the Court of Appeals, which found that "the statute in question does not directly prohibit John Doe and Mary Roe from having the child as planned. It acts instead to prevent plaintiffs from paying consideration in conjunction with their use of the state's adoption procedures."[21] Far from being obtuse legalese, the message is clear: in states with laws similar to Michigan's (about twenty-five), surrogate mothering is illegal when it is done as work-for-hire. This does *not* mean that surrogate mothering cannot take place, it means only that the contract must not be construed as containing payment clauses.

While the issue of payment is the greatest legal impediment to surrogate mothering, it is hardly the only interesting legal issue. Other unresolved questions include: How do our adoption laws apply to such cases? Just how strictly can such contracts control the surrogate's behavior? What remedies are available in cases of contract violations? What happens if the surrogate decides to keep the baby? Can the father be forced to pay support? What are the rights of the child who is the unwitting subject of the agreement? It seems clear that surrogate mothering will be in the courts, and in the headlines, for some time to come.

The problem is that it is unlikely that the courts will ever be able to adequately resolve these problems. The only legal model for surrogate mothering is contractual: the parties to the agreement draw up a contract specifying everyone's rights and obligations. But what happens when one of the parties wants to breach the contract? What if the surrogate decides she wants to get an abortion? Or keep the child? What if the couple decide they no longer want the child? Or the child is born with severe birth defects?

The law really has only two remedies for breach of contract: monetary compensation for damages, and *specific performance*—forcing the defaulting party to perform the services specified in the contract. Quite clearly, neither of these remedies is likely to apply. Money will never be adequate compensation for a couple who want a child, and it is ludicrous to think the court might be willing to force a couple to accept a child they do not want or lock up a pregnant woman for nine months in order to monitor her compliance with a contract.

It is problems like these that led Britain's Warnock Commission (analogous to our President's Bioethics Commission) to recommend that surrogate-mother contracts not be enforced by the courts. But that leaves the issue of regulation wide open. If reproductive technologies in general, and surrogate mothering in particular, are too personal to legislate, how should society regulate them? Since we don't have a Solomon on the bench, one option might be a careful combination of laws (for practices in which there is a clear consensus), community standards (for administrative regulations at the hospital level), and public- and private-agency cooperation (for family counseling services). However the issue is decided in this country, reproductive technologies present ample evidence that bioethical problems extend well beyond legal solutions.⁹²

A much different, and potentially more serious, public-policy problem is our inability to regulate *in vitro* fertilization research. Because we all stand to benefit from medical breakthroughs, almost all biomedical research, from artificial hearts to replaceable hip joints, is initially funded by the government. This gives government an opportunity to establish priorities, exert some control, and protect human subjects.

The glaring exception is *in vitro* research. Ten years ago the Department of Health, Education and Welfare announced that it would not fund any proposal for research on human embryos or on the external fertilization of human eggs unless it was reviewed and approved by its ethics board. Although that board never approved a single proposal, its final report in 1979 concluded that such research was ethically acceptable as long as it was applied to solving problems of infertility. But six years later the moratorium has not been lifted.

The effect has been the growth of an unregulated "test tube baby" business. Since the birth of Elizabeth Carr in 1981, more than one hundred children have been conceived outside the womb in the United States, and we still have no program to study and improve the technique. For example, doctors currently have no way of knowing which fertilized eggs have the best chance of developing into a fetus. This means that they must implant all the eggs, a practice which leads to unwanted multiple births. In a society that regulates everything from over-the-counter eardrops to genital vibrators, it is ridiculous that the technology used to create life should escape meaningful oversight.

In 1929 E. B. White and James Thurber published their satirical classic *Is Sex Necessary?* Little did they know that within fifty years we would be able to give an emphatic No! as the answer. But having the technological capability to answer "No" has raised many social, political, legal, and psychological questions. Yet, as the following case demonstrates, the most important questions are ethical.

CASE 51: THE EMBRYO AS PROPERTY

By 1973 John and Doris Del Zio had been married for five years. Unfortunately, all their attempts to conceive children had failed. When it was finally determined that Doris had blocked fallopian tubes, they were referred to Columbia Presbyterian Hospital, New York, where they first heard about research into *in vitro* fertilization. Although researchers had been able to fertilize human egg cells outside the body, there had been no attempts to reinsert the cells back into the womb. The Del Zios pleaded that this was their only chance to have a child, and they convinced Drs. William J. Sweeney and Landrum Shettles to perform the procedure.

Although the egg capture and *in vitro* fertilization went well, Dr. Shettles was summoned to appear before his superior, Dr. Raymond Vande Wiele, the next day. Shettles found the sterile Del Zio flask sitting on Vande Wiele's desk with its seal broken, an action that effectively terminated the experiment before insertion could take place. He was told that because the procedure did not have the approval of the Human Experimentation Review Board, and since it bore the risk of producing a "monstrosity," Vande Wiele had unilaterally pulled the plug.

When the Del Zios found out about this action, they sued the hospital for $1.5 million, claiming wrongful deprivation of property and psychological harm.[23] As a member of the jury, would you:

    A. find for the Del Zios in the full amount?
    B. find for the hospital on grounds that an experimental procedure does not guarantee success?

    C. reject the claim regarding wrongful deprivation of property but grant damages for psychological harm?

It took five years for the Del Zios' case to work its way through the justice system, a period of time during which Louise Brown, the first *in vitro* baby, was born. In picking option C and awarding the Del Zios $50,003 (the final digit of which represented $1 for the husband from each of the three defendants), the jury chose to avoid the obvious questions surrounding the status of fertilized human eggs. But as the following catalog so clearly indicates, the list of bioethical issues raised by *in vitro* fertilization is so broad that we will not be able to avoid them for long:

1. Presuppositions
    a. The moral status of the early embryo
    b. The naturalness or artificiality of laboratory-assisted reproduction
2. Ethical issues related primarily to individual research subjects
    a. The need for clinical IVF research
    b. The need for and adequacy of prior laboratory research, including animal research, on IVF and embryo transfer
    c. Risks of clinical IVF research to the potential product of IVF
    d. Risks of clinical IVF research to the ovum donor
    e. Informed consent by participants in clinical IVF research
    f. Liability or compensation for IVF-research-related injury
3. Broader social and public policy issues
    a. Potential long-term social consequences of clinical IVF research
    b. Appropriate allocation of research and clinical resources to clinical IVF research and to other areas of research or health care
    c. Appropriate institutional frameworks for the pro-

      vision of advice on or monitoring of clinical IVF
      research
4. Special case: potential problems resulting from the donation and receipt of sperm, ova, or embryos
5. Future issues
    a. The sexing of embryos
    b. Preimplantational genetic screening
    c. Preimplantational repair of genetic defects
    d. The creation of human-animal hybrids
    e. Cloning
    f. Ectogenesis[24]

Some of these issues (e.g., human experimentation pro-
tocols, allocation of medical resources) simply exacerbate
already difficult problems. But the extension of IVF techniques to sex selection, chimeras, and cloning raises a new
problem: the fear that society will be unable to resist new
technologies that lead to dire consequences for our species. Such a fear is expressed in Howard and Rifkin's *Who
Should Play God?*:

> Over a period of time (the next twenty-five to fifty
> years) the cumulative effect of this step-by-step pro-
> cess will be the emergence of a kind of corporate
> Brave New World, not unlike the one Huxley fantas-
> ized over forty years ago. It is a much less dramatic
> approach to the ultimate enslavement of the human
> species, but the results are no less terrifying than if
> they had been ruthlessly imposed by some mad po-
> litical dictator. The only real difference is that with
> this approach we will march passively and in some
> cases even willingly into this new reality without
> pain, without inconvenience, and without aware-
> ness.[25]

Just how serious is this threat?

While it would be foolish to underestimate the potential
effect that biotechnology may have on our lives, an anal-

ysis of this slippery-slope argument turns up very little that is compelling. The logical form of the argument is a syllogism:

> Once we allow exceptions to a general principle, we cannot stop granting exceptions until the principle is destroyed.
> Standard human sexual reproduction is an important principle.
>
> ---
>
> Therefore, any deviation from this principle (e.g., artificial insemination, *in vitro* fertilization) endangers standard human sexual reproduction.

Although the argument is valid (i.e., once you accept the premises, you must accept the conclusion), it should be clear that the first premise is far from self-evident. In fact, there are hundreds of cases in which we grant exceptions to general principles without rendering the principle moot. Doctors must report cases of infectious disease to public-health officials, but this has not devalued the principle of confidentiality. Capital punishment sanctions the killing of selected convicted criminals, but this has not led to an orgy of state-sponsored murder. The use of prisoners as research subjects under tightly controlled conditions has not undermined the basic principle of voluntary, informed consent. It is simply not true that exceptions always erode general principles, or that because we have the technological knowledge to achieve some end, that end is inevitable.

The most important point overlooked by those who wield the slippery-slope argument is that science is directed by human goals. Reproductive technologies currently serve the function of helping to overcome infertility. They may also have the potential to replace biological reproduction, but that is not their current purpose. As long as society is open and clear about its uses for these technologies, there is no reason to anticipate a Brave New World. That scenario can occur only if citizens neglect their responsibility to monitor and direct science and technology, and that is why our current head-in-the-sand attitude is dangerous and unconscionable.

GENETIC ENGINEERING

CONCEPT: Modern medicine is on the threshold of some radically new forms of therapy. Although certain conditions (e.g., albinism, hemophilia) had long been recognized to occur within families (most notoriously in the royal families of Europe, where intermarriage was a political necessity and generations of kings suffered from the "bleeders disease"), it wasn't until the dawn of the twentieth century that Sir Archibald E. Garrod deduced the real, underlying cause of such ailments. By applying the work of Mendel to the metabolic disorder *alkaptonuria*—a condition that turns the urine black and leads to crippling arthritis—Garrod was able to conclude:

> We are dealing with individualities of metabolism and not with the results of morbid [disease] processes.... These are merely extreme examples of variations in chemical behavior which are probably everywhere present in minor degrees and that just as no two individuals of a species are absolutely identical in bodily structure neither are their chemical processes carried out on exactly the same lines.[26]

While the gene would still not be discovered for several decades, Garrod had recognized that certain disorders are genetically caused and transmitted.

Today, we know quite a bit about genes and disease: Each human somatic cell contains twenty-three pairs of chromosomes constructed from the DNA molecule. (The sole exceptions are human germ cells—sperm and ova—

which contain only twenty-three chromosomes; during fertilization the chromosomes pair up so that the *zygote*, a fertilized egg, gets half of its genetic complement from the male, half from the female.) The chromosomes are like beaded necklaces, with the individual genes lining up as beads, and a single cell having upward of 100,000 genes.

Since the pioneering work of Garrod, researchers have catalogued more than two thousand disorders that are caused by a single gene variation. They have even begun to develop gene maps so that faulty genes may be recognized and located. This has fostered the practice of genetic screening: couples may be counseled about the probabilities that their child will be born with a genetic disorder, and early detection of such conditions may enable treatment that can forestall the effects of the disease. But all current treatments for genetic disorders are palliative, not curative—they treat symptoms rather than the underlying cause.

Genetic engineering, the direct manipulation of a cell's genetic contents, is a radically new technology because it will allow physicians to actually enter a cell and change its genetic makeup. Recombinant-DNA techniques that merge human and bacterial DNA are already being used to mass-produce vital substances like human growth hormone and interferon. Gene therapy promises that instead of the physician's having to artificially replace an enzyme via drug therapy, the faulty gene will be "fixed" so that the cell will begin to produce the enzyme naturally on its own. And some futurists even believe that the prospect of human cloning suggests a possible world where every human will have his own, identical "spare-parts alter ego." Although research in these areas is less than twenty years old and much of its direct application to humans lies in the future, there are no in-principle scientific objections against altering the genes in a human cell.

But such a development does raise a number of possible

bioethical objections: Are there any ethical bounds to medical therapies? What about therapies that may affect future generations? If it is acceptable to alter genes for therapeutic purposes, is it also acceptable to alter them for eugenic purposes? Does man's ability to alter the evolutionary process amount to his playing God, and is this a type of knowledge he should not have? What happens to the image of Man when we have the power to change men at will?

PRACTICE: The idea that some knowledge may be forbidden is as old as the Bible; one standard interpretation of the Adam and Eve parable is that they were punished for partaking of the fruits of the tree of knowledge. In fact, for most of mankind's recorded history, knowledge has been more feared than revered. It was the jealously protected province of shamans and priests who were often less interested in discovering new knowledge than in preserving the old, and in using it to control their minions.

The Renaissance changed that perspective. Visionaries like Bacon and Descartes actually produced systems to aid in the development of new knowledge; scientists like Galileo and Newton demonstrated how knowledge could be used to control and predict nature. Awakening from the Dark Ages, society embraced a new cultural paradigm, the idea of progress, and knowledge was perceived to be its handmaiden. In a very real sense, the last five hundred years may be characterized as the Age of Knowledge.

To be sure, not everyone has always applauded the results obtained from that knowledge. Whether it was the Luddites protesting the mechanization of factory work, or the peace movement decrying the proliferation of atomic weapons, citizens have always found some aspects of technology troubling. But few in this age of knowledge actually questioned its ultimate worth until the discovery of *recombinant DNA*—a molecular biological technique in which genetic material from one organism may be inserted into the chromosomal structure of another organism. What is it about this technological advance that leads so many citizens (according to a recent poll, almost two thirds of the public think that studies in this area should not be pursued[27]), as well as some of our brightest scientists, to now question the absolute worth of knowledge?

Answering that question can be as easy as mumbling a few buzz words, or as difficult as trying to understand the societal implications of a scientific puzzle of enormous complexity. Those who adopt the first approach usually begin with a literary allusion: The great tragedy of *Frankenstein* was not the monster's, but that of Dr. Frankenstein himself:

> Sometimes I endeavoured to gain from Frankenstein the particulars of his creature's formation: but on this point he was impenetrable. "Are you mad, my friend?" he said; "or wither does your senseless curiosity lead you? Would you also create for yourself and the world a demoniacal enemy? Peace, Peace! learn my miseries, and do not seek to increase your own."[28]

This "knowledge leads to devastation" scenario is usually updated with a few new words like "algeny," "cloning," "orthobiosis," "designer genes," prognostications about the threat of an Andromeda Strain bacterium or the creation of man-animal hybrid slaves, and a strict, concluding injunction that there is knowledge man was never meant to possess. Man must never play God.

More thoughtful critics skip the sloganeering and focus instead on the hard scientific facts and their potential societal consequences. The first pertinent fact is that the DNA of all organisms, from bacteria to men, is composed of the same chemical *bases*—the four nitrogenous rings (adenine, guanine, cytosine, and thymine) that are paired in an infinity of ways to specify an individual's unique genetic code. This means it is possible to transplant the genes responsible for producing insulin in humans into a strain of bacteria, and to then harvest large quantities of that vital biochemical product as the bacteria rapidly multiply. But it also means that scientists now have the ability to produce new life forms in the laboratory, and this capacity raises concerns about the unpredictable future evolutionary development of such human-engineered life forms.

A second fact is our recently developed ability to isolate specific, defective genes in multicell animals (e.g., fruit flies) and to then correct the defect through *gene therapy*—transplanting a healthy gene to supplement the faulty one. Although this medical technology is not yet available for humans, it promises to dramatically change the way we treat the more than two thousand single-gene (e.g., sickle cell anemia, hemophilia) disorders. While few people object to this therapeutic use of genetic engineering, many are concerned about the possibility that such techniques will be used for eugenic purposes with disastrous consequences: a blurring of the concept of genetic defect (e.g., Tay-Sachs) with the notion of a simply undesirable trait (e.g., big nose), a homogenization of the gene pool leaving it vulnerable to new diseases, and the ability of the state to prescribe citizen characteristics.

A final fact is the possibility of *cloning*—the production of an organism or group of genetically identical cells descended from a single common ancestor and produced by a process of asexual reproduction. Farmers have known about cloning for centuries, and if you've ever grown a house plant from a cutting, you've nurtured a clone. But cloning an animal is much more difficult, and it is only in the last few years that animal research (e.g., mice and frogs) has met with some success. Human cloning, which involves enormously difficult problems of developmental biology, is much more difficult still, and to date we have only been able to clone human genes, a necessary step for the production of the healthy genes needed for gene therapy. Looking toward the distant future, however, many worry about the specter of human clones: the production of individual replicas in order to ravage them for spare parts, the risk that clones will weaken the gene pool as sexual reproduction, along with its needed mixing of genes, is replaced by the asexual reproduction of cloning, and Lewis Thomas' concern that cloning will lead to the elimination of sex with only a metaphoric elimination of death as compensation.[29]

Reviewing all the evidence has led more than one scientist to agree with the distinguished biologist Dr. Robert Sinsheimer when he denounces genetic engineering in words similar to those of Dr. Frankenstein: "Do we want to assume the basic responsibility for life on this planet— to develop new living forms for our own purposes? Shall we take into our hands our own future evolution?... Perverse as it may, initially, seem to the scientist, we must face the fact that there can be unwanted knowledge."[30] Do the facts really justify an about-face from our five-hundred-year-old tradition characterizing knowledge as an intrinsically worthwhile goal?

CASE 52: FROM "ANDROMEDA STRAIN" Bacteria to Frankenstein

In 1980 the United States Supreme Court heard a case unlike any other in its two-hundred-year history. At issue was the patentability of a new life form—a genetically engineered bacterium named *Pseudomonas* capable of digesting oil slicks. General Electric, the company that had developed the bacterium, argued that patents were devised to protect the legal rights of anyone inventing something new and useful. Since *Pseudomonas* was certainly new—it had not existed until a GE researcher applied recombinant-DNA techniques to create it—and obviously useful, the case for granting a patent was clear.

The opposition adopted two approaches. The U.S. government argued that genetically engineered bacteria were merely rearrangements of components already existing in nature. Because patents are automatically denied on "products of nature," the government concluded that while the process used to develop the bacterium might be patentable, *Pseudomonas* itself certainly was not. Amicus briefs filed on behalf of lobbying groups employed a much broader, public-policy perspective. They argued that genetic engineering posed such substantial health, environmental, and moral risks that the Court should decide against the patentability of all life forms.[31]

As a Supreme Court justice, would you:

  A. find for GE by holding that life forms may be man-made?
  B. find against GE by asserting that all life forms are, by definition, of nature?
  C. find against GE on grounds that the risks of genetic engineering far outweigh the expected benefits?

As it usually does, the Court chose to decide this case on narrow, legalistic grounds. In a five-to-four vote, the Court asserted that *Pseudomonas* was a live, human-made microorganism, that it was the result of human ingenuity and research, and was, therefore, patentable. (Perhaps the Court was swayed by GE's ad line, "We bring good things to life.") Writing for the majority, Chief Justice Burger also cautioned opponents of genetic engineering that the deeper moral issues would not have been resolved even if the Court had voted the other way; "...legislative or judicial fiat as to patentability will not deter the scientific mind from probing into the unknown any more than Canute could control the tides."[32] Once again, the deeper bioethical issues proved to be immune from legal solution.

Those issues are embodied in two main arguments against recombinant-DNA research. The first is based on contingent, risk-benefit reasoning:

> Man can never be certain about all the properties of new life forms that he might create.
>
> If a new form of cancer or other deadly virus should escape the laboratory, it could wipe out a genetically defenseless population
>
> _____
>
> Since the potential risk is so great, we should not allow recombinant-DNA research.

While both of these premises are true, the conclusion does not necessarily follow. What is missing is some probability estimate. We must ask ourselves how likely this "worst-case" scenario really is, and what we would have to give up if we banned this type of research.

As more and more recombinant-DNA research is conducted without incident, much less catastrophe, it becomes harder to believe the "Andromeda Strain" scenario. After ten years of productive research, we have both physical containment and biological containment mechanisms (e.g., many organisms are engineered to live only under certain laboratory conditions; leave the lab and they instantly die). On the benefit side, we also have new organisms that eat oil and other pollutants, as well as those that produce insulin and interferon. While it would be foolish to neglect the possibility of health and environmental risks, the burden of proof has really shifted to the other side. Proponents of recombinant-DNA research need no longer defend themselves against every imagined risk; opponents must now demonstrate that specific, positive dangers really exist.

The second argument is an in-principle, ethical one:

The ability to create new life forms is a Godlike power.

Man does not have the wisdom to guide this power.

Man should not create new life forms.

Unlike the contingent argument, this one is deductively valid. Accept the premises and you must logically accept the conclusion. However, the premises are open to doubt. If creating new life forms is a Godlike power, it is a power man has had for hundreds of years. Thousands of new botanical life forms, from roses to tangelos, are the product of man's handiwork. And it is certainly difficult to argue that man has not used this power wisely.

A more charitable view of this argument sees it directed not at all new life forms, but only at those involving the mingling of human and nonhuman DNA. Seen in this way it is a variant of the slippery-slope argument: If we even start creating new life forms (bacteria), we may pass on to creating new species, and may eventually end up creating half-human, half-animal creatures that might serve as a race of acquiescent robots for an evil master. It may be the possibility of this "Frankenstein scenario" that is the driving force behind the injunction that man should not create new life forms.

The first response to such an argument is similar to the one used to rebut the "Andromeda Strain" scenario. Our scientific knowledge is so far removed from the possibility of such a creature that it is impossible to even assign it a probability. The second response is the general reply to all slippery-slope arguments: it seems foolish to deny ourselves the benefits of the current recombinant-DNA research because, if unchecked, it could lead to an undesirable situation. The most reasonable attitude seems to be the one suggested by the theologians who advised the President's Bioethics Commission: "... contemporary developments in molecular biology raise issues of responsibility rather than being matters to be prohibited because they usurp powers that human beings should not possess."[33]

CASE 53: THE GENETIC SUPERMARKET

In the mid-1960s two German sisters were diagnosed as suffering from *hyperargininemia*—a genetic defect that allowed the substance *arginine* to accrete in the blood and the spinal fluid, causing mental retardation. Although there was no known cure, a researcher working on a different project had noted that individuals exposed to *Shope papilloma virus* exhibited a marked decrease in their arginine level. He hypothesized that this was the result of *viral transduction*, the use of a virus to transfer new genetic material into a cell, and suggested that the girls' genetic defect might be cured by injections of the Shope virus. Because the virus had no known harmful effects, and because there was no other hope, the experiment was conducted. Although it failed, this was the first reported attempt of gene therapy in humans.[34] Is gene therapy just a logical extension of other medical therapies, or does it carry with it some special ethical concerns?

It is difficult to see what rational objection might be made to the procedure described above. If the purpose of medicine is the therapeutic healing of patients, then we should applaud each increase in the doctor's healing power. The argument is sometimes made that gene therapy is "unnatural." But we now know that the exchange of genetic material occurs in nature, and we certainly see nothing "unnatural" about a doctor treating an infection with antibiotics or even transplanting a heart. Furthermore, since we are part of nature, it is difficult to understand how something that humans do could be unnatural.

Jacob Bronowski pointed out that human beings are

distinguished by our ability to shape, rather than simply being shaped by, the environment. This defining characteristic applies as much to ourselves as it does to our crops, our animals, or our living conditions. Unless one is willing to put limits on this aspect of human nature, it seems unreasonable to object to this type of gene therapy.

A more serious objection surfaces with the possibility of using genetic-engineering techniques for eugenic purposes. For some, like the Nobel laureate H. J. Muller, this is a wonderful opportunity to better mankind:

> And so we foresee the history of life divided into three main phases. In the long preparatory phase it was the helpless creature of its environment, and natural selection gradually ground it into human shape. In the second—our own short transitional phase—it reaches out at the immediate environment, shaking, shaping, and grinding to suit the form, the requirements, the wishes, and the whims of man. And in the long third phase, it will reach down into the secret places of the great universe of its own nature, and by aid of its evergrowing intelligence and cooperation, shape itself into an increasingly sublime creation— a being beside which the mythical divinities of the past will seem more and more ridiculous, and which, setting its own marvelous inner powers against the brute Goliath of the suns and planets, challenges them to a contest.[35]

For other, equally prominent thinkers, such a suggestion is fraught with danger:

> If any one age really attains, by eugenics and scientific education, the power to make its descendants what it pleases, all men who live after it are patients to that power. They are weaker, not stronger: for though we have put wonderful machines in their hands we have preordained how they are to use them. ...Man's conquest of Nature, if the dreams of the

scientific planners are realized, means the rule of a few hundreds of men over billions upon billions of men.[36]

Who's right?

Embedded in this sometimes florid prose are three important issues: (1) Can a sharp distinction be made between the therapeutic and eugenic purposes of genetic engineering? (2) Who should decide how genetic engineering is applied to human beings? (3) What are the possible consequences of the eugenic use of such technology? The answer to the first question is a qualified No. Like therapy and research, the distinction between therapy and eugenics can get awfully fuzzy (e.g., would a procedure to eliminate the genetic marker for alpha-1-antitrypsin deficiency be therapy or eugenics?). Yet the concepts are distinct at their cores, and everyone can agree that a medical procedure to eliminate the sickle cell gene is therapy while a procedure to insure a blond, blue-eyed baby is eugenics. What is really at issue is not the words, but the purposes to which we apply genetic engineering.

But who should get to decide those purposes? One major theme running through many anti-technology arguments is the "Big Brother, Brave New World scenario"—the idea that powerful new technology may be centrally controlled by a few who will use it to control the many. While this is a legitimate concern, it has more to do with the political climate than with any given technology. There is no in-principle reason why the power to use such a technology would have to reside with the state. Instead of central control, social philosopher Robert Nozick envisions a laissez-faire system:

> Many biologists tend to think the problem is one of *design*, of specifying the best types of persons so that biologists can proceed to produce them. Thus they worry over what sort(s) of person there is to be

and who will control this process. They do not tend
to think, perhaps because it diminishes the importance of their role, of a system in which they run a
"genetic supermarket," meeting the individual spec-
ifications (within certain moral limits) of prospective
parents.... This supermarket system has the great virtue that it involves no centralized decision fixing the
future human type(s).[37]

Whether or not we embrace the idea of a "genetic supermarket," we can all agree that citizens should choose the
constitution of their government; government has no business dictating the genetic constitution of its citizens.

But what would the consequences be if everyone had
free license to alter their own, as well as their potential
children's, genetic makeup? The answer really depends
on which traits would be manipulable. If the technology
never progresses past the point where personal characteristics like hair color or a disposition to be tall are con-
trollable (and we are a long way from even this), it is
unlikely that much will change. Some parents, like those
who today opt for cosmetic surgery for the least perceived
"flaw," may insist that their child have just that certain
"look." Most will simply ignore the opportunity. Our current experience with sex selection techniques may be instructive. For years, dire predictions have been made about
an impending imbalance among the sexes if we ever
achieve the power to choose the sex of our children. Yet
we now have that technology, and there is no evidence of
a male, or female, baby boom.

Before anything like Muller's scenario could occur, it
would have to be possible to select for polygenic traits
like intelligence, creativity, loyalty, and ambition. But such
a possibility seems extremely remote because of the environmental component of these traits as well as Peter
Medawar's observation regarding the "zero sum game"
aspects of eugenics. But what if we could? Any wholesale

rush to make a dramatic change in the human gene pool would have to be resisted. If the human species is to remain robust and capable of coping with future environmental changes, it must maintain a diverse genetic stock. Like any supermarket, the "genetic supermarket" can function only as long as not all the customers are clamoring for the same goods.

CASE 54: THE CLONETRONICS CORPORATION

For Immediate Release   **Date: JANUARY 15, 2084**

Clonetronics Corporation

The Clonetronics Corporation is proud to announce that it has been awarded patent #5,198,484 for its human-cloning process. After a decade of careful animal and human experimentation, the Corporation is commencing this day to offer the general public the opportunity to have themselves rendered immortal through cloning. The process requires only that the "clonor" make a brief visit to our offices in order to have a few sample body cells painlessly removed in our sterile laboratory. Following a nine-month period of *ectogenesis*—the extracorporeal gestation of the cells—a genetically identical clone will be ready to be taken home and reared exactly as one would a child produced via sexual union. Clonetronics believes today is the dawn of a new age in the history of human beings.

There is little doubt that if cloning of human beings could ever be accomplished (and it is the most complicated, and perhaps least likely, of the various genetic-engineering techniques), it would certainly usher in the "dawn of a new age." But is that an age we should embrace or resist? Many of the arguments already discussed—that it amounts to Godlike knowledge, that it has the potential for state control of reproductive freedom, that it would lead to a weakening of genetic diversity—apply in spades to cloning, and they need not be reiterated here. Yet cloning, more than any other genetic-engineering technique, forces us to face the ultimate value question: What is a human being?

The name we've given to ourselves, *Homo sapiens*, or "wise man," presents a final paradox. By placing a premium on thinking and reasoning, we seem to be saying that the essence of being human involves the acquisition of knowledge. With such knowledge we can improve ourselves and hope to make a better world. Yet, if we are truly "wise men," we must also recognize that other values, like the preservation of the species, are equally important, and that the unbridled quest for knowledge may sometimes conflict with these other goals. Having the wisdom to make the proper value choices today will determine our quality of life tomorrow.

In striving to make those choices we are trapped in a Zenlike riddle: it is only through increased knowledge, both of the world and ourselves, that we will be capable of making decisions about knowledge. As the ethicist Daniel Callahan reminds us, this is no less true of bioethics than it is of biology:

> If the essence of good scientific research is to leave no stone unturned, it is no less pertinent to moral thought. A scientific researcher would, in strictly scientific terms, be considered poor if he did not allow his mind to roam in all directions during the phase of hypothesis development, taking seriously any idea that might produce a promising lead.... The same is true of moral thinking, particularly when it bears on the future consequences of our actions. We are obliged to explore all possibilities, however vague and remote; and the moral person will also end by throwing most of them out—most, finally, but not all. Since we surely now know that scientific research, whether

basic or applied, is a source of enormous power for both good and ill, the scientific researcher has, then, an obligation to be as active in his moral imagination as in his scientific imagination. We ask the same of any person in a position of power.[38]

But we must also demand the same of ourselves. When it comes to our own well-being, we are that person in power. The essential message of *Life Choices* is first and foremost a challenge to assume that power and to use it wisely.

NOTES

II. THE DOCTOR–PATIENT RELATIONSHIP

1. International Code of Medical Ethics, reprinted in Robert M. Veatch, *Case Studies in Medical Ethics* (Cambridge, Mass.: Harvard University Press, 1977), pp. 355–56.
2. Schloendorff v. Society of New York Hospital, 211 N.Y. 125, 105 N.E. 92, 93 (1914)
3. *Personal Privacy in an Information Society: The Report of the Privacy Protection Study Commission* (Washington, D.C., July 1977).
4. Hippocratic Oath, reprinted in Veatch (1977), pp. 351–52.
5. American Medical Association Principles of Medical Ethics, reprinted in Veatch (1977), pp. 354–55.
6. Simonsen v. Swenson, 177 N.W. 831 (1920).
7. Ronald L. Williams, "Using Birth and Death Certificates to Describe Maternal and Child Health Risks in California: Past, Present, and Future," *Möbius*, Vol. 4, No. 3 (July 1984), pp. 81–93.
8. Tarasoff v. Board of Regents, 551 P.2d 334 (1976).
9. *Ibid.*
10. Mohr v. Williams, 95 Minn. 261, 104 N.W. 12 (1905).
11. Natanson v. Kline, 186 Kan 393, 350 P.2d 1093 (1960).
12. Canterbury v. Spence, 464 F.2d 772 (D.C. Cir. 1972).
13. Oliver Wendell Holmes, *Medical Essays, 1842–1882* (Boston: Houghton Mifflin, 1891).
14. William T. Fitts, Jr., and I. S. Ravdin, "What Philadelphia Physicians Tell Patients with Cancer," *JAMA*, Vol. 153 (1953), p. 903; Donald Oken, "What to Tell Cancer Patients," *JAMA*, Vol. 175 (1961), pp. 1120–28. Doctors' attitudes toward informing terminal patients may be beginning to change. A more recent study has found that an astounding 97 percent of physicians now have a policy of disclosure. Novack et al, "Changes in Physicians' Attitudes Toward Telling the Cancer Patient," *JAMA*, Vol. 241 (1979), p. 897.

15. W. D. Kelly and S. R. Friesen, "Do Cancer Patients Want to be Told?," *Surgery*, Vol. 27, June 1950, pp. 822–26; Robert J. Samp and Anthony R. Curreri, "A Questionnaire Survey on Public Cancer Education Obtained from Cancer Patients and their Families," *Cancer*, Vol. 10, March–April 1957, pp. 382–84; C. H. Branch, "Psychiatric Aspects of Malignant Disease," *CA: Bulletin of Cancer Progress*, Vol. 6, (1956), No. 3, pp. 102–4.

16. B. S. Hulka, J. C. Cassel, et al., "Communication, Compliance, and Concordance between Physicians and Patients with Prescribed Medications," *American Journal of Public Health*, September 1976, pp. 847–53; L. D. Egbert, G. E. Batitt, et al., "Reduction of Postoperative Pain by Encouragement and Instruction of Patients," *New England Journal of Medicine*, Vol. 270 (1964), pp. 825–27; H. Waitzskin and J. D. Stoeckle, "The Communication of Information about Illness," *Advances in Psychosomatic Medicine*, Vol. 8 (1972), pp. 185–215.

III. ALLOCATING MEDICAL RESOURCES

1. Too many facts and figures, and MEGO—my eyes glaze over. Yet the statistics regarding health care in this country are so staggering that an informed citizenry needs to be briefly acquainted with them. See *Health, United States, 1980*, DHHS pub. no. (PHS) 81–1232 (Hyattsville, Md.: U. S. Public Health Service, December 1980), and the most recent *Federal Budget*.

2. Illich sees this medicalization of life as a grave social threat. See Ivan Illich, *Medical Nemesis* (New York: Random House, 1976).

3. President's Commission for the Study of Ethical Problems in Medicine and Biomedical and Behavioral Research, *Summing Up: The Ethical and Legal Problems in Medicine and Biomedical and Behavioral Research*, March 1983, p. 27.

4. This medical paradox is documented in Gerald Leach, *The Biocrats* (New York: McGraw-Hill, 1970), ch. 11.

5. John Hersey, *My Petition for More Space* (New York: Knopf, 1974).

6. Title 18 of the Social Security Act, PL 89–97, 42 U.S.C. sec. 1395 *et. seq.*

7. Wilmington General Hospital v. Manlove, 54 Del. 15, 174 A. 2d 135 (1961).

8. Memorial Hospital v. Maricopa County, 415 U.S. 250 (1974); Edward V. Sparer, "The Legal Right to Health Care: Public Policy and Equal Access," *Hastings Center Report*, Vol. 6, No. 5 (1974), p. 39.

9. President's Commission for the Study of Ethical Problems, *Summing Up*, p. 29.
10. *Ibid.*, pp. 29–30.
11. U.S. Department of Health, Education and Welfare, Public Health Service, *Forward Plan for Health: FY 1977–81*, DHEW pub. no. OS-76–50024, p. 15.
12. James F. Childress, "Who Shall Live When Not All Can Live?," *Soundings*, Winter 1970, pp. 339–55.
13. Tom Christofell, *Health and the Law* (New York: The Free Press, 1982), p. 179.
14. Tom L. Beauchamp and Ruth R. Faden, "The Right to Health and the Right to Health Care," *The Journal of Medicine and Philosophy*, Vol. 4 (1979) No. 2, p. 121.
15. International Code of Medical Ethics, in Robert M. Veatch, *Case Studies in Medical Ethics* (Cambridge, Mass.: Harvard University Press, 1977), p. 355.
16. Jeremy Bentham, *An Introduction to the Principles of Morals and Legislation*, in *Utilitarianism*, ed. Mary Warnock (New York: Meridian Books, 1962), p. 34.
17. Aristotle, *Nicomachean Ethics* (New York: Bobbs-Merrill, 1962), pp. 118–19.
18. Ayn Rand, *Atlas Shrugged* (New York: Signet, 1957), p. 958.
19. Robert M. Veatch, "Voluntary Risks to Health," *JAMA*, Vol. 243, No. 1 (Jan. 4, 1980), pp. 50–55.
20. President's Commission for the Study of Ethical Problems in Medicine and Biomedical and Behavioral Research, *Securing Access to Health Care*, Vol. 1, March 1983, p. 20.
21. Russell Scott, *The Body as Property* (New York: Viking, 1981), ch. 5.
22. See Alfred M. Sadler, Blair L. Sadler and E. B. Stason, "The Uniform Anatomical Gift Act: A Model for Reform," *JAMA*, Vol. 206, Dec. 9, 1968, pp. 2501–6.
23. Nicholas Rescher, "The Allocation of Exotic Medical Lifesaving Therapy," *Ethics*, Vol. 79 (1969), p. 178.
24. Childress, p. 149.
25. Bureau of National Affairs, *Occupational Safety and Health Reporter*, Vol. 8, No. 16 (Sept. 14, 1978), p. 463.
26. Joyce C. Lashoff, "Risk and Healthy People," *Möbius*, Vol. 4, No. 3 (July 1984), p. 8.
27. W. W. Lowrance, *Of Acceptable Risk: Science and the Determination of Safety* (Los Altos: William Kaufmann, 1976), p. 8.
28. Gail Bronson, "Issue of Fetal Damage Stirs Women Workers at Chemical Plants," *Wall Street Journal*, Feb. 9, 1979, p. 1.

29. Wright v. Olin Corp., No. 81–1229 (4th Cir. Dec. 23, 1982).
30. Mary P. Lavine, "Industrial Screening Programs for Workers," *Environment*, Vol. 24, No. 5 (June 1982), p. 32.
31. Wright v. Olin Corp.
32. *Science*, Feb. 20, 1981, p. 799.
33. Marc Lappé, "Ethical Issues in Testing for Differential Sensitivity to Occupational Hazards," *Journal of Occupational Medicine*, Vol. 25, No. 11 (November 1983), pp. 797–808.

IV. LIFE AND DEATH

1. *Black's Law Dictionary*, 4th ed. (St. Paul: West Publishing Co., 1968), p. 488.
2. "A Definition of Irreversible Coma," Report of the Ad Hoc Committee of the Harvard Medical School to Examine the Definition of Brain Death, *JAMA*, Vol. 205, No. 6 (Aug. 6, 1968), pp. 337–40.
3. President's Commission for the Study of Ethical Problems in Medicine and Biomedical and Behavioral Research, *Defining Death*, July 1981, p. 160.
4. Barbara J. Culliton, "Manslaughter: The Charge Against Edelin of Boston City Hospital," *Science*, Vol. 186, Oct. 25, 1974, pp. 327–30; *ibid.*, "Abortion and Manslaughter. A Boston Doctor Goes on Trial," *Science*, Vol. 187, Jan. 31, 1975, pp. 334–35; *ibid.*, "Edelin Trial: Jury Not Persuaded by Scientists for the Defense," *Science*, Vol. 187, March 7, 1975, pp. 814–16; *ibid.*, "Edelin Conviction Overturned," *Science*, Vol. 195, Jan. 7, 1977, pp. 36–37.
5. Roe v. Wade, 410 U.S. 113 (1973).
6. Doe v. Bolton 410 U.S. 179 (1973).
7. Tom Christoffel, *Health and the Law* (New York: The Free Press, 1982), pp. 350–51.
8. Griswold v. Connecticut, 381 U.S 479 (1965).
9. Jeff Lyon, *Playing God in the Nursery* (New York: Norton, 1985), ch. 1.
10. Raymond S. Duff and A. G. M. Campbell, "Moral and Ethical Dilemmas in the Special-care Nursery," *New England Journal of Medicine*, Vol. 289 (1973), pp. 890–94.
11. Dr. Richard Gross et al., "Early Management and Decision Making for the Treatment of Myelomeningocele," *Pediatrics*, Vol. 72, No. 4 (October 1983), pp. 450–58.
12. President's Commission for the Study of Ethical Problems in Medicine and Biomedical and Behavioral Research, *Deciding to Forego Life-Sustaining Treatment*, March 1983, pp. 225–27.
13. In the Matter of Karen Quinlan, 70 N.J. 10, 355 A.2d.

14. *Time*, April 9, 1984, p. 68.
15. Richard Polenberg, "The Second Victory of Anthony Comstock," *Society*, May/June 1982, p. 32.
16. Eisenstadt v. Baird, 405 U.S. 438 (1972).
17. Roe v. Wade, 410 U.S. 113 (1973).
18. "The Human Life Bill—S. 158," Report of the Subcommittee on Separation of Powers to the Senate Judiciary Committee, U.S. Senate, 97th Congress, First Session, December 1981.
19. Robert M. Veatch, *Case Studies in Medical Ethics* (Cambridge, Mass.: Harvard University Press, 1977), p. 170.
20. Judith Blake and Jorge H. Del Pinal, "Predicting Polar Attitudes Toward Abortion in the United States," in *Abortion Parley*, ed. James T. Burtchaell (New York: Andrews & McMeel, 1980), pp. 27–56.
21. Exodus 1:16.
22. Plato, *The Republic*, transl. Francis MacDonald Cornford (London: Oxford University Press, 1945), p. 160.
23. Aristotle, *Politics*, in Richard McKeon, ed., *The Basic Works of Aristotle* (New York: Random House, 1941), p. 1302.
24. A. Jonsen et al., "Critical Issues in Newborn Intensive Care: A Conference Report and Policy Proposal," *Pediatrics*, Vol. 55 (1975), pp. 756–68.
25. A. Shaw et al., "Ethical Issues in Pediatric Surgery: A National Survey of Pediatricians and Pediatric Surgeons," *Pediatrics*, Vol. 60, Supp. 1977, p. 588.
26. *The Gallup Poll: Public Opinion 1983* (Wilmington: Scholarly Resources Inc., 1983), p. 102.
27. Dr. C. Everett Koop, quoted in President's Commission, *Deciding to Forego Life-Sustaining Treatment*, pp. 219–20.
28. Maine Medical Center v. Houle, No. 74–145, Superior Court, Cumberland, Maine, Feb. 14, 1974.
29. *Ibid.*
30. Edward W. Keyserlingk, *Sanctity of Life or Quality of Life* (The Law Reform Commission of Canada, 1979), p. 60.
31. Anthony Shaw, "Defining the Quality of Life," *Hastings Center Report*, October 1977, p. 11.
32. President's Commission, *Deciding to Forego Life-Sustaining Treatment*, pp. 214–15.
33. See *ibid.*, Appendix D, for a listing and comparison of all current natural-death statutes.
34. William G. Blair, "Poll Backs 'Right to Die' Ruling," *New York Times*, March 17, 1985.
35. Natanson v. Kline, 186 Kan. 393, 350 P.2d 1093 (1960).

36. Bouvia v. County of Riverside, No. 159780, Superior Court, Riverside County, Calif., Dec. 16, 1983, Tr. 1238–1250.
37. George J. Annas, Leonard H. Glantz, and Barbara F. Katz, *The Rights of Doctors, Nurses, and Other Allied Health Professionals* (New York: Avon Books, 1981), pp. 83–85.
38. Superintendent of Belchertown State School v. Saikewicz, 370 N.E.2d 417, 426 n.11 (1977).
39. *San Francisco Chronicle*, Aug. 27, 1985, p. 15.
40. Robert M. Veatch, *Death, Dying, and the Biological Revolution* (New Haven: Yale University Press, 1976), p. 93. For more on the passive–active distinction see Veatch, pp. 77–115, and President's Commission, *Deciding to Forego Life-Sustaining Treatment*, pp. 60–90.
41. Leo Alexander, "Medical Science Under Dictatorship," *New England Journal of Medicine*, Vol. 241 (1949), pp. 39–47.

V. EXPERIMENTATION WITH HUMAN BEINGS

1. William L. Shirer, *The Rise and Fall of the Third Reich* (New York; Simon and Schuster, 1960), p. 985.
2. M. H. Papworth, *Human Guinea Pigs: Experimentation on Man* (London: Routledge & Kegan Paul, 1967); Alan W. Scheflin and Edward M. Opton, Jr., *The Mind Manipulators* (London: Paddington Press, 1978); James Jones, *Bad Blood: The Tuskegee Study of Untreated Syphilis in the Negro Male* (New York: The Free Press, 1981).
3. *Trials of War Criminals Before the Nuremberg Military Tribunals* (Washington, D.C.: Government Printing Office, 1948). See Robert M. Veatch, *Case Studies in Medical Ethics* (Cambridge, Mass.: Harvard University Press, 1977), Appendix 2, for the text of other Guidelines for Human Experimentation.
4. E. Langer, "Human Experimentation: Cancer Studies at Sloan-Kettering Stir Public Debate on Medical Ethics," *Science*, Vol. 143, Feb. 7, 1964, pp. 551–53; *ibid.* "Human Experimentation: New York Verdict Affirms Patients' Rights," *Science*, Vol. 151, Feb. 11, 1964, pp. 663–66.
5. Talcott Parsons, *The Social System* (New York: The Free Press, 1951), pp. 428–79.
6. 45 C.F.R. 46.116.
7. Sissela Bok, "The Ethics of Giving Placebos," *Scientific American*, Vol. 231, November 1974, pp. 17–23.
8. Declaration of Helsinki, reprinted in Veatch (1977), p. 361.
9. Comptroller General's Report to the Congress, *Federal Control*

of New Drug Testing Is Not Adequately Protecting Human Test Subjects and the Public (Washington D.C.: GAO, July 15, 1976).

10. Baldor v. Rogers, 81 So.2d 658, 660 (Fla. 1955).

11. 42 U.S.C. Secs. 2891–3(a).

12. Tom Christoffel, *Health and the Law* (New York: The Free Press, 1982), p. 295.

13. James J. McCartney, "Encephelitis and Ara-A: An Ethical Case Study," *Hastings Center Report*, December 1978, pp. 5–7.

14. Gina Bari Kolata and Nicholas Wade, "Human Gene Treatment Stirs New Debate," *Science*, Vol. 210, Oct. 24, 1980, p. 210; Nicholas Wade, "UCLA Gene Therapy Racked by Friendly Fire," *Science*, Vol. 210, Oct. 31, 1980, pp. 509–11; Nicholas Wade, "Gene Therapy Caught in More Entanglements," *Science*, Vol. 212, April 3, 1981, pp. 24–25.

15. Declaration of Helsinki, reprinted in Veatch (1977), p. 361.

16. George Bernard Shaw, *The Doctor's Dilemma* (New York: Dodd, Mead, 1941), p. 33.

17. *Black's Law Dictionary*, 4th ed. (St. Paul: West Publishing Co., 1951), p. 377.

18. Jessica Mitford, *The Prison Business* (New York: Knopf, 1973), pp. 138ff.

19. J. C. McDonald, "Why Prisoners Volunteer to Be Experimental Subjects," *JAMA*, Vol. 202, No. 6, (1976), pp. 511–12.

20. Arnold S. Tannenbaum and Robert A. Cooke, "Research in Prisons: A Preliminary Report," DHEW Publication No. (OS) 76–132, 1976, pp. 10–46.

21. National Commission for the Protection of Human Subjects of Biomedical and Behavioral Research, *Research Involving Prisoners, Report and Recommendations*, DHEW Publication No. (OS) 76–131, 1976.

22. Antti Vaheri et al, "Isolation of Attenuated Rubella-vaccine Virus from Human Products of Conception and Uterine Cervix," *New England Journal of Medicine*, Vol. 286, May 18, 1972, pp. 1071–74.

23. Geoffrey Chamberlain, "An Artificial Placenta: The Development of an Extra Corporeal System for Maintenance of Immature Infants with Respiratory Problems," *American Journal of Obstetrics and Gynecology*, Vol. 100, March 1, 1968, pp. 615–26.

24. DHEW, "Protection of Human Subjects: Policies and Procedures," *Federal Register*, Vol. 38, Nov. 16, 1973, pp. 31738–49.

25. *Report and Recommendations: Research on the Fetus*, DHEW Pub. No. (OS) 76–127, 1975.

NOTES 271

27. Declaration of Helsinki, reprinted in Veatch (1977), p. 359.
28. William Bennet and Joel Gurin, "Science that Frightens Scientists," *The Atlantic*, February 1977, p. 62.
29. The whole story of the recombinant-DNA controversy is well told in Bennet and Gurin. In fairness, it must be pointed out that it was a group of scientists who first called attention to the safety issues involved with this type of research and then pushed for stringent measures to insure that safety. Nevertheless, and despite an enviable safety record, such research is still hotly debated today, and author Jeremy Rifkin has instituted a number of lawsuits to block such research.
30. Robert L. Sinsheimer, "The Presumptions of Science," *Daedalus*, Vol. 107, No. 2 (Spring 1978), pp. 23–326; Robert S. Morison, "Misgivings about Life-extending Technologies," *Daedalus*, Vol. 107, No. 2 (Spring 1978), pp. 211–26.
31. Sheila M. Rothman and David J. Rothman, *Willowbrook Wars: A Decade of Struggle for Social Justice* (New York: Harper & Row, 1984).
32. See Henry K. Beecher, "Ethics and Clinical Research," *New England Journal of Medicine*, Vol. 274 (1966), pp. 1354–60, for a cataloguing of real-life cases with unethical research designs.
33. See D. T. Campbell and J. C. Stanley, *Experimental and Quasi-experimental Design for Research* (Chicago: Rand McNally, 1966), for a compendium of research designs and their uses.
34. Beecher (1966).
35. Clark C. Havighurst, "Compensating Persons Injured in Human Experimentation," *Science*, Vol. 169, July 10, 1970, pp. 153–57.
36. This argument is elaborated on in James F. Childress, "Compensating Injured Research Subjects: I. The Moral Argument," *Hastings Center Report*, December 1976, pp. 21–27.
37. *Report, HEW Secretary's Task Force on the Compensation of Injured Research Subjects*, DHEW Publication No. (OS) 77–003 (1977), VI-9.

VI. GENETIC INTERVENTION AND REPRODUCTIVE TECHNOLOGY

1. James D. Watson and Francis Crick, "Molecular Structure of Nucleic Acids," *Nature*, Vol. 171, April 25, 1953.
2. The exact workings of the DNA molecule have been chronicled in hundreds of works. Two of the best are by Nobel Prize–winning scientists: James D. Watson, *The Double Helix* (New York: New American Library, 1968); Jacques Monod, *Chance and Necessity* (New York: Vintage Books, 1972).

3. Peter Medawar, "Science and the Sanctity of Life: An Examination of Current Fallacies," *Encounter*, December 1966, pp. 96–104.

4. Ernest B. Hook, "Behavioral Implications of the Human XYY Genotype," *Science*, Vol. 179, Jan. 12, 1973, pp. 139–50; Herman A. Witkin et al., "Criminality in XYY and XXY Men," *Science*, Vol. 193, Aug. 13, 1976, pp. 547–55.

5. Gina Kolata, "Huntington's Disease Gene Located," *Science*, Vol. 222, Nov. 25, 1983, pp. 913–15; James F. Gusella et al., "DNA Markers for Nervous System Diseases," *Science*, Vol. 225, Sept. 21, 1984, pp. 1320–26.

6. Immanuel Kant, *Foundations of the Metaphysics of Morals* (Indianapolis: Bobbs-Merrill, 1959), p. 18.

7. "The XYY Controversy: Researching Violence and Genetics," *Hastings Center Report Special Supplement*, August 1980.

8. Report of the Cambridge Experimentation Review Board, reprinted in June Goodfield, *Playing God* (New York: Harper & Row, 1977), Appendix II (emphasis added).

9. The history and science of genetics is explained in many sources. For three different approaches see R. P. Levine, *Genetics* (New York: Holt, Rinehart & Winston, 1962); Jonathan Miller, *The Body in Question* (New York: Random House, 1978); ch. 7; Larry Gonick and Mark Wheelis, *The Cartoon Guide to Genetics* (New York: Barnes & Noble, 1983).

10. Yvonne Baskin, *The Gene Doctors* (New York: William Morrow, 1984), p. 39.

11. Marc Lappé, "Genetic Knowledge and the Concept of Health," *Hastings Center Report*, Vol. 3, No. 4 (September 1973), pp. 1–3.

12. Barbara J. Culliton, "Genetic Screening: States May be Writing the Wrong Kinds of Laws," *Science*, Vol. 191, March 5, 1976, pp. 926–29.

13. Dr. Leon Kass, reported in Richard M. Restak, *Premeditated Man* (New York: Viking, 1975), p. 90.

14. Dr. Glenn Seaborg quoted in Howard Rheingold and Howard Levine, *Talking Tech: A Conversational Guide to Science and Technology* (New York: William Morrow, 1982), p. 9.

15. For more about the new infertility treatments see Lori B. Andrews, *New Conceptions* (New York: St. Martin's Press, 1984); R. H. Glass and R. J. Ericsson, *Getting Pregnant in the 1980s: New Advances in Infertility Treatment and Sex Preselection*

(Berkeley: University of California Press, 1983).

16. President's Commission for the Study of Ethical Problems in Medicine and Biomedical and Behavioral Research, *Summing Up*, 1983, pp. 84–85.
17. *Ibid.*, p. 85.
18. Doornbos v. Doornbos, 23 U. S. L. W. 2308 (1954).
19. Doe v. Kelly, No. 78–815–531CC (Circuit Court Wayne County, Jan. 28, 1980).
20. 6 Family Law Reporter 3013.
21. 106 Mich. App. 169, at 173–74.
22. See Noel Keane and Dennis Breo, *The Surrogate Mother* (New York: Everest House, 1981), for the proposals of a lawyer who believes that the contractual model can work; see Peter Singer and Deane Wells, *Making Babies: The New Science and Ethics of Conception* (New York: Charles Scribner's Sons, 1985), ch. 4, for arguments opposed to a legalistic approach and in favor of a surrogacy board modeled after private adoption practices.
23. Del Zio v. Presbyterian Hospital, 1974, Civ. 3588 (S. D. N. Y. 1978).
24. Leroy Walters, "Human In Vitro Fertilization: A Review of the Ethical Literature," *Hastings Center Report*, Vol. 9, No. 4 (August 1979), pp. 23–43.
25. Ted Howard and Jeremy Rifkin, *Who Should Play God?* (New York: Dell, 1980), p. 206.
26. Archibald E. Garrod, "The Incidence of Alkaptonuria: A Study in Chemical Individuality," *The Lancet*, Vol. 2, Dec. 13, 1902, pp. 1616–20.
27. John Walsh, "Public Attitude Toward Science Is Yes but...", *Science*, Vol. 215, Jan. 15, 1982, pp. 270–72.
28. Mary Shelley, *Frankenstein* (New York: New American Library, 1965), p. 199.
29. All of these genetic-engineering techniques, as well as many of the ethical concerns, have been explained in June Goodfield, *Playing God* (New York: Harper Colophon, 1979); President's Commission for the Study of Ethical Problems in Medicine and Biomedical and Behavioral Research, *Splicing Life*, November 1982; Yvonne Baskin, *The Gene Doctors* (New York: William Morrow, 1984).
30. Robert L. Sinsheimer as reported in Bernard Dixon, "Tinkering with Genes," *Spectator*, Vol. 235 (1975), p. 289.
31. Diamond v. Chakrabarty, 447 U.S. 303 (1980).
32. *Ibid.*

33. President's Commission, *Splicing Life*, p. 53.
34. The particulars of this case are drawn from President's Commission, *Splicing Life*, p. 44, and Robert Veatch, *Case Studies in Medical Ethics* (Cambridge, Mass.: Harvard University Press, 1977), pp. 208–9.
35. H. J. Muller, *Out of the Night* (London: V. Gollancz, 1935).
36. C. S. Lewis, *The Abolition of Man* (New York: Collier-Macmillan, 1965), pp. 70–71.
37. Robert Nozick, *Anarchy, State, and Utopia* (New York: Basic Books, 1974), p. 315.
38. Daniel Callahan, "Ethical Responsibility in Science in the Face of Uncertain Consequences," *Annals of the New York Academy of Science*, Vol. 265, Jan. 23, 1976, p. 6.

INDEX

275